August 26, 2009

To Father Steven Hawkes-Teeples, S.J.

with love

[signature, illegible]

IN THE IMAGE OF GOD

Maximos Aghiorgoussis
Metropolitan of Ainou

In the Image of God

Studies in Scripture, Theology, and Community

Holy Cross Orthodox Press
Brookline, Massachusetts

© Copyright 1999 Holy Cross Orthodox Press
Published by Holy Cross Orthodox Press
50 Goddard Avenue
Brookline, Massachusetts 02445

Library of Congress Cataloging-in-Publication Data
Aghiorgoussis, Maximos.
In the Image of God : studies in scripture, theology, and community / Maximos Aghiorgoussis.
    p.   cm.
Includes bibliographical references.
ISBN 1-885652-11-9 (pbk.)
1. Orthodox Eastern Church—Doctrines. 2. Theology, Doctrinal.
I. Title.
BX320.A36   1998
230'.19—dc21   98-39682
                                              CIP

We are grateful for permission to reprint these articles from the following journals:

The Church as a Presupposition for the Proclamation of the Gospel, *Greek Orthodox Theological Review* 25 (1980) pp. 371-376.

Image as "Sign" (Semeion) of God: Knowledge of God Through the Image according to Saint Basil, *Greek Orthodox Theological Review* 21 (1976) pp. 19-54.

Applications of the Theme "Eikon Theme" (Image of God) According to Saint Basil the Great, *Greek Orthodox Theological Review* 21 (1976) pp. 265-288.

The Theology and Experience of Salvation, *Greek Orthodox Theological Review* 22 (1977) pp. 405-415.

Orthodox Soteriology, *Epistemonike Parousia Estias Theologon Chalkes* Tomos 2 (1991)

"Sister Churches:" Ecclesiological Implications, *Epistemonike Parousia Estias Theologon Chalkes* Tomos 3 (1994) Ekatonpentekontaeteris Ieras Theologikes Scholes Chalkes 1844-1994

TABLE OF CONTENTS

Dedicated to My Parents of Blessed Memory
Protopresbyter Evangelos
and Presbytera Lemonia Aghiorgoussis

Introduction

This collection of essays represents the work of many years of study, teaching, and involvement in the movement which aims at the "rapprochement" of divided Christians. Thus, the collection, which is mostly based on articles published in *The Greek Orthodox Theological Review*, includes articles on the image of God according to the teaching of Saint Basil the Great, and papers prepared for and presented to meetings of the dialogues between Christians.

The present volume includes only part of these papers. It is my hope that more of these articles, some already published and some still unpublished, will appear in a next volume. I am happy to share my thoughts on topics of God's image in man, theology, salvation, and Christian community with the reader. I am happy to offer a modest contribution to the Orthodox Christian understanding of these topics.

The first article, "The Church as Presupposition for the Proclamation of the Gospel," was written at the beginning of the international Orthodox-Lutheran Dialogue. It is a brief explanation of the importance of the Gospel for the Orthodox and the instrumentality of the church in keeping and teaching Christ's Gospel. The church, "pillar and bulwark of truth"(1 Tim 3:15), gifted with a hierarchical structure with the "charisma veritatis" bestowed upon its episcopacy in continuity with the apostolic ministry, is charged with the same responsibility as the apostles: to preserve the integrity of the Gospel and proclaim it through word and sacraments for the salvation of the world.

The second article, which gave the name to this book, is an excerpt from my doctoral thesis, "La Dialectique de l'Image de

Dieu d'Après Saint Basile le Grand" (Louvain, 1964). "Image as 'Sign' (Semeion) of God: Knowledge of God through the Image According to Saint Basil," deals with the second aspect of the image of God in man, which is the image's instrumentality of knowing God, "the same by the same." This knowledge is not a matter of our intellect only. It is also a matter of our entire being: it is the result of our experience of God in communion with Him, a knowledge by "familiarity" with God, known in the West as "connaturality." The Eastern Fathers speak of the life of *theosis*. This second, more profound level of knowledge belongs to the realm of ontology (communion of human and divine natures).

The third article, "Applications of the Theme 'Eikon Theou' (Image of God) According to Saint Basil the Great" is yet another chapter from my doctoral thesis. It deals with the specific applications of the theme of the image of God to the doctrines of the Holy Trinity, Angelology, and Anthropology. Special topics are also considered: the distinction between image and likeness, image and grace, image and gender, image and evil, and image and glory. Image and Christology and Ecclesiology, and Image and End-Times (Eschatology) are also part of this chapter.

The fourth article is being published for the first time. "Some Preliminary Notions of 'Baptismal Ecclesiology': Baptism and Eucharist, Constitutive of the Church as Communion," is an essay submitted to the Orthodox-Roman Catholic Theological Consultation of North America. Its intention is to consider "Baptismal Ecclesiology" as a corrective to an one-sided "Eucharistic Ecclesiology." The work of Fr. Alexander Schmemann, *Of Water and the Spirit*, was summarized in order to serve as a basis of the discussion of Baptism from an Orthodox point of view. Articles of prominent Roman Catholic liturgists, such as Aidan Kavanagh, were also utilized for the same purpose. The second part of the article considers all three sacraments of initiation (Baptism, Chrismation, and Eucharist) as creators of communion in the life of the church. Patristic arguments are added to the liturgical ones. The next section deals with the Trinitarian foundation of the sacraments. The balance of the article discusses the distinctiveness and interrelatedness of Baptism and Eucharist, and how the ecclesiologies based on these two sacraments are complementary, both of them serving the unity of the church as communion.

Article five discusses "The Theology and Experience of Salvation." Orthodox theology is characterized by its experiential dimension. Theology cannot be separated from life and experience. Theology of salvation cannot be separated from the experience of salvation in the sacramental life and practice of the church. Salvation, which in Orthodoxy is understood both as freedom from eternal death and as the life of *theosis* through Christ and in God's Holy Spirit is only experienced and meditated upon in the concrete life of the church, centered around the sacraments.

Article six is a paper on "Orthodox Soteriology" presented to the second phase of the Orthodox-Lutheran Dialogue in the U.S.A. The article deals with the Orthodox understanding of salvation in Christ and its presuppositions; the ancestral fall and its consequences; the person and the work of the Savior; the work of the Holy Spirit; justification and sanctification; justification by faith; faith and works; sanctification and *theosis;* the communion of saints; fulfillment of salvation in Christ (eschatology). One of the special problems discussed is the Lutheran teaching of "simul iustus et peccator" (simultaneously righteous and sinner). The Orthodox response is that one cannot mix light and darkness.

The last (seventh) article deals with "Sister Churches: Ecclesiological Implications." The essay was submitted to the Orthodox-Roman Catholic Theological Consultation of North America. It deals extensively with the concept of "sister churches," its Scriptural and patristic foundations, its use in history, up to the 20th century, when, following the second Vatican Council, the concept abounds in the official literature, especially in documents signed by the Popes of Rome and the Patriarchs of Constantinople.

The paper utilizes the findings of Frs. Yves Congar, Emmanuel Lanne, and John Meyendorff. It concludes that, even if the concept applies mostly to churches which are in full communion with one another, like the Eastern Orthodox Churches amongst themselves, the concept can also be extended to churches which are sisters from the very beginning of the Christian era; "estranged" through schism, they are still sisters, with the responsibility to fully rediscover one another as such, and strive for the restoration of full communion with one another. Such is the call addressed to the Orthodox and Roman Catholic Churches by the Lord.

I am pleased to present the above essays to the reader, both Orthodox and non-Orthodox. According to Fr. Georges Florovsky, Orthodox theologizing is supposed to be done "from the heart of the church." I had that in mind, as I was dealing with the above topics. I cannot say that I have succeeded. If I failed, I ask for the indulgence of my readers.

Maximos Aghiorgoussis, Th. D.
Metropolitan of Ainou,
President of the Diocese of Pittsburgh

October 1, 1998
Feast of the Holy Protection
of the Mother of God

One

The Church as a Presupposition for the Proclamation of the Gospel[1]

This brief essay does not pretend to exhaust the topic under discussion. It only offers a few basic views and remarks in the Orthodox Tradition. Hopefully, it will be of some use to my readers.

As I try to answer the question how the Church is a presupposition to the preaching of the Gospel, I deem it necessary to respond first of all to the question: What is the Gospel, and what is the Church?

WHAT IS THE GOSPEL ?

Evangelion is the good announcement, the good news. It is the good news of our salvation in Christ, announced and proclaimed first by Christ and then by Christ's disciples.

The message of our salvation in Christ, whose kernel is to be found in Saint Peter's preaching on the day of Pentecost, is the basic message of the entire revelation of God, treasured in the Holy Bible. It is the unique message of the entire Bible, that of the old covenant, and that of the new. The God of our fathers, the God of the prophets and the patriarchs, reveals himself in history as the God of our salvation. He prepares that salvation through the setting apart of the old chosen people, the old Israel. He gives that salvation to the new chosen people, the new Israel, through his Christ, the author of the new covenant of God, sealed by His own redeeming blood. Christ is the center of the history of God's salva-

1

tion. The Christ event, completed with the event of the descent of the Holy Spirit, makes God's salvation a reality and a possibility for the entire fallen human race.

The Gospel proclaims and celebrates the message of salvation in Christ: the message that God gave humankind the possibility of participating in his glory through Christ's exaltation and glorification and through the operation of the Holy Spirit of God. The Gospel is thus the announcement of this new order of things in Christ, the proclamation of the kingdom of God being inaugurated in Christ and through Christ, the kingdom coming in power through the descent of the Spirit, and accompanied with specific signs, the mighty works of the Holy Spirit (Mk 16:17).

It is those *magnalia Dei,* the mighty works of God throughout history, as completed by his Christ and as revealed and given by the Holy Spirit for participation by all of humankind that the disciples announce on the day of Pentecost. The Risen Christ sends the disciples to teach all nations about these mighty works of God, and to call them to fully associate themselves with these deeds, through baptism of the water and the Spirit. The disciples accept the order which they execute with the assistance and guidance of the Holy Spirit. They are the witnesses *(martyres)* of the *magnalia Dei,* and especially of Christ's death and Resurrection, in the Holy Spirit. Sent by the Risen Lord to be his witnesses, "to Judea, and Samaria, and Galilee and to the extreme parts of the earth" (Acts 1:8), the disciples accepted this missionary responsibility for the salvation and transfiguration of humankind and of the entire created and fallen world: everything is restored in Christ; everything is new in Christ; there is a new creation in Him. Things of the old have passed away, new things have been created in Christ! (2 Cor 5:17). This is the message of the Apostles, and especially of Paul. Along with the proto-apostles, he is sent to announce and proclaim salvation in Christ: he best expresses the feelings of every apostle-proclaimer of the Gospel when he says: "Woe is me, if I do not preach the Gospel!" (1 Cor 9:16).

The apostolic community followed the example of the proto-apostles and Paul. The proclamation of the Gospel is always central in its life. Witnesses like the *Didache of the Twelve Apostles*, Saint Irenaios, and almost all the fathers of the Church, of both East and West, testify to this concern of the community established by the Apostles, following their example. It is this community that we call the Church.

WHAT IS THE CHURCH?

The Church is specifically that covenant and apostolic community, to which salvation in Christ is revealed, through which this salvation is proclaimed and attained.

God reveals himself and his mighty works including salvation in Christ not to individuals only, but to a people, His chosen people, to a community, the covenant community, both the old and the new. God calls a people to be set apart and to be used as an oasis in the midst of the fallen world, as a means through which God's salvation is given to the world. These people are His people, and He is their God. He is their Father, and they are His sons and daughters (2 Cor. 6.18). It is this chosen people of God, the people of the covenant, that fully participate in the blessings of God's salvation in Christ. It is this people that becomes part of the new order of things in Christ, of the new reality, new creation, new life in Christ. For these people are organically associated with Christ, having Christ as head and as cornerstone while they are Christ's body and living stones of the holy temple of God, gathered together, inhabited, and enlivened by the Holy Spirit of God.

The Church as *ekklesia* (*qahal*) *is* a corporate reality, a unity of persons called together by God which reflects the kind of society that the Holy Trinity is. For the Church is created after the image of the Holy Trinity, in whose life it participates. As there is hierarchy in the Holy Trinity, there is hierarchy and structure in the Church. As there is equality of persons in the Holy Trinity, there is equality of persons and personal destinies in the life of the Church. The Church is only one communion of saints, in which all saints, all Christians, are called to respond to the common call to holiness. At the same time, hierarchy and structure in the Church is part of the being of the Church as instituted by Christ. The people of God is not left without leaders; the Body of Christ is not an amorphous accumulation of cells, but an organic body, with distinct parts having distinct functions. The holy construction, the holy temple of God is not without foundations, columns, and cornerstones. The Apostles lie in those foundations, having Christ as the cornerstone, and having the Apostle's successors as pillars which hold the temple standing and united.

The Church is apostolic, which means that the Church not only is founded on the Apostles, but also follows the life, mission, and doctrine of the Apostles. It continues to proclaim the apostolic message and to live the life of the Apostles, a life renewed by Christ, a new life in Christ. The Church continues the apostolic witness to this new, healed, resurrected, transfigured, glorious and powerful life in Christ and the Holy Spirit, the life of the kingdom which is to come fully, but which is at the same time inaugurated through Christ the King and His royal Spirit.

Being the body of Christ, Christ's extension, and according to Saint Augustine, being "Christ perpetuated into the ages," the Church assumes all those functions which are in Christ: Christ is the Savior of the Body, the only Savior of this world. The Church makes Christ present to the world, mediates Christ's salvation to the world; through it Christ continues to reconcile the world with God, to enlighten and enliven it with His truth, to govern and direct everything to achieve salvation in Him.

According to an old scholastic distinction, which goes back to Eusebios of Caesarea, Christ is the great priest, the prophet, and the king. The Church continues this threefold ministry of Christ, mediating salvation to the world, proclaiming the Gospel of salvation, and leading people to this salvation through this proclamation, and through its sacramental life.

Thus, the Church proves itself to be the pillar and bulwark of truth (1 Tim 3:15), as it fully identifies itself with Christ, the living truth (Jn 14:6), and as it leads human persons to an existential encounter with this living truth.

How is the Church a Presupposition
for the Proclamation of the Gospel?

The Church, as the covenant community, is the place where the word of God is to be found, for it is to the holy people of God, "His own possession," that God revealed His truth, His salvation in His Christ. It is to this community that the announcement of this salvation was given; it is through this community that this announcement was proclaimed and is proclaimed to the world; it is in that community that "faith which was once delivered unto the saints" is to be found, sustained, and propagated.

As the body of Christ, as an extension of Christ, even as "Christ perpetuated into the ages," the Church reflects the truth of Christ, being the "pillar and bulwark of truth." Christ, the living, incarnate truth, is present in the Church, calling each human person to a personal encounter and relationship with Him. Thus, the Church not only calls to salvation in Christ (which is the content of the Gospel), but also communicates this salvation, allowing a personal experience of this salvation in Christ and through Christ.

Being a structured community, after the image of the Holy Trinity, and an apostolic community, in continuity with the proto-Christian community, the Church has in its leaders (specifically, bishops as successors to the Apostles) the guarantees of continuity in the proclamation of the apostolic message of salvation in Christ. The bishops, among other tasks, have the responsibility of "proclaiming aright the word of truth" (Divine Liturgy). They are the teachers and prophets *par excellence* in the community, reflecting and embodying the teaching ministry of Christ and of the Church.

Since the Church is also a charismatic community, being the temple of the Holy Spirit and receiving His gifts, it experiences special gifts of teaching, not only in its bishops and other clergy, but also in lay teachers, who, under the authority and direction of the bishop share also in the bishop's responsibility to "teach aright the word of truth" and proclaim the Gospel.

The Church is also a *communio sanctorum,* not only as communion of saints, but also as communication in holy things, or a communion of holy things. These "holy things" (*sancta*), are the word of God, the Holy Bible, the Holy Gospel itself. The proclaimed word of God, the Gospel, is a sacrament in itself, inasmuch as a sacrament is a means of grace which leads to salvation in Christ through the work of the Holy Spirit. Also, the rest of the sacraments and other messianic gifts in the life of the Church, are the other "holy things" in which members of the messianic community (the Church) share together. Three of these sacraments have a special significance in terms of the proclamation of the Gospel: Baptism, Chrismation (Confirmation), and Holy Eucharist.

It is through these three sacraments that we are fully incorporated in the new life in Christ, and we bear its fruits. According to the late Fr. Georges Florovsky, "The true proclamation of the Gospel would be precisely the practice of this new life: to show faith by deeds" (cf. Mt 5:16). And also: "The Church is more than a company of preachers, or a teaching society, or a missionary board. It has not only to invite people, but also to introduce them into this new life, to which it bears witness. It is a missionary body indeed, and its mission field is the whole world. But the aim of its missionary activity is not merely to convey to people certain convictions or ideas, nor even to impose on them a definite discipline or a rule of life, but first of all to introduce them to the new reality, to *convert* them, to bring them through their faith and repentance to Christ himself, that they should be born anew in him and into him by water and the Spirit. Thus the ministry of the Word is completed in the ministry of the sacraments."[2]

Baptism, the sacrament of water and the Spirit, is of course, much more than a ritual: it is the sacrament of repentance, of renouncing Satan and the fallen world, renouncing one's old self in order to be fully incorporated into Christ, to fully participate in the new life in Christ, the life of resurrection. At the same time, one is fully a participant in the royal priesthood of all the believers, thus sharing in Christ's threefold ministry, including the prophetic one.

Chrismation (Confirmation), our new Pentecost, is the sacrament of the gifts of the Holy Spirit, among which is the gift of teaching and proclaiming the Gospel.

Finally, the Holy Eucharist is the sacrament which gives to the Church the strongest presupposition of proclaiming the Holy Gospel. The Eucharist is Christ himself, as the Eucharist is also the sacrament of the Church. It is at the Holy Eucharist that the Church is fully present in its apostolic faith, doctrine, and practice, in the fullness of its apostolic and ecclesial life. Celebrated by the bishop or the priest in continuity with the Apostles, the Eucharist is the celebration of the Word of God coming to the world and preaches the Gospel of salvation (Liturgy of the Word), and also the actualization of the Lord's death and resurrection (Liturgy of the Sacrament). Christ the King is present on the altar, through the operation of the Holy Spirit. The Eucharist is the actualization of Christ's resurrection and Pentecost since the Spirit, the *eschaton* breaks through into history, allowing us to participate in the kingdom of God anticipated and made present. The foretaste, the present reality of the kingdom which is to come fully, is experienced by the faithful at the Eucharistic celebration. The gifts are consecrated to become Christ's presence, and the faithful are sanctified through the operation of the Holy Spirit of God. The gifts, and through them the faithful, are transfigured; in this the transfiguration of the whole cosmos is anticipated. It is in the Holy Eucharist that the mystery of Christ, "who is, who was, and who is to come" (Rev 1:4; 8:11,17), is proclaimed in the most dramatic terms. One of the most ancient liturgical rites of the Orthodox Church includes this chant during the anaphora: "Thy Death we proclaim, O Lord, and Thy Resurrection we confess" (Saint James Liturgy).

The proclamation of the Gospel in various ways pertains to the essence of the Church. The Church cannot be the Church unless it is holy, set apart in the world, and is apostolic, missionary, proclaiming Christ's salvation to the world. It is the responsibility of the Church always to hand down and proclaim the revealed truth once given to the saints, and to live and experience. This truth is Christ himself, not as an abstract idea, but as a living reality. The Church always has had, and also has now one main function: to proclaim the Gospel of salvation and restore all things in Christ "for the life of the world" (Jn 6:51). What the Church lives and proclaims in its preaching is an abundant life in Christ and the Holy Spirit (Jn 10:10), a glorious life in God (cf. Rom 8:17).

ENDNOTES

[1] A paper prepared for the first session of the international Orthodox-Lutheran dialogue.

[2] Georges Florovsky, *Bible, Church, Tradition: An Eastern Orthodox View* (Belmont, MA: Nordland Publishing Company, 1972). p. 69.

Two

Image as "Sign" (Semeion) of God: Knowledge of God through the Image According to Saint Basil[1]

The dialectic of the image of God according to the doctrine of the great Cappadocian Father Saint Basil contains four important aspects, going from the more simple to the more profound. What are these aspects? The first is that of the image as a "portrait" of the Prototype, that is the image as a "picture" depicting the Prototype in a rather external way. It does not exhaust the "raison d' être" of the image. Completely the opposite, its role is purely functional, and thus leaves intact the essential aspect. The second aspect is the image as a "sign" (σημεῖον) of the Prototype. The image not only depicts, but also "signifies" its Prototype. The image makes its Archetype manifest and known, through reflection in the image of essential qualities of the divine Prototype. These qualities are known in the theological tradition of the Christian East as the attributes, or energies of God. Through their presence in the image, the latter becomes a means of knowledge of God. The third aspect is that of the image as belonging to the Archetype, and as the basis of personal relationships with the Archetype. These relationships develop on the basis of knowledge of the Archetype through the image. They are the vision, desire, and love of the Archetype and ultimately union with Him. The fourth and last aspect of the image's dialectic is that of the image as "presence" of the Archetype. The image makes the Prototype present, seen, and felt by all those who have the spiritual eyes to see Him, and have the spiritual "extrasensory perception" to feel Him present.

Unlike the Christian West – which sees in the image a mere representation of the Prototype and thus stops at a rather external and static aspect of the image – the Christian East puts much more into this doctrine of the image of God. The image is an instrument of knowing God; it is the seal of belonging to Him, the means of entering into personal relationships with Him, of being in communion with Him, and ultimately of having Him present and making Him present in a very dynamic way.

It is my intention to develop one of the four aspects mentioned above, the image as a "sign" of God, which constitutes one of the important themes in the theology of the great Cappadocian pastor and theologian, Saint Basil the Great. At the same time this doctrine touches the very heart of Orthodox theology and spirituality.

To attempt a synthesis of Saint Basil's thought on a given theme, as of any of the Fathers, is not an easy task. The Fathers themselves did not always feel the need for this synthesis. They spoke and wrote quite casually, according to the needs – mostly pastoral – of the moment. Yet, there is order in their thought. We can find enough hints for a synthesis, as they occasionally offer them to us.

In attempting such a synthesis, we should follow generally accepted principles and guidelines, such as the following: the historical context in which the texts have been delivered must be taken into consideration; the chronological order of the Father's writings must be respected as indicative of the development of his thought; the literary character of the texts should be taken into account; a thorough study of all the authentic works of the Father is required; doubtful works may be quoted as extra references in the notes. These principles are respected in this study of Saint Basil's thought.

By way of introduction, a definition should be given of the image as a "sign" of God. In Saint Basil's thought, one can define the image as the "intermediary between beings which look for one another." There are two such "images" of God, one perfect and one imperfect. The Son of God is the perfect image of the Father.

Christ fully manifests God. He fully shares the whole divine reality with Him. His essence and energies are those of the Father. The Son is not only fully oriented towards the Father, but He also fully "knows" the Father; He is wholly in the Father and the Father is in Him. The second image of God is man. He is an imperfect reflection of God. Only some of His "qualities," or "attributes" – or more precisely "energies" – are manifested through the image. It is this image, this "particle of grace" of God in man, which orients him towards God; through it man knows God, "the like by the like." It is important to see what the problems of this knowledge are. This knowledge is seen as a "journey from man's conscience to God." This "journey" has as its point of departure the image of God in man; and as its goal, knowledge of God as a response to His call.

The nature of the "object" of this knowledge of God calls for a special kind of knowledge. This knowledge cannot be a merely intellectual one. In His more intimate reality, His essence, God is fully unknown by man; He is wholly unreachable. Yet, He is partially known and available in His energies. As an "object" of knowledge, He is thus both transcendent and immanent, known and unknown, present and absent. As an "object" of knowledge, He becomes the real "subject," offering Himself to man for knowledge. This knowledge is more than intellectual; it is moral, affective, experiential, "ontological," and by "connaturality" (communion of natures).

The intellectual knowledge of God presents us with limitations, both on the part of the subject and on the part of the object. The subject is finite, not being able to have a true comprehension of God. The body is a kind of "veil," an obstacle for the human spirit to clearly see God. Fully in His essence, the object is infinite, transcendent, inaccessible, and incomprehensible. Thus, an immediate knowledge of God is impossible for man.

But there are intermediate ways of reaching God in His energies; the "knowable" of God is present in the creation as a whole and more particularly in man made in the image of God. Some divine attributes are reflected both in the whole creation and in man-in-the-image-of-God. These attributes are nothing other than God's energies, which reach us – which "descend to us" to use St. Basil's own term – in different ways. One of these is the image of God in man.

There are special instances of this kind of knowledge of God through God's energies. There is a superior degree of knowledge of God, of a conceptual and intellectual character, which is the knowledge in the "faith-belief." Yet this knowledge remains partial, or rather, half-way, without the moral, affective, experiential knowledge of God which complements the conceptual and intellectual.

This experiential, affective, and moral knowledge of God is the *true knowledge* of God. Only people who know God in this sense, who have the experience of God as he offers Himself to them in union and communion, are considered by St. Basil to be really alive. They participate in true Life and Existence, which is that of God.

As far as the *fact* of this knowledge is concerned, this experiential knowledge of God proves to be commitment to God, observance of His commandments, and also "familiarity" with Him, in union and communion with Him.

As for the explanation of this fact, there are two things to consider: the preliminary conditions, and the way of this knowledge in communion with God. Preliminary events explaining this affective knowledge of God are: firstly, the creation of man in God's image – man is called to preserve God's image in him, which is to preserve "life according to nature," a life in communion with God; secondly, the fall of man, which is the cause of degeneration of human nature; and thirdly, the plan of divine economy, which is the restoration of the fallen image in man through Christ and the Spirit. The grace of God given through Christ in the Spirit fulfills the *via descensiva* of God, so that the *via ascensiva* becomes possible for men. The way of this ascension to God through the restored image in man and the way of true experiential knowledge of God in communion with Him is the one of purification and *askesis*. Free from the will of the flesh, free from sin, renewed according to the image of His creator, man achieves life in communion with God. Then the three persons of the Holy Trinity dwell in man.

The "blessed end" of this way of ascension to God is the vision and contemplation of God. It is the "understanding" of God, not in a merely intellectual way, but also in an affectionate and experiential manner. To the purified soul, the Spirit shows the Blessed Light of the Ineffable Image of the Invisible God: Christ. In this Image we contemplate the Ineffable Beauty of the Archetype, the Father of Lights. Ultimately, the image-"sign" of God in us proves to be the "earnest" of this beatific knowledge of God experienced in union with Him. Through the image of God in us, we receive a partial knowledge of God "as in a mirror, and enigmatically." We are expecting the "perfection" of this knowledge according to God's promise. Then we will see God "face to face" (1 Cor 13:10,12), in the full splendor of His blinding Glory.

Having these main ideas of Basilian thought in mind, let us examine St. Basil's texts.

Before discussing the main theme of the image as "sign" of God in Saint Basil's thought, the following items should be considered: (1) a tentative definition of this image-"sign," (2) the case of man as an image-"sign," (3) the case of the Son of God, (4) particular problems for man: the "journey from the conscience to God," and finally, (5) two kinds of knowledge of God through the image-"sign" of God: intellectual and experiential.

The image as the "portrait," a mere representation of the Prototype, has no meaning unless it refers to the Archetype on which it depends and of which it is a manifestation. Oriented thus wholly towards this manifestation, it is, to use the expression of Roger Leys, "the intermediary between beings which look for one another,"[2] which "declares" its Archetype and is its "sign."[3]

The case of the Son of God, the Image of the Invisible God, presents us with this aspect of the image as a "sign" of God in an eminent degree. The Son "shows us the Father in Himself."[4] The Son is the "imprint of the substance" of the Father, the "effulgence of His glory,"[5] having the same attributes in common with the Father in numeric identity of essence. He has the same will and

energies, showing to us in Himself all the beauty of the Archetype, who is the Father.[6] The Son as the image of the Father is not
simply just "turned towards" the Father, "oriented" towards Him
from whom He receives origin; He *is* in Him. The Son of God has
no need to "possess" the Father, since there is no "distance" between them; the one is in the other. The Son is the Wisdom of the
Father; there is the identity of "knowing" as there is the identity of
will.[7]

The concept of man as an image of God is much more complex. When we gaze upon man as the image of God, we behold
those qualities of the transcending Archetype which are propor-
tionately present in man.[8] Through our knowledge of the qualities
of man we know by analogy those of the Archetype. However there
are two problems which must be considered: how the created image manifests the transcending Archetype and how this same image
leads to the knowledge of God. To reply to these questions we will
follow the "spiritual journey" that leads from the image to the Archetype, from the human conscience to God, as Basil describes it
in his works. As we have noted, Saint Basil does this not system-
atically, but occasionally and by aspects, emphasizing first one and
then another of these aspects according to the concerns of the
moment.

The starting point of this "spiritual journey" is the very image
of God in man-made-in-the-image-of-God. This "image" which
encompasses our faculties of perception and knowledge is wholly
oriented towards its objects of knowledge and discernment – God
and the divine realities. To begin with, the image is oriented towards its Archetype, God. In the act of knowledge by
man-in-the-image-of-God, the Archetype while being "objecti-
fied," becomes the true "subject" of knowledge, "objectifying" His
image. Thus, the knowledge of God through this image is a *sui
generis* knowledge, as we will subsequently see.

According to Saint Basil, if God conferred upon us reason, in
which we have the image of the Creator, it is to know the truth. To
know the truth means to know God, because God is the existing
Truth. Thus, our mind is oriented towards the knowledge of God,

on the basis of its very foundation, which is the image of God in us; this is so from the very beginning of the mind's existence. Saint Basil states in one of his letters to Amphilochios of Iconion:

> The mind is a wonderful thing (χαλὸν μὲν ὁ νοῦς), and therein we possess that which is after the image of the Creator (χαὶ ἐν τούτῳ ἔχομεν τὸ χατ᾽ εἰχόνα τοῦ κτίσαντος). And the operation of the mind is wonderful; in that, in its perpetual motion, it…is frequently carried straight to the truth…
>
> The judgment of our mind is given us for the understanding of the truth. Now our God is the very Truth (ἡ αὐτοαλήθεια). So the primary function of our mind is to know our God (ὥστε προηγούμενόν ἐστι τῷ νῷ τὸν Θεόν ἡμῶν ἐπιγινώσκειν).[9]

This knowledge of God, proportional to the cognitive power of the mind,[10] is surely not just "intellectual" and "philosophical." It is a knowledge which aims at assimilation, at "resemblance" to the known "object,"[11] and at the "enjoyment" of this Knowable Good. This happens when in the act of knowledge man is possessed by God. The subject then paradoxically becomes the object, while remaining the subject.[12]

Thus, in the act of knowing God by man-made-in-the-image-of-God there are two continuous and concomitant aspects: one is sensorial, intellectual, and philosophical; the other is extrasensorial, ethical, and experiential. In Saint Basil's terms, there is the intellectual understanding which he views as a good means to lead to knowledge "by faith,"[13] that is to say, a knowledge by consent and confidence in the Revealer of the revealed truth.[14] Therefore, "intellectual" knowledge, a philosophical knowledge, is good in spite of its inferiority to revelation, and is even able to be delivered to us by the wisdom of "those from outside."[15] But it is the aspect of "knowledge in faith," knowledge "lived," by "connaturality" as the Scholastics would say,[16] is knowledge by faithfulness to the commandments of God and the "familiarity" (οἰκείωσις) with Him, which is the principal aspect of the act of knowing God, by man-made-in-the-image-of-God.[17]

Both of these aspects, intellectual and experiential, constitute the one act of knowing God, which leads to union and communion with Him. At the same time, knowledge of God is nourished by the experience of God, obtained by man in this union and intimate communion with Him. What follows is an analysis of these two aspects on the basis of Basilian thought.[18]

1. "Intellectual" Knowledge of God – Transcendence of "Object"

The fact of the creation of man in the image of God, that is to say, the fact that God "accorded to man reason," is the basis and the beginning of the "spiritual journey" which the human conscience must make to its Archetype. The human conscience is thus capable of this knowledge of God, inasmuch as it is He who wanted it so, creating us in His image.[19] Knowledge of God is thus possible for man.

Transcendence of God

There are two obstacles to an intellectual knowledge of God: the first is the limitation of our mind in understanding God; the second is the nature of the "object" of our knowledge, God Himself who in His essence totally transcends our capacity for knowledge and understanding. Let us examine these obstacles as Saint Basil describes them to us.

Limitations of the Human Mind

The measure of our knowledge of God is directly proportional to the capacity of our reason, according to that measure which was granted to it. To show the extent of this human knowledge, Saint Basil tells Amphilochios: "Reason knows God in such a way as the infinite Grandeur is able to be known by a lowly subject."[20] Basil insists as much on the reality of this knowledge as on its minuteness.[21]

The minuteness of the human knowledge of God is not only due to the limited capacity of our reason; it is also due to the limitation of our present bodily existence. The body with which we are clothed and in which our soul dwells,[22] is occasionally seen by Saint Basil as a "prison" (δεσμωτήριον)[23] for the soul. Thus the body becomes a kind of "veil" (περικάλυμμα) for the immaterial soul. Without this veil the soul would have knowledge similar to that of the angels.[24] It is therefore quite normal that sensorial perception is precluded as a means of true knowledge of God.[25] Inasmuch as the soul is tied to this "veil," we are prevented from "seeing the grandeur of the glory of God" without an intermediary as the angels see it.[26]

Transcendence of the "Object" of Knowledge

But in our act of knowing God it is especially in considering the "object" of knowledge that the difficulty arises; in the short treatise *On Faith,* preceding the *Moralia,* Basil says that "before making a confession of faith, it is important to know what follows. Just as the majesty and glory of God is unexplainable in words and incomprehensible by reason, it is impossible to express it in a single word or a concept, or to understand it."[27] Thus we must approach the mystery of faith and be prepared to receive it without being able to understand or to articulate everything of its content, knowing that it surpasses the cognitive abilities of the mind. We find the same ideas expressed by Saint Basil in his *Homily On Faith,* where he, says:

> It is consistent with piety to remind one's self of God, the soul that loves God is never saturated with Him. But it is bold to talk about that which is of God by words, firstly, because our intelligence is much inferior to the grandeur of (divine) things; and secondly, because the word is equally inferior to intelligence... How would it not be necessary to remain silent, for fear that one will diminish the dignity of "theologia"[28] by the mediocrity of words (through which it is expressed)? The desire to glorify God is sown in the nature of beings endowed with reason. But all are equally incapable of speaking in a fashion worthy (of God). No one is so blinded and fools himself so much that he believes himself to have arrived at the peak of comprehension.[29]

After this avowal of the incapability of the mind to understand the mysteries of "theologia" and the inadequacy of words to express them,[30] Basil gives an excellent discourse on divine transcendence. He describes the trudging progress of thought until it attains the contemplation of the "qualities" of divine nature in its transcendence and the contemplation of the three persons of the Holy Trinity as faith shows them to us.[31] Precautions are taken by Basil before he goes on to express the mysteries of faith. Basil must speak about faith. Yet he realizes that he is not able to say "all that God is, but all that he is capable of saying about Him."[32] Even "the tongues of the angels and archangels, whatever their nature might be, if gathered together with all rational nature, would have attained but very little of the total Reality." All the more, if man wants to say or to hear something about God, he must devote himself to *askesis* to go beyond himself. He must rise above his earthly condition, he must "pass beyond everything by his mind, surpass even the sky, and once being above the sky, he must contemplate all the beauty that is found there by intelligence alone."[33] There he will contemplate upon the divine nature "beyond all things,"[34] there he will contemplate upon "the uncreated Nature, the natural Goodness," the Father, the Son, and the Holy Spirit.[35]

But if we dare to make this "spiritual journey" by thought, and if we dare to talk about it, as is only right, in the end we must "concede victory to the majesty of the (divine) Nature, against all rational expression."[36] We must understand that the mysteries concerning the divine nature and the divine Persons are "inexpressible and inconceivable for the human mind,"[37] and they "exceed all human conception."[38] In another text on the transcendence of God taken from his *Hexaemeron,* Basil compares the "hidden-mysteries" of God to the Holy of Holies of the temple of Jerusalem. Standing in front of the *propylaeum,* Basil envisions the Beauty hidden in the Sanctuary:

> If the entrance of the Holy is such, if the *propylaea* are venerable at this point, elevated and of a beauty the excess of which blinds our intelligence with lightning, what will the Holy of Holies be? And what man is capable of confronting the Sanctuary? Who will medi-

tate upon the hidden mysteries? For even the sight of them is inaccessible; and in any case, it is difficult to put into words what the spirit understood of them.[39]

We are thus amazed by the sight of the "entrance" and the *"propylaea"* of the knowledge of the mysteries of God. We would not dare enter into the Holy of Holies, seeing that access to it is impossible. The divine mysteries are hidden and inaccesible even to the sight; if by grace we understand something of them, we are incapable of translating it into speech.

In that case, if God as an "object" of knowledge is unreachable in His transcendence, if our faculty of knowledge is so weak and powerless, does this mean that we must confess "agnosticism"?

We have just seen in the texts cited on God's transcendence that Basil does not come to this conclusion. He is obligated to speak about the mysteries of faith. He speaks of God and the divine realities, while he is conscious that our intellect is incapable of understanding the Incomprehensible.[40] It is thus possible to see, to comprehend, to say something in spite of everything.

KNOWLEDGE OF GOD

In the act of knowing God, if an immediate grasp of the "object" is impossible for us because the "object" is transcendent to the conscience, there is nevertheless a means to grasp it in a certain way, albeit inadequate and mediate.

Intermediaries

Basil speaks about the intermediate way of knowing God through the creation – a partial knowledge of the artist by his work of art, and of God by his creatures.[41] Amphilochios of Iconion asks the question, "Which one preceeds the other: faith or knowledge?" Basil answers that conceptual knowledge preceeds knowledge by faith. In his words, "In faith concerning God the concept of the existence of God is the first. This concept we obtain from creation."[42] Thus, the creation initiates the knowledge of God. This Pauline theme[43] is taken up several times in the different works of Basil. We read in the *Hexaemeron:*

> The world is conceived by the Creator in the best in-
> terest of beings. It responds to their ultimate needs in
> becoming the school where rational souls educate
> themselves, the place where they learn to know God;
> He offers Himself in effect to our spirit to guide it by
> visible and sensible objects, as far as the contempla-
> tion of invisible things, according to what the apostle
> says: Ever since the creation of the world, the invisible
> perfections of God are offered for contemplation by
> our spirits by means of His works.[44]

It is in creation that we contemplate the wonders of God: beauty
and order, grandeur, strength, goodness, wisdom, and providence.[45]

Creation as a whole is thus a good "intermediary" to give us the
first idea of God, to manifest God to us in a certain way. But it is
rational creation especially, and man in particular, that "microcosm"[46] who summarizes creation in himself, who makes us know
God in a way far superior to that of irrational creatures. In the
homily *On Observe Yourself,* Saint Basil states:

> If you gaze upon yourself attentively, that will ad-
> equately lead you to the knowledge of God. If you
> reflect upon yourself, you will not have need of the
> structure of the universe to look for the Demiurge, but
> in yourself, as in a microcosm, you will clearly see the
> great wisdom of your Creator.[47]

The same idea returns in the *Hexaemeron.* In the latter homily,
Basil vows that "it seems that this is of all things the most difficult
– to know one's self." In fact, "the eye which sees the exterior, does
not enjoy its own view;" furthermore, "our spirit itself, prompt to
perceive the sins of others, is slow to recognize its own imperfec-
tions." Saint Basil claims that this is why his discourse on the
Hexaemeron, "after having examined with speed the entirety of other
beings, shows itself to be lazy and hesitant in the search of what
touches us personally." Basil however began his commentary on
the creation of man just the same; unfortunately he was not able to
finish it before his death. Saint Basil powerfully gives the reason
for which he continues his discourse on the creation of man on the
sixth day:

> Nevertheless, for whoever examines himself with in-
> telligence, the sky and the earth are less suited to make
> us know God than is our own constitution. This is what
> the prophet says: 'Admirable the knowledge of Thee
> that I have taken from myself', that is to say: To know
> myself, I have learned the infinite wisdom which is in
> Thee.[48]

In knowing ourselves, we know our Creator. This is due to the
fact that God made us in His image, bestowing reason upon us.[49]
Basil stresses this in his commentary on Psalm 48 (49). The "image" is the great "natural" prerogative of man. It constitutes his
grandeur, his honor; it is his "dignity in his natural constitution."[50]
Just as the angels are able to know God, man also has this power.
This is the consequence of his creation in the image of God, this
"bit of His grace which God deposited in man, in order that the
latter might know the like by the like."[51]

Basil explains how we obtain this knowledge of "the like by the
like:"

> Understand God as incorporeal, on the basis of the
> incorporeal soul which dwells in you. God is not cir-
> cumscribed in a place just as the soul's intelligence has
> no residence in a place, before the soul is joined to your
> body. Having gazed upon your soul, which is inaccesible
> to sight, believe in God as being invisible.[52]

God is thus knowable in a certain way by the knowledge we have
of ourselves. "Therefore pay attention to yourself, so that you might
pay attention to God."[53]

Therefore we know God in a certain fashion through the entire
creation, and more particularly through the creation of
man-the-microcosm. We know something about God; Basil affirms this against the Eunomians, who accused him of
"agnosticism."[54]

Knowledge of the Divine Attributes or Energies of God

We have already seen that what we know of God is that which
is "knowable" (γνωστὸν) by our intellect and is proportional to
our capacity to know.[55] In this stage of "intellectual" knowledge

this "knowable" consists of certain attributes which can be deduced by means of syllogism, by reflection upon creatures and especially upon man.

We know the wonders of God, their beauty, their order, and the grandeur of created beings; we behold in them the magnificent attributes of God which correspond to Him: Intelligence, Beauty, Infinite "Grandeur." We reflect upon the goodness, the wisdom, the strength, the providence, the justice of God in created beings. Moreover, in contemplating the human soul, we know attributes of God such as omnipresence, invisibility, and knowledge by the energies alone. By way of affirmation (ὑπαρχόντων ὁμολογία) we attribute to God that which is suitable to his Divine Majesty, according to Basil in his *Against Eunomios*. But it is especially by way of negation (ἀπεμφαινόντων ἄρνησις) that we know the "magnificent attributes" which "surround" the divine essence (περιθεωρούμενα ἰδιώματα), the "energies" of God.[56]

Unknowability of the Divine Essence

But even if we succeed in knowing the "magnificent attributes" of the divine substance, we are never able to enter into the fathomless mystery. We have already seen the foundation of this ignorance: the "like" reality to God set in us by creation in His image is not the essence of God, but only certain qualities of God accorded to man in a proportionate measure. Only the Son and the Spirit know all of the Father absolutely and know each other mutually by reason of identity of essence. The divine essence remains inaccessible to human knowledge. Basil repeats this several times to the rationalists of his time, Eunomios and the Eunomians.[57]

It is in the letters to Amphilochios that Basil presents us with the best of his passages on the inaccessibility of the divine essence. He says:

> The information that one is able to have on the divine essence is the realization of its incomprehensibility. That which is respectable, is not to comprehend *what* the essence is, but to comprehend *that* the essence *is*.[58]

In the same letter, Basil summarizes all his thoughts on what we are able to know of God:

> We assert that we know our God by his 'energies.' We do not promise to attain His very essence. For it is His energies which descend to us, whereas His essence remains inaccessible.[59]

Human intelligence is not able to pass beyond the borders marked out by its condition, its created standard. It is not able to penetrate beyond the περιθεωρούμενα (attributes surrounding the divine essence) up to the mystery of the very essence of God, on pain of no longer being human, or as Basil says to Eunomios, on pain of being struck with "apparent madness" (μανία σαφής).[60]

Privileged Instances of Knowledge of God

Moreover, Basil speaks to us about special instances of privileged knowledge on the part of some righteous and holy men of the Old and New Testaments. Such were Abraham and Moses, the Prophet Elijah, David, Isaiah, Saint Peter, and Saint Paul.

Basil presents Abraham and Moses as having advanced very much in the knowledge of God – but without having gone past the human standard. According to this standard we are not able to attain the summit of comprehension, the knowledge of the divine essence; we are not foolish enough to believe it! On the contrary, the more we advance in the knowledge of God, the more we realize our own weakness. This is precisely what happens in the case of Abraham and Moses:

> When they had seen God as it is possible for a man to see Him, it is then that each one humiliated himself the more: the former, Abraham, called himself clay and dust; the latter, Moses, described himself as being of few words and stammering.[61]

Moses sees God "face to face," equally as the angels. But while still being elevated to the dignity of the angels, he does not exceed his human state. He sees God as it is possible for a man to see Him.

The case of the Prophet Elijah is similar. In his cave on the same mountain as Moses, he is found "worthy of seeing the Lord, as a man is able to see Him."[62]

With regard to David, Isaiah, and Saint Paul, the case is very clear: David receives the grace of the "manifestation of hidden and unknown things of the wisdom of God." Isaiah gazes upon "the glory of God." Saint Paul "is carried off to the third heaven and hears unutterable words which he is not permitted to repeat to men." But not one of these three, not even Saint Paul who has the greatest "measure of knowledge," gazes upon the essence of God. Since the divine essence stays inaccessible to created understanding, not one of them declares or teaches anything concerning the essence of God.[63]

The case of Saint Peter is equally very clear: the knowledge which he receives by revelation is not knowledge of the divine essence.[64]

Thus there are special instances of knowledge of God in the sense that a person finds himself before a superior degree of knowledge; but the "human measure" is always kept – the divine essence always remains impenetrable.

Knowledge in Faith-Belief: Its Progress and Achievement

With these privileged instances of knowledge, we also have progressed in the description of the "journey from the human conscience to God." We are no longer in the domain of the mind alone, which bearing within it the image of God is capable of knowledge of Him and gives us our first knowledge of God. Neither is it the domain of "common sense" (κοινὴ ἔννοια), as Basil says in his *Against Eunomios*.[65] In these special instances we find ourselves in the domain of the "instruction of the Spirit" (διδασκαλία τοῦ Πνεύματος),[66] in the domain of Revelation to which man is invited to reply by faith.

Basil makes the distinction between the two domains of philosophy and faith, but he places them in continuity: the "philosophical" domain or that of the "κοινὴ ἔννοια" prepares man very simply for the reception of faith, and at the same time it strengthens the faith.[67] The domain of philosophy – which is also the philosophy of "those from outside," the non-initiated, is not separated from the domain of faith. There is continuity and concordance between the two. As there is elsewhere a knowledge which leads to faith, faith equally leads to higher knowledge:

> If you affirm that whoever believes knows at the same time, it is on the basis of what he believes that he knows. Or vice versa, it is on the basis of what he knows that he believes. For we know God by his strength. All things considered, we believe in Him whom we have known, we worship Him in whom we have believed.[68]

It is thus that Basil concludes one of his letters to Amphilochios, treating *ex professo* the question of the relation between knowledge and faith.

This knowledge in faith is likewise a knowledge in progress. Its dynamism is inexhaustible in this life. Not only does the "sage from outside" become wiser in placing himself in the school of the Wisdom of God, but those who are already instructed from Christ the True Wisdom, whatever might be the stage of progress, are also able to grow in wisdom:

> The word "wise" (σοφὸς) applies equally to whomever desires (ὁ ἐπιθυμῶν) Wisdom, to whomever already finds himself in progress (ὁ ἐν προκοπῇ) in the contemplation of wisdom, and to whomever is already perfected (ὁ τετελειωμένος) in this contemplation by habituation (ἕξις). Now, all of them, including the lover (ἐραστὴς) of wisdom and the one who has already advanced in wisdom, having heard wisdom, will become wiser... [always progressing in the knowledge of] divine dogmas (θείων... δογμάτων).[69]

This progress will not end until our actual earthly condition changes. It is only by the separation of the soul and the body at death that the dynamism ceases to exist, and that the progress has no reason to be. There will no longer be "circumstances" (περιστάσεις) which will necessitate this "becoming" (ἀλλοίωσις). In the "land of the living" (χώρα τῷ ὄντι ζώντων) we stay "always identical with ourselves" (ὁμοίων ὄντων ἀεὶ αὐτῶν ἑαυτοῖς).[70] It is in the life of the age to come that the actual condition of "partial knowledge" (ἐκ μέρους) will yield its place to the condition of "perfection" (τὸ τέλειον).[71] It is then that as "sons of resurrection" (υἱοὶ ἀναστάσεως), we shall have transformed, "spiritualized" bodies which will no longer be like "veils."[72] It is then that we will no longer see, as in our earthly condition, "through a mirror and enigmatically," but we will see God face to face, like the angels. We will see the "depths in the treasures of God," if we show ourselves worthy of it at the end of our "journey."[73]

Intellectual knowledge of God does not represent the entirety of our act of knowing God. At this point, we are led to examine the second aspect of this act, which is complementary and concomitant to the intellectual: the aspect of knowledge which, transforming us by the known object, renders us worthy of God, worthy of participating in Him and being united to Him. The object God, becomes the subject, and the human subject objectifies itself. Here is a knowledge no longer intellectual but experiential, a knowledge by "connaturality" with God, as we participate in Him through His energies.

2. Knowledge – "Experienced" or by "Familiarity:" The Immanence of the Known "Object"

The "philosophical" knowledge of God must lead us to the knowledge of God "by faith." This "faith" is not only a simple "belief;" it is belief, for the "intellectual" element is present. Yet there is more than just belief in this faith: there are also elements of the emotional and moral order. It is that aspect of faith which we can call "faith-faithfulness" – that response to the call of God to know Him both through the image which He placed in us and through Revelation. Knowledge leads us to faith-faithfulness in which we worship God.[74]

This faith-faithfulness is an active response, expressing itself by fidelity to the commandments of God. It is this faithfulness which makes us known by God, which familiarizes us with Him, which "wins us over" to Him, which "makes us like Him," and which "fashions us after Him."[75] It is this faithfulness which makes the very life of our soul:

As our body cannot live without breathing (μὴ

ἀναπνέοντι), so our soul cannot keep alive without
knowing the Creator (μὴ γνωριζούσῃ τὸν κτίσαντα);
for the ignorance of God [in the sense of the absence
of knowledge by 'familiarity' with Him] is the death of
the soul (Θεοῦ γὰρ ἄγνοια θάνατός ἐστι ψυχῆς).[76]

Moreover,

those who are not united to the truly existing God by
faith (οἱ τῷ Θεῷ τῷ ὄντι μὴ ἡνωμένοι κατὰ τὴν
πίστιν) – being accustomed to lies... due to the depri-
vation of the truth (διὰ τὴν στέρησιν τῆς ἀληθείας)
and the alienation of life (ἀπὸ τῆς ζωῆς ἀλλοτρίωσιν)
– have been called 'nonexistent' (μὴ ὄντες). On the
contrary, when Paul writes to the Ephesians who are
genuinely united to the truly Existing through the
knowledge (ὡς γνησίως ἡνωμένους τῷ Ὄντι διὰ
τῆς ἐπιγνώσεως), he calls them 'beings' par excellence
(ὄντας αὐτοὺς ἰδιαζόντως ὠνόμασεν).[77]

Thus the object of this knowledge always remains the Truth as it is
in "intellectual" knowledge.[78] Being equally the Life and Source of
existence, this Truth makes those who are united to it exist and
truly live. It is in this sense that we speak of "experienced knowledge," knowledge by "familiarity" (οἰκείωσις) with God, by "union"
(ἕνωσις), and thus "connaturality" with Him.

The Fact of Experiential Knowledge

Both intellectual and experiential knowledge have two compo-
nents. In a letter to Amphilochios, Basil gives us these constituent
parts. Intellectual knowledge consists of "the understanding of the
marvels of God" in the creation and "the comprehension of our
Creator" through His creatures. Experiential knowledge encompasses "the observance of God's commandments" and the
"familiarity" or "intimate communion with Him," which God offers us Himself.[79]

Observance of the Commandments

Basil calls the observance of the commandments of God "knowledge of God:"

See how one understands God; to understand God is

to hear His commandments. It is to observe them after hearing them. That is the knowledge of God: the
observance of the commandments of God (τοῦτο
γνῶσις Θεοῦ, τήρησις ἐντολῶν Θεοῦ).[80]

Evidently it is not a matter of "intellectual" knowledge. To observe the commandments of God is to testify faithfulness to Him,
to entrust ourselves to Him, to follow Him wherever He leads us.

To not know God in the above fashion is "to know Him
half-way" (ἐξ ἡμισείας),[81] it is to stop ourselves at the beginning
of knowing God, or before we have started to know Him at all.
The practical consequences of knowing or not knowing God are
significant: as Basil understands it, to truly know God means to be
a participant in true Life; it means "to preserve life according to
nature" (κατὰ φύσιν ζωήν), a nature which God created in his
image in order to endow us with both intellectual and experiential
knowledge of Him.[82] To know God is "to perfect one's life by the
commandments, to walk towards God by precepts."[83] It is to return to the state of the "original good" from whence we are fallen,
"the residence beside God and union with Him by love."[84] Not to
know God through the observance of the commandments is to
allow our nature to degenerate,[85] to be given over to "dishonoring
passions,"[86] "to resemble irrational beasts instead of resembling
God."[87]

Experiential knowledge gained by observance of the commandments makes us participants in the true life. It is then that
the object of our knowledge, God, being the true subject, objectifies us in acknowledging us among His own:

'What have you that you did not receive? If then you
received it, why do you boast as if it were not a gift?' It
is not you who has known God by your justice. It is
God who has known you through His kindness. [Scrip-
ture] says: 'You have come to know God, or rather to
be known by God.' It is not you who have taken hold
of Christ by your virtue. It is Christ who has taken
hold of you by His coming.[88]

It is obvious that in this text Saint Basil stresses the fact that everything comes from God and that in the act of knowing God, God Himself is the principal agent, offering Himself to be known by man. God takes up man into communion with Himself in spite of human unworthiness. The latter is quite emphatically underlined in the above text. There are no "meritorious" works whatsoever for man. Knowledge of God is offered to man as a free gift from God.

In the above text, Basil minimizes the human factor in man's "synergy" with God in salvation[89] due to his pastoral concerns. But he affirms this human factor in his letter to Amphilochios; although the human is evidently subject to the divine, the two agents find themselves in harmonious cooperation: "The Lord has known His own; that is to say, He has received them into His intimacy (οἰκείωσιν) by good works" (διὰ τῶν ἀγαθῶν ἔργων).[90]

Familiarity with God

God offers us His intimacy on account of our Good Works. This "intimacy," "intimate communion," or "familiarity" (οἰκείωσιν) with God, is the result of our "affective" and "moral" knowledge of God (ἐπίγνωσις). Moreover, this intimacy or familiarity with God *is* true knowledge of God, in the sense of a personal experience of God's energies when in communion with Him.[91] Based on kinship through the image of God in us[92] – a particle of His grace which makes us like Him – this familiarity finds its maturation in our education through the instruction of Wisdom "in the knowledge of God." Thus we are always becoming more what we already were from our creation in God's image: "Children of Wisdom."[93] The moral and affective element is inseparable from this knowledge in intimacy. Faith – here not only as belief, but moreover as confidence and faithfulness – is tied to the love of God,[94] to the "enjoyment" (ἐνευφρανθῆναι) of God.[95] It is this moral and affective knowledge of God, which the "fire" (πῦρ τῆς γνώσεως) that the Bridegroom asks of the "wise virgins," that they might be received into His "intimacy" (συνάφεια).[96] Here we are then at the summit of our "journey from the human conscience to God."

Explanation of the Fact of Experiential Knowledge

What are the preliminary conditions explaining the fact of experiential knowledge of God? Three events must be considered: firstly, the creation in the image of God which enables us to know God through intimacy with Him; secondly, the fall which weakens the potential of the image in man; and thirdly, the divine Economy through which the potential of the image is fully restored and new possibilities of knowing God in the life of grace are offered to man. God's coming to us in His Christ and His Spirit (*via descensiva*) explains our return to Him and the possibility of an experiential knowledge of God in union and communion with Him (*via ascensiva*).

Creation of Man in the Image of God

The image of God is destined to make us know God, rendering us alike with God.[97] This knowledge, which is not only of a conceptual order but also of a moral and emotional order, has as a consequence "residence beside God and union with Him through love" (προσεδρία τοῦ Θεοῦ καὶ διὰ τῆς ἀγάπης συνάφεια).[98] "Reason" with which we are gifted by the image is necessarily oriented towards the First Knowable, the Truth.[99] This Truth, opposed to the nonexistence of falsehood, is veritable Existence. In knowing this Truth, man participates in It, or rather is known by It.

The Fall: Degeneration of the Image

Man is called to become more what he is, to display the dynamism included in the "particle of grace" of God, to arrive at a greater resemblance to the Creator. Created and finite, the "rational nature" is called to a ceaseless perfecting; in his possibilities and in his created and finite measure, man is called to resemble the Infnite Perfection. "Rational nature" means nature "delivered of all necessity." It is God who grants this grace to man, creating him in His image. This freedom from all necessity or this liberty, imperfect as it is, and destined to perfection by habit, is also a negative power (ἐξουσία): man is able either to progress in his perfection or "to turn himself away from good at a certain moment," thus no longer preserving life "according to nature" (κατὰ φύσιν).[100] In fact Adam chooses the second alternative: he misuses his power of liberty, he "transposed his desire of the divine glory. Hoping for more things and running headlong towards that which he was not able to receive, he lost that which he was able to keep."[101] He makes himself wicked, "not by necessity, but by the lack of will."[102] As much as he separates himself from authentic Existence, he goes towards unauthentic existence. He asks for his well-being outside of God, outside of life. Separated from life, he finds death: "the more he separated himself from life, the more he drew near to death. For God is Life, and the loss of life is death."[103] That is the error of Adam which degenerates and depraves his nature; in that is the "fall." Adam was mistaken in his act of the knowledge of God: instead of choosing God, he chose the glory of resembling God, separating himself from Him who is the source of life; he chose falsehood in the place of Truth,[104] death in the place of life.

Divine Economy, Restoration of the Image: "via descensiva"

In the strict sense, the plan of Economy is the plan of restoration of the depraved nature, the plan of "return to that which we had in the beginning" (πρὸς τὸ ἐξ ἀρχῆς ἐπάνοδος).[105]

It is the possibility of new "intimacy" (οἰκειότης) with God, which He offers to his ungrateful creation.[106] The Creator's work of salvation is based on the restoration of the image of the Celestial in a "new creation."[107] The plan of God-the-friend-of-men is to again teach man the truth by his Revelation,[108] to give man the possibilities of a new "proximity (with God) by true knowledge" (διὰ τῆς ἐπιγνώσεως ἐγγύτητα)[109] which leads to intimacy with Him. This work conceived by the Father is accomplished by the sending of the Son and the Spirit.[110] God prepared the accomplishment of this work through the history of the chosen people. Through symbols and shadows He accustomed the eyes to greeting the "full light of the truth" (μέγα φῶς τῆς ἀληθείας).[111]

The Son, the eternal light whose origin is the unbegotten Light, is He who dispels the darkness of ignorance. He makes the morning rise in the soul by the growing appearance of spiritual light, giving men the possibility to become again "sons of light" (τέκνα φωτός).[112] It is the Son, who by the "rays of His divinity" illuminates "those who are seated in darkness and the shadow of death" and "illumines (them) in the truth."[113] The "Sun of Righteousness ("Ήλιος δικαιοσύνης), enlightens us with His rays through His precepts. [In effect,] without Him, man remains blind and in darkness."[114]

It is "the fall from truth which is the blinding and the blindness of the soul."[115] This Truth is Christ Himself, who allows us to participate in Him, thereby illuminating us with His truth.[116] Christ, Treasure of knowledge, "establishes those who by their faith take refuge in Him, in the well-being of gnosis" (γνώσεως ἀγαθόν).[117] Christ, the Bread of Life which came down from heaven, is the food of the rational soul:

> If the Scripture calls Him Bread (ἄρτον), it is because He is a very familiar food of the mind (οἰκειοτάτη τροφὴ τοῦ λογικοῦ). In fact, it is He who sustains the constitution of the soul, who preserves its characteristics. It is He who fills that which is missing (in the soul) with Himself and does not let it collapse in illness which arises from the lack of reason (ἀλογία).[118]

This "reason" is not only our faculty for thinking; by "reason" Saint Basil understands all that is extraordinary in man, that which makes his grandeur. Inasmuch as this grandeur depends on God, since it is from Him that man receives it, our faculty of affective knowledge makes us intimate with God and allows us to reside near Him, to participate in Him. In effect, Basil tells us:

> The foolish person (ἄνους) is he who does not have that which is extraordinary (ἐξαίρετα) in man, that is to say, the understanding (κατανόησις) of the Father, the acceptance (παραδοχή) of the Word which in the beginning was with God, and the illumination (φωτισμός) effected in us by the Holy Spirit. Those who have this reason (νοῦν) are able to say with Paul: 'We have the mind of Christ.'[119]

This "reason" thus contains, with the understanding of the Father and the acceptance of the Son, the illumination of the Spirit. This illumination does not happen except by participation in the Spirit: to those who are worthy the Spirit distributes the charismata, among which is that of "gnosis."[120]

> If [reason] turns itself towards the divine side (θειοτέραν μερίδα) and receives the gifts of the Spirit (τοῦ Πνεύματος ὑποδέξηται χάριτας), then it understands the most divine things (τῶν θειοτέρων καταληπτικὸς) to the measure prescribed by its nature... Reason, then, being intermingled (ἀνακραθεὶς) with the divine reality (θεότης) of the Spirit, is already able to behold grand things for contemplation (μεγάλων θεωρημάτων ἐποπτικὸς) and reflects upon divine beauty, in the measure which grace accords to it and which its make-up is able to sustain (ὅσον ἡ χάρις ἐνδίδωσι καὶ ἡ κατασκευὴ αὐτοῦ ὑποδέχεται).[121]

The *"divine side"* "leads up to the likeness of God" (Θεοῦ ὁμοίωσις).[122] This "resemblance" is incomprehensible without holiness, moral perfection, and affective knowledge.

This knowledge is offered by the Spirit in baptism. In his homily *On Baptism* Saint Basil states: "He who is not baptized is not illuminated: and without light, neither is the eye able to see the things which affect it, nor is the soul able to be qualified for the contemplation of God (Θεοῦ... θεωρία)."[123] It is in the mystagogy of baptism that one is received in the "gnosis" of God (θεογνωσία).[124] We are able "to know the truth" (ἐπίγνωσις... ἀληθείας)[125] only in the Church of God, for which Christ died, and upon which He abundantly bestowed the Holy Spirit. It is the Spirit in the Church which, if we choose the Good, makes us participate in Goodness (μέτοχος... ἀγαθότητος),[126] in Holiness (ἁγιάζον),[127] and in the Divine Reality (θεοποιοῦν).[128]

"Experienced" Knowledge of God: Purification and Askesis

Up to this point we have spoken of the initiative of God in the creation of man in His image and of the restoration of this image by Grace as the basis of the affective knowledge of God. This knowledge is accomplished by man's response to God's initiative.

In his commentary on Psalm 44 (45), Basil sees Christ Himself in the "Beloved One" of the Greek title of the Psalm.[129] Basil applies the philosophical theme of the ultimate Good, which is at the same time the ultimate Desirable. This ultimate Good and Desirable is God in Christ. Basil also applies the biblical theme of Christ-the-Bridegroom with direct reference to John 3:29: the true friend of Christ-the-Bridegroom, who is worthy of Christ's friendship, is he who constantly remains loyal and faithful to this friendship:

> It is not for anyone to advance in the perfection of love, and to know Him who is truly lovable. But it is for him who casts off the old man that corrupts him in the thread of delusive desires and who clothes himself with the new man – he who plods towards true knowledge in renewing himself in the image of his Creator... Thus it is the characteristic of him who achieves perfection to really know the One who is truly lovable. In fact the only true friends of God, who are also friends among themselves, are the holy people; for none of the wicked and ignorant are really friends.[130]

In order for us to be worthy of the friendship of God, to encounter the ultimate Good and Desirable – God as He offers Himself to us in His Christ – to be able to enter the marriage feast together with the Bridegroom, we must adequately prepare ourselves through a continuous renewal and enhancement of our inner selves. We must abandon the man aged by sin and reclothe the new man; we must renew and restore the fallen image, so that we might again trudge toward true knowledge of God. We must continually progress in this renewal and knowledge so that we become able to progress in likeness with God by image. We must achieve that Christian perfection in which we really know the One who is truly lovable and become true friends of God, taken up into fellowship and communion with Him.[131]

How is this continuous renewal and this progress in the knowledge of God conceived in Saint Basil's thought? What are the different stages of this continual "becoming" in Christian perfection and life in fellowship with God, in which He "knows" His friends and they truly know Him?

Purification and askesis is the first step in this renewal, leading towards Christian perfection and knowledge of God. A *katharsis* of both soul and body is required for man to be able to receive the truth of God which is revealed in His Christ. *Askesis* is the proper characteristic of the Christian who accepts this revelation, enabling himself to become worthy of God.

"The words of God are not written for all, but for those who have the ears of the interior man" (ὦτα κατὰ τὸν ἔσω ἄνθρωπον).[132] To hear the voice of God, an indispensable condition of the response to it, there is need of a whole preparation of "receptivity."

This preparation consists of two steps: firstly, in the "destruction of sophisms and of all haughty power (ὕψωμα) which rise up against the knowledge of God" (κατὰ τῆς γνώσεως τοῦ Θεοῦ); secondly, "in capturing all thought to lead it to obey Christ."[133] Thus the first part in this preparation is negative; we must cast off the "whims of understanding (διανοιῶν θελήματα), all thought which does not conform to Scripture," and all "sophism" which prevents our access to the knowledge of God. We next rid ourselves of the "desire of the flesh" (φρόνημα τῆς σαρκὸς) which is equally "an enmity toward of God" (ἔχθρα εἰς Θεόν).[134] In brief we cast off all the "haughty power" of sin, which "through contempt for the divine commandment one calls the 'haughty power' which rises up against the knowledge of God."[135] The positive aspect of preparation is to undertake immediately in "the desire for perfection, any possible good thing which leads to the knowledge of God."[136]

This double movement of casting off on the one hand and the "return" to knowledge on the other finds its crowning at baptism,[137] when he who comes "from outside" approaches the knowledge of God. But throughout the new life of baptism in Christ, he must continue at the School of Wisdom, progressing in Wisdom and virtue.

For the Christian this "progress" (προκοπή) comprises the following elements: in the negative step, we must rid ourselves from

all "the anxiety of life (βιωτικὴ μέριμνα),"[138] from all slavery to
the senses and to the passions (πάθη) of the body,[139] and, finally,
we must concern ourselves with the "purification of the heart"
(καθαρότης καρδίας), for only those who have a pure heart will
be able to see God.[140]

As for the positive step, we must "occupy the mind with necessary things," taking into consideration the presence of God
(παρεῖναι τὸν Θεόν),[141] having the "fear of God" (φοβουμένους
Θεόν),[142] and loving God in affectionate contemplation.[143] What
makes the veritable knowledge of God possible is the arrange-
ment of our "inner selves" worthy (ἀξίοις)[144] of receiving the Spirit
and "permitting" Him to dwell in us and to illumine us. By this
affective knowledge we participate in Him (μετεχόμενον).[145] With
the indwelling (ἐνοίκησις) of the Spirit comes that of the Son
(προενοικήσαντες διὰ τοῦ Πνεύματος τὸν Χριστόν).[146] The
Son in turn leads us to the Father (ἐπάνοδος εἰς οἰκείωσιν
Θεοῦ).[147] In this way we arrive at the summit of affective knowledge of God.

Contemplation and Vision of God: "via ascensiva"
The ultimate step in our way towards Christian perfection, and
the last stage in our "journey from the conscience to God," is the
vision and contemplation of God. This contemplation is followed
by the understanding which God offers of Himself to those who
are worthy of Him. Indeed, the "understanding of God" (Θεοῦ
κατανόησις) is "the blessed end" (μακάριον τέλος) of the "advancement," which is continual and ordered towards perfection –
thanks to works of justice and the illumination of gnosis – going
"always ahead, stretched out towards that which is still left to travel."
The Lord grants this comprehension of Himself to those who believe in Him.[148] Faith in the fullest sense of the word (not only
belief but also confidence in and faithfulness to the Lord) and its
accompanying affective knowledge are communicated to us by the
Holy Spirit through our participation in Him.

For the purified soul, the Spirit is "the strength to see in a healthy
eye."[149] It is in the Spirit that we see the Son. "It is impossible to

see the Image of the Invisible God except in the illumination of the Spirit (φωτισμὸς τοῦ Πνεύματος)." Through the "illumination of the Spirit" we perceive the "effulgence of the glory of God." Through the "Imprint," the Son, "we are led to the glory of Him to whom belongs the seal of the same shape."[150]

Thus "the way of the knowledge of God" (ὁδὸς θεογνωσίας) leads upward toward God, whereas the blessings through which we obtain this knowledge descend to us from God. These blessings originate in the Father and reach man by the Son in the Spirit: whereas, the way of the knowledge of God climbs "from the unique Spirit, through the unique Son, up to the unique Father."[151] It is in God that the conscience "takes refuge, realizing that its only rest is residence in Him."[152]

How much does this experiential aspect of our act of knowing God advance us in the knowledge of God? In this aspect we "feel" God in His moral perfection and in His holiness much more than we "understand" Him. God as an object of knowledge is immanent to us and is experienced as such by us. Nevertheless, even this experiential knowledge of God is not less obscure and imperfect than the parallel intellectual knowledge of Him. We cannot surpass the limiting standard of our actual human condition. We see God "as in a mirror and enigmatically." Commenting on Psalm 33 (34) Basil tells us:

> 'Taste,' he says, 'and do not satisfy yourselves,' for now we partially know the truth, as in a mirror and enigmatically. But there will come a certain time where the present 'earnest' (ἀῤῥαβὼν) and the actual banquet of grace (γεῦμα τῆς χάριτος) will attain completion and perfection for us (εἰς τελειότητα ἡμῖν καταντήσει).[153]

Conclusion

Saint Basil's doctrine of the knowledge of God through the image-sign (σημεῖον) of God in us presents us with a paradox: God as an object of knowledge for man presents Himself as infinitely distant but, at the same time irresistibly close. God is transcendent, incommunicable, and hidden in His essence: "His essence remains unapproachable."[154] The human intellect cannot comprehend Him. His essence totally escapes our mind as an object of knowledge. Yet, He is close to us and makes Himself present to us in His energies: "His energies descend towards us."[155] We experience them in the creation just as we experience them in us: in the very image of God in us. Through this "bit of grace" which He put in us at our creation, we are first able to know God intellectually in the measure that our intellect can understand Him. Subsequently, this knowledge which begins with our intellect becomes committment to God; it becomes faithfulness to Him and observance of His commandments. This knowledge finally becomes a means of union and intimate communion with God as we accept full participation in His Life, which He offers to us in Jesus and in His Holy Spirit.

The process of our knowledge of God begins with the image of God in us and ends with our union with Him, in participation in His veritable Life and Existence. Thus the image of God in us becomes both the promise and the partial fulfillment of the promise of knowing God. We look forward to the complete fulfillment of this promise in the age to come, when we will see God "face to face" (1 Cor 13:12).

ENDNOTES

[1] This study originally appeared as part of my dissertation entitled "La dialectique de l'image de Dieu chez Saint Basile le Grand" submitted to the school of Theology of the University of Louvain, in June 1964, in partial fulfillment of the requirements "pro gradu Doctoris in Sacra Theologia." It has been revised and modified, especially with regard to the references. I offer this study as a contribution to a better understanding of Saint Basil's doctrine. I am thankful to all those who have made this modest contribution possible. Specifically, I am deeply appreciative of the care and diligence which Mr. Nicholas Pissare exercised in translating this study from the French. I would like to also express my gratitude to the Rev. Dr. Nomikos M. Vaporis for his helpful remarks and suggestions concerning the revision of the original text.

[2] Roger Leys, *L'image, de Dieu chez Saint Grégoire de Nysse* (Brussels, 1951), p. 27.

[3] Saint Basil gives the following definition of sign: "Sign *is* the indication of a paradoxical and hidden reality; it is merely seen by simple people, but it *is* understood by those who have a trained intelligence." *Letter* 260,7; PG 32:965B.

The image of God is exactly this kind of "sign."

⁴ *Adversus Eunomium*, 2,16; PG 29:605B; "῞Ολον ἐν ἑαυτῷ δείχνυσι τὸν Πατέρα." See also *Homilia de fide*, 2; PG 31:468B; *Letter* 105; PG 32:513A; *In illud, in principio erat Verbum*, 3; PG 31:447BC; also *Liturgy* ed. F. E. Brightman, in *Liturgies Eastern and Western, Being the Texts Original or Translated of the Principal Liturgies of the Church* (Oxford, 1896), p. 322, lines 29-30; and p. 402, lines 18-19.

⁵ *Letter* 38,6-7; PG 32:336C-40A; ed. Yves Courtonne (Paris, 1957), pp. 89-91. Cf. *De Spiritu Sancto*, 7,16; PG 32:96AB: "One conceives the effulgence with the glory, the image with the model, the Son with the Father."

⁶ *De Spiritu Sancto*, 8,19; PG 32:101C-04B; ibid., 8,21; PG 32:104BD.

⁷ *Adversus Eunomium*, 1,23; PG 29:564AB; ibid., 2,21; PG 29:617C-20A. See also *Letter* 236.1; PG 32:877AB; and *De Spiritu Sancto*, 8,20; PG 32:104AD.

⁸ See, for instance, what Saint Basil has to say on this specific point in *In Illud, attende tibi ipsi*, 7; PG 31:213C-16B: "Observe yourself, so that you discover in you the great wisdom of your Creator. Conceive God as bodiless, for your soul is bodiless. Believe in God as invisible, for your soul cannot be seen by your bodily eyes...it is known through its energies only. Thus do not ask to see God with your bodily eyes.

⁹ *Letter* 233, 1-2; PG 32:864C-65C. Cf. *Regulæ fusius tractatæ*, 2,3; PG 31:913B; see also homilies *Dicta tempore famis et siccitatis*, 5; PG 31:317AB; *In illud, attende*, 6; PG 31:212B; and *De gratiarum actione*, 2; PG 31:221C. Here, the translation is that of *The Nicene and Post-Nicene Fathers*, ed. Philip Schaff and Henry Wace (Grand Rapids, 1955), vol. 8, p. 273, columns 1 and 2. On the basis of the Greek original, the ending of this translation has been adjusted to read "our God," instead of "one God."

¹⁰ *Letter* 233,2; PG 32:868B. Cf. ibid., 1; PG 32:865C; and *Letter* 235,1; PG 32:872B.

¹¹ *De Spiritu Sancto*,1,2; PG32:69B. Cf. *Regulæ fusius*, 2,3; PG 31:913B; *Letter* 233,1; PG 32:865A; and *Letter* 159,1; PG 32:620B.

¹² *De humilitate*, 4; PG 31:532B. Cf. *Quod Deus non est auctor malorum*, 6; PG 31:344BC; and *Letter* 235,3; PG 32:876A.

¹³ Here, by "faith" Basil understands "faithfulness."

¹⁴ *Letter* 235,1; PG 32:872AB. Cf. *Ad adolescentes*, 2; PG 31:568BC; ed. Fernand Boulenger (Paris, 1952), 3; p. 44, lines 11-15.

¹⁵ *In principium Proverbiorum*, 7; PG 31:401A; see also ibid., 6; PG 31:397BC-400B; and ibid., 14; PG 31:416C.

¹⁶ The term *connaturalitas* was created in the Christian West on the basis of 2 Peter 1.4, to indicate our union with the nature of God. Eastern Christianity interprets this union as a participation in the energies of God which together with the essence are the one nature of God (see Lossky, *The Mystical Theology*, pp. 67-70). I use the term 'connaturality' with the Eastern understanding of divine nature in which we are called to participate. In this participation we know God in the measure that He is knowable by us, that is in His energies.

¹⁷ *In Psalmum XIV*, 1, 3; PG 29:256BC; see also ibid., 1,3; PG 29:256CD. Cf. *In principium Proverbiorum*, 14; PG 31:416C.

¹⁸ In a letter to Amphilochios of Iconion, Saint Basil makes the synthesis of

the two aspects, when he speaks of the many facets of the knowledge of God. This knowledge is at the same time "understanding of our Creator (τοῦ κτίσαντος ἡμᾶς σύνεσις), comprehension of His marvelous things (τῶν θαυμασίων αὐτοῦ κατανόησις), observance of His commandments (τήρησις τῶν ἐντολῶν), and familiarity with Him" (οἰκείωσις πρὸς αὐτόν). *Letter* 235,3; PG 32:873C. The translation of *The Nicene Fathers*. vol. 8, p. 275, column 2, renders "οἰκείωσις" (*familiarity*) with "intimate communion." I would agree with this translation, less literal than mine, as an alternative meaning of "οἰκείωσις" in the given context of the letter.

[19] *Dicta tempore famis.* 3; PG 31:317AB: "Who forced (the Creator) to endow man with reason, according to His own image (κατ᾽ εἰκόνα ἰδίαν τὸν λόγον τῷ ἀνθρώπῳ χαρίσασθαι), so that beginning his journey from there (ἐκεῖθεν ὁρμηθείς) he may be versed in arts and may learn how to contemplate the highest realities, which he cannot reach through his senses?" (μάθῃ περὶ τῶν ἀνωτάτω φιλοσοφεῖν ὧν αἰσθητῶς οὐχ ἅπτεται.)

[20] *Letter* 233,2; PG 32:865C-868A.

[21] Ibid., 2; PG 32:868A, where Saint Basil brings the example of the sky. We cannot see everything in it, he says, yet we cannot say that the sky is invisible. The same goes with the knowledge of God.

[22] See, for example, *Letter* 46,4; PG 32:376C; ed. Courtonne, p. 121, lines 7-8: We are "living bodies, inhabited by a soul made in the image of God" (σωμάτων ζώντων... ψυχὴν ἔνοικον ἐχόντων, κατ᾽ εἰκόνα Θεοῦ πεποιημένην). See also R*egulae fusius*, 1; PG 31:104A; *In Psalmum XXXIII*, 6; PG 29:337D; *In Psalmum CXIV*, 5; PG 29:493C; and *In illud, attende*, 1-8; PG 31:197-217 (*passim*). One should note that in all these texts, Saint Basil sounds dualistic regarding the constitution of man. Yet, this dualism is very much different from the one of Plato and Origen. Actually, Saint Basil speaks of a duality of principles in man, without being Aristotelian either. His doctrine is that of the Holy Scripture: there is a duality of principles in man, one spiritual, another material. The two make the one man, who is a "psycho-physical," or "psycho-somatic" unity. In this Saint Basil is more in line with Makarios of Egypt rather than with Evagrios Pontikos, both of them his contemporaries. In spite of the appearances, Saint Basil's general doctrine supports a rather "wholistic" view of man. If Saint Basil considers the body dangerous, it is because of its "passions," a result of the fall, which are "against nature." But once the soul-in-the-image-of-God wins the battle over these passions, the body becomes the best co-worker of the soul. The body serves in the best interests of the soul and with it ultimately achieves "theosis" (see next note). With regard to the theology and anthropology of Makarios and Evagrios, see the recent work of John Meyendorff, *Byzantine Theology* (New York, 1974), pp. 67-69.

[23] On some rare occasions Saint Basil speaks of the body with some disdain. This makes him sound very much like Plato. Yet in Saint Basil's texts the emphasis is not on contempt for the body "the prison of the soul," but on the soul's priority over the body. In Saint Basil's thought the body is never seen as a penalty for the fallen soul, as we see it in Plato's thought (see Plato's *Cratylus*, 400C; and *Phaedo*, 62B, 82D). Even in the text which denotes the strongest Platonic

influence, Saint Basil does nothing but attempt to establish this priority of the spiritual and immortal soul over the mortal and material body. Here is an excerpt from this text, where Saint Basil tells his young nephews: "You should not be slaves of your body, unless this is absolutely necessary. As far as your soul is concerned, make certain to obtain for it whatever is best. Also, as from a prison (ὥσπερ ἐκ δεσμωτηρίου) try to liberate your soul from the body's passions. Make your body the winner of the battle over these passions." *Ad adolescentes*, 7; PG 31:581A; ed. Boulenger, 9; pp. 54-55, lines 3-7. Cf. ibid., 7; PG 31:584C; ed. Boulenger, 9; p. 57, lines 77-80. In the fallen nature our material body hinders the movements of our spiritual soul. Saint Basil is sensitive to this fact and seeks for remedies which we can fnd in ourselves: we can make our own bodies the winners of the battle over the passions.

[24] *In Psalmum XXXIII*, 11; PG 29:377BC. See also *In illud, attende*, 1; PG 31:197C.

[25] *Adversus Eunomium*, 1,9; PG 29:532C-33A. See also *In illud, attende*, 7; PG 31:216A; and *Dicta tempore famis*, 5; PG 31:317B. Cf. *In Psalmum XXXIII*, 3; PG 29:329B.

[26] *In Psalmum XXXIII*, 11; PG 29:337C. Cf. *De Spiritu Sancto*, 22,53; PG 32:168AB.

[27] *De fide*, 2; PG 31:681A.

[28] "Θεολογία" is a technical term in Saint Basil's theological language. The term indicates "word on God," that is "word on the Holy Trinity." Saint Basil distinguishes "Θεολογία" from "Οἰκονομία" as "word on God in His transcendence and His intimate life"; from "word on God as He manifests Himself to the world," specificaily through His plan of salvation in Christ. See *Homilia de fide*, l; PG 31:464A; ibid., 2; PG 31:468BC. See also *De Spiritu Sancto*, 7,16; PG 32:93C; ibid., 15,35; PG 32:128C; and ibid., 16,39; PG 32:140B.

[29] *Homilia de fide*, 1; PG 31:464BC.

[30] Saint Basil is one of the many exponents of apophatic theology in the great patristic tradition of the East. Basil's attitude is not to discredit human reason and/or human expression, but to stress God's transcendence, incomprehensibility, and ineffability. On other occasions, Saint Basil expresses confidence in our reason, a gift that God gave us to use for knowledge of Him (see *Letter* 233, 1-2; PG 32:864C-68B). He also expresses confidence in our expression, even if he does this in an apologetical context; The Son of God, he says, being Word of God, is fully whatever the Father is in His divinity, "as our spoken word reflects the full content of our mind" (ὁ ἡμέτερος λόγος ὅλην ἡμῶν ἀπεικονίζει τὴν διάνοιαν) *In illud, in principio erat Verbum*, 3; PG 31:477BC.

[31] *Homilia de fide*, 1; PG 31-163AC; and ibid., l; PG 31-165C.

[32] "Ἐροῦμεν δέ, οὐχ ὅσος ἐστιν ὁ Θεός, ἀλλ᾿ ὅσον ἡμῖν ἐφικτόν" Ibid., l; PG 31:465A.

[33] Ibid., 1; PG 31:465B.

[34] "Ἐπέκεινα τούτων" Ibid., 1; PG 31:465C. see also *De Spiritu Sancto*, 22, 53 PG 32 165D.

[35] *Homilia de fide*, 2; PG 31:465C.

[36] Ibid., 1; PG 31:465A.

[37] *Letter* 52,3; PG 32:396A.

[38] *De Spiritu Sancto*, 22,53; PG 32:165D. The text refers to the Holy Spirit, being in His nature "beyond human understanding" (ἐπέκεινα ἀνθρωπίνης ἐννοίας), like the Father and the Son. On several other occasions in his writings, Saint Basil develops the theme of divine transcendence and incomprehensibility. He often attacks the rationalism of his opponents, the Arians and the Sabellians. Basil tries to reason with them. He tells them that there is no shame not to know the mysteries of God, pertaining to the essence and the mode of existing of the persons of the Holy Trinity. There are so many mysteries, he says, pertaining to this world and to our earthly existence, which we still ignore. If it is so, he asks, what is wrong with confessing our ignorance concerning the mysteries of God? see *Adversus Eunomium* 1,13; PG 29:541BC; ibid., 3, 6; PG 29:668AB; *Contra Sabellianos*, 6; PG 31:613AB; *In Hexaemeron*, 2,2; PG 29:32B; ed. Giel, p. 144; and ibid., 2,2; PG 29:33AB; ed. Giet, p. 148.

[39] *In Hexaemeron*, 2,1; PG 29:28C; ed. Giet, p. 138-39. see also *De Spiritu Sancto*, 27,26; PG 32:189AB. This theme of the Tabernacle where the divine mystery is hidden is also very dear to Saint Gregory of Nyssa. To describe it, Gregory uses the same terms as his brother and teacher (Saint Basil) those of mystery religions: ἄδυτα, ἐπόψεται, ἀπόρρητα, ἀπρόσιτος. See Gregory of Nyssa, *De vita Moysis*; PG 44:380B. Cf Leys, *L'image de Dieu*, p. 32.

[40] *In Hexaemeron*, 2,1; PG 29:28 CD; ed. Giet, pp.138-39.

[41] See, for instance, what Saint Basil says in his *Adversus Eunomium*, 4,32: PG 29:648A: "For the created things show forth (the Creator's) power, wisdom, and art" (Δυνάμεως γὰρ, καὶ σοφίας, καὶ τέχνης... ἐπιδεικτικά ἐστι τὰ ποιήματα).

[42] *Letter* 235.1; PG 32:872B. *The Nicean Fathers*, vol. 8, p. 275, column 1, renders "δημιουργήματα" (created things) with "works." I feel that this translation is not specific enough. In my estimation, the Greek text refers to Rom 1.20. Evidence of this should be found in the English translation.

[43] See for example Rom 1.19,20.

[44] *In Hexaemeron*, 1, 6; PG 29:16BC; ed. Giet, pp. 110-111. see also ibid., 1,5; PG 29:13B; ed Giet, p. 106; ibid., 3,10; PG 29:77BC; ed. Giet, p. 242; ibid., 6,1; PG 29:117BC; ed. Giet, p. 326; and *In Psalmum XXVIII*, 3; PG 29:289BC. The quotation comes from Rom 1. 20.

[45] *In Hexaemeron*, 7,6; PG 26:161B; ibid., 1,7; PG 29:17B; ibid., 9,5, PG 29:200B; *In ebriosos*, 6; PG 31:456B; *In Psalmum XXXII*, 3; PG 29:329B, *In martyrem Iulittam*, 3; PG 31:224C; *In Psalmum XXXIII*, 3; PG 29:357A; *Letter* 235,1; PG 32:872A; *Adversus Eunomium*, 1,14; PG 29:544BC; *In principium Proverbiorum*, 3; PG 31:389C-92B. A complete list of all Saint Basil's passages on this theme is given in my thesis, *La dialectique*, pp. 77-78.

[46] "Microcosm" (μικρόκοσμος) stands for "small world." It is a philosophical term of Stoic origin. In the time of Saint Basil it was used by philosophers to indicate that man is a summary of the whole world. Being such he is at the same time the representative of the world unity and the witness to it. From an epistemological point of view, man is able to understand the world because he contains the world in him [See Christos Androutsos, Λεξικὸν τῆς Φιλοσοφίας, 2nd

ed. (Thessalonike, 1965), p. 241]. Saint Basil adjusted this philosophical doctrine from a Christian point of view. He uses the term to indicate that man, inferior by little to the angels, constituted of two principles, material and spiritual, is a summary of the whole creation, both visible and imisible. At the same time man himself is a means of knowing the whole creation, especially as revealing God's wisdom and splendor. See the text from the Saint's homily *In Illud, attende* which follows this note.

[47] *In illud. attende,* 7; PG 31:213D-16A

[48] *In Hexaemeron,* 9,6; PG 29:204BC; ed. Giet, pp. 512-14; cf. ibid., 6, 1; PG 29:120A; ed. Giet, p. 828. cf. also *Ad adolescentes,* 7; PG 8l:908BC; ed. Boulenger, 9; p. 55, lines 30-33; also, *In illud, attende,* 8; PG 3l:217B. The text upon which Saint Basil comments is from Ps 138 (139):6. Saint Basil makes use of the text of Septuagint, substantially different at this point from the original Hebrew.

[49] *In Hexaemeron,* 6,1; PG 29:117D-20A; ed. Giet, p. 828.

[50] *In Psalmum XLVIII.* 8; PG 29:449B.

[51] "Μοῖράν τινα τῆς ἰδίας αὐτοῦ χάριτος ἐναπέθετο τῷ ἀνθρώπῳ, ἵνα τῷ ὁμοίῳ ἐπιγινώσκῃ τὸ ὅμοιον." Ibid., 8; PG 29:449BD. Cf. *Dicta tempore famis,* 5; PG 31:317AB.

[52] *In illud, attende,* 7; PG 31:216A. Cf. *Regulae fusius,* 2,1; PG 31:908BC. Here there is an explicit attack against Plato's doctrine on the pre-existence of "souls-intelligences," incarnated only after their fall [See references from Plato's works given above. Also, on Platos's doctrine on the origin of the soul and its relation to the body, see the recent work by Athenagoras Zakopoulos, *Plato on Man* (New York, 1975), pp. 49-53, and pp. 73-74].

[53] *In illud, attende* 8; PG 3l:2l7B.

[54] *Letter* 234,1; PG 32:868C; cf. *Letter* 235, 2; PG 32:872CD.

[55] "Εἰδέναι… ὁμολογοῦμεν τὸ γνωστὸν τοῦ Θεοῦ." *Letter* 235,2; PG 32:872D. Reference to Rom 1:19.

[56] *Adversus Eunomium,* 1,10; PG 29:533C-36D; ibid., 2,24; PG 29:625C. Cf. *Letter* 52, 3. PG 32:396A; ed. Courtonne, 3; p. 136, lines 10-20. These attributes of God, which "surround" the essence, are not the "propria personarum" (ἰδιαζόντως ἐπιθεωρούμενα); see *Letter* 38,6; PG 32:336C; ed. Courtonne, p. 89, line 7; see also my thesis, *La dialectique* p. 57). These attributes are the energies of God, which are the divine reality as it is accessible to us. The divine essence remains incommunicable inaccessible and unapproachable. See Vladimir Lossky, *The Mystical Theology of the Eastern Church,* 2nd ed. (Cambridge, England, 1968), pp. 67-90.

[57] *Adversus Eunomium,* 1,13-14; PG 29:544A. See also ibid., 1,13; PG 29:541BC; and ibid., 2,24; PG 29:628A.

[58] *Letter* 234.2; PG 32:689C.

[59] "Αἱ μὲν γὰρ ἐνέργειαι αὐτοῦ πρὸς ἡμᾶς καταβαίνουσιν, ἡ δὲ οὐσία αὐτοῦ μένει ἀπρόσιτος", *Letter* 234,1; PG 32:689AB. See also *Letter* 235,2; PG 32:872C-73A Cf. *Letter* 234,2; PG 32:689B; *Adversus Eunomium,* 1,14; PG 29:544BC-45A; *Letter* 38,3; PG 32:328C-29A; ed. Courtonne, pp. 83-84, lines 33-41. See comments by Lossky, *The Mystical Theology,* pp. 71-72, where the author quotes the first of these texts. Saint Gregory Palamas makes an extensive

use of this text in this *Contra Acindynum* [Πρὸς Ἀκίνδυνον ἀντιρρητικοί, ed. Leonidas Contos-Basil Fanourgakis (Thessalonike, 1970), pp. 42-45]. On the development of this distinction between essence and energies by Saint Gregory Palamas see John Meyendorff, *A Study of Gregory Palamas,* trans. George Lawrence (London, 1964), pp. 202-26.

[60] *Adversus Eunomium,* 2,4; PG 29:580B. Cf. *Letter* 234,2; PG 32:869B

[61] *Homilia de fide,* 1; PG 31:464C. Cf. *In Mamantem martyrem,* 3; PC 31:593B; *De Spiritu Sancto,* 26,62; PG 32:131CD. See also *In Hexaemeron,* 1,1; PG 29:5BC; ed. Giet, p. 90; ibid., 6,l; PG 29:117B; ed. Giet, p. 326.

[62] *De ieunio,* 1,6; PG 31:172BC. Cf. *In Gordium martyrem,* 2; PG 31:496B.

[63] *Adversus Eunomium,* 1,12; PG 29:540BC. Cf. ibid., 2,4; PG 29:540A.

[64] Ibid., 2,7; PG 29:534C.

[65] Ibid., 1,12; PG 29:540A.

[66] Ibid., 1,12; PG 29:540AB.

[67] *In Psalmum XXXII,* 3; PG 29:329B. See also *Letter* 235,1; PG 32:872BC; cf. *Letter* 234,2; PG 32:869B.

[68] *Letter* 234,3; PG 32:869D-72A.

[69] *In principium Proverbiorum,* 14; PG 31:416CD; cf. ibid., 14; PG 31:417A. See also: *De fide,* 2; PG 31:681B; and ibid., 3; PG 31:684A.

[70] *In Psalmum CXIV,* 5; PG 29:492C-93C.

[71] *De fide,* 3; PG 31:684A; also, *Letter* 233,2; PG 32:868B. Quote from 1 Cor 13.10.

[72] *In Psalmum XXXIII,* 11; PG 29:377BC.

[73] *De fide,* 2; PG 31:681A; also: ibid., 2; PG 31:681C; *Adversus Eunomium,* 3.7; PG 29,669C; *In Psalmum XXXII,* 5; PG 29:337A. Quote from 1 Cor 13.12.

[74] *Letter* 284,3; PG 32:869D-872A.

[75] *Letter* 204,6; PG 32:753A; also *Letter* 235,3; PG 32:876A; *De Spiritu Sancto,* 1, 2; PG 32:69As; and *Letter* 159, 1; PG 32:620B.

[76] *In Sanctum Baptisma,* 1; PG 31 424C.

[77] *Adversus Eunomium,* 2,19; PG 29:612C. See also ibid., 2,19; PG 29:613A. Reference is made to Eph 1:1.

[78] *In Psalmum XIV,* 1,3; PG 29:256CD.

[79] *Letter* 235,3; PG 32:873C. See also the translation of the *The Nicene Fathers,* vol. 8, p. 275, column 2.

[80] *In Mamantem martyrem,* 4; PG 31:597A.

[81] *Regulae fusius,* Prooemium, 4; PG 31:897CD.

[82] *Quod Deus non est auctor malorum,* 6; PG 31:344BC.

[83] *In illud, attende,* 6; PG 31:213A.

[84] *Quod Deus,* 6; PG 31:344B. Cf. Moralia, 80, 9; PG 31:864A; *De gratiarum actione,* 6; PG 31:244A.

[85] *Quod Deus,* 6: PG 31:344B; cf. ibid., 6; PG 31:344C.

[86] *Regulae brevius tractatae,* 20; PG 31:1097A; see also *De iudicio Dei,* 3; PG 31:656C-657AB. Quote from Rom 1:28-32.

[87] *In Psalmum XLVIII,* 8; PG 29:449D-452A. Cf. *Letter* 233,1; PG 32:865A.

[88] *De humilitate,* 4; PG 31:532B. Quotations from 1 Cor 4:7 and Gal 4:9. The translation is that of the Revised Standard Version.

[89] See for example *In Psalmum XIV,* 1,3; PG 29:256C, where, probably on the basis of 1 Cor 3:9, Basil speaks of man as a "co-worker of salvation" (συνεργὸν σωτηρίας) with God.

[90] *Letter* 235,3; PG 32:876A.

[91] In some instances, Saint Basil understands "ἐπίγνωσις" and "οἰκείωσις" as cause and effect. For example, in his work *On the Holy Spirit* one can gather this kind of relation between "true knowledge" and "closeness" (familiarity) with God: Basil says that Gregory the Wonder-worker, being himself familiar (ᾠκειωωμένος) with God, brings close to God (προσήγαγε τῷ Θεῷ) the people entrusted to him, through true knowledge (διὰ τῆς ἐπιγνώσεως), *De Spiritu Sancto,* 29,74; PG 32:205BC. Also in *Adversus Eunomium,* 2,19; PG 29:612C (quoted above) there is an interesting parallelism established between "knowledge of God-union with God," and "lack of truth-familiarity with the nonexistence of falsehood." Basil says that holy men are considered to be "united with the truly Existing through true knowledge" (ἡνωμένοι τῶ Ὄντι διὰ τῆς ἐπιγνώσεως), whereas wicked people are "familiar" with the non-existance of falsehood by lack of truth" (τῇ ἀνυπαρξίᾳ τοῦ ψεύδους οἰκειωθέντες... διᾶ τὴν στέρησιν τῆς ἀληθείας).

In other instances, the two terms, ἐπίγνωσις and οἰκείωσις are seen as interdependent. They are used as quasi-synonymous terms: the distinction one can establish between the two is that ἐπίγνωσις is a cause which contains its effect (οἰκείωσις), whereas the latter (οἰκείωσις) is an effect which contains its cause (ἐπίγνωσις). An example of this is found in the letter to Amphilochios quoted in the previous note. In this letter, ἐπίγνωσις, or simply "γνῶσις Θεοῦ" is the kind of cause which contains its effect οἰκείωσις. Vice versa, οἰκείωσις Θεῷ is the effect containing its cause, ἐπίγνωσις Θεοῦ. One of the meanings that Saint Basil finds in γνῶσις Θεοῦ is that of οἰκείωσις Θεῶ. For Basil, this is the usual Scriptural meaning of "knowledge;" it implies the experience of intimate union between persons, and, at the same time, it is this experience of communion between them. This is also true of the knowledge of God. Here is the text: "Is it not the custom of the Scripture to use the word 'know' (ἔγνω) of nuptial embraces (ἐπὶ τῶν γαμικῶν συμπλοκῶν)? The statement that God shall be known from the mercy seat means that He will be known to His worshippers. And the Lord knoweth (ἔγνω) them that are His, means that on account of their good works He receives them into intimate communion (οἰκείωσις) with Him." *Letter* 235, 3; PG 32:876A. The translation here is that of *The Nicene Fathers,* 8:275-76.

[92] On this "kinship" see *Regulae fusius,* 2,2; PG 31:912BC.

[93] *In Psalmum VII,* 1; PG 29:229C.

[94] *Letter* 236,1; PG 32:876C. Cf. *Regulae fusius,* 55,3; PG 31:1048C.

[95] *Regulae fusius,* 37,3; PG 31:1013B; Saint Basil exhorts his monks not to begin their day without "enjoying" God through the rememberance of Him: "Do not undertake any care before enjoying the understanding of God which comes from Him (τῇ παρὰ τοῦ Θεοῦ ἐννοίᾳ ἐνευφρανθῆναι), according to what it is written: I have remembered God, and have rejoiced (Ἐμνήσθην τοῦ Θεοῦ, καὶ ηὐφράνθην). Quotation from Ps 76(77).4.

[96] *Dicta tempore famis,* 8; PG 31:325D-28A. The theme of mystical marriage

with Christ, the Bridegegroom, is very dear to all mystics and mystic theologians of our Christian tradition. Saint Basil is no exception to this rule. For example, here is what he says in the homily quoted here: "Do not present the Bridegroom with a bride who is ugly (ἄμορφον) and without ornaments (ἄκοσμον). In seeing her in this condition, He might dislike her (or hate her: μισήσῃ) and refuse to take her into His intimacy... But keep her beautiful (or pretty: εὔμορφον)...so that she can light her candle together with the wise virgins, keeping alive the fire of knowledge, and not being short in the oil of good deeds" (μὴ λείπουσα τῶν κατορθωμάτων τὸ ἔλαιον). Here reference is made to Mt 25.4.

[97] See *In Psalmum XLVIII*, 8; PG 29:449C. Cf. *De gratiarum actione*, 2; PG 31:221C.

[98] *Quod Deus*, 6; PG 31:344B.

[99] *Letter* 233, 1-2; PG 32:864C-65C.

[100] *Quod Deus*, 6; PG 31:344BC.

[101] *De humilitate*, 1; PG 31:525B.

[102] *Quod Deus*, 7; PG 31:345A.

[103] Ibid.

[104] See *De humilitate*, 1; PG 31:525AB.

[105] Ibid.

[106] See *De gratiarum actione*, 2; PG 31:224A.

[107] See *De Spiritu Sancto*, 14,32; PG 32:124D-125A; ed. Giet, p. 32. Ibid., 15-35; PG 32:129D; ed. Giet, p. 32. Ibid., 15, 36; PG 32:132B. See also *In Sanctum Baptisma*, 2; PG 31:428A.

[108] See *Regulae brevius*, Prooemium; PG 31:1080A. See also *De iudicio Dei*, 8; PG 31:673B, and *Liturgy*, ed. Brightman, p. 322, lines11-12; p. 402, lines 9-10.

[109] *In Psalmum XLV*, 7; PG 29:425D-28A.

[110] See *Regulae brevius*, 258; PG 31:1248CD. See also *De gratiarum actione*, 2; PG 31:224A; In *Psalmum XLVIII*, 8; PG 29:452B; and *In illud, attende*, 6; PG 31:213A.

[111] *De Spiritu Sancto*, 14.33; PG 32:125D-28A.

[112] *In Psalmum XLV*, 5; PG 29:424CD. Cf. *Adversus Eunomium*, 1,7; PG 29:525A. Reference is made to Eph 5:8.

[113] *In Psalmum XIII*, 4; PG 29:460B. Reference is made to Mt. 4:16; Lk 1:78-9; and Jn 1:9.

[114] *Regulae brevius*, 1; PG 31:1081AB.

[115] *Adversus Eunomium*, 2,16; PG 29:604B.

[116] See *In Psalmum XIV*, 1,3; PG 29:526D. See also *In Psalmum XLIV*, 6; PG 29:401B.

[117] *De Spiritu Sancto*, 8,17; PG 32:97B.

[118] *Adversus Eunomium*, 1,7; PG 29:525B. Saint Basil hints to Jn 6:48-58, where Christ speaks of Himself as the "Bread of Life." Saint John's context is eucharistic. Here, for apologetical reasons, Saint Basil reduces this doctrine of Christ being the Bread of Life to only one aspect of it, that of Christ being the "familiar food of our mind." Yet, Saint Basil's doctrine concerning the nature

and function of the human mind obviously differs from the Eunomian, Neoplatonic, and Origenistic view of the intellect having the power to fully know God in reaching God's essence itself (cf. Meyendorff, *Byzantine Theology*, pp. 26-28). For Saint Basil, this knowledge of God and the encounter with Him as Truth revealed in Christ, Bread of the human mind, is an act of the whole being of man. Through it, man achieves Communion with God without reaching His essence, and without losing his human, "created" identity. On the contrary, through a eucharistic reception, as it were, of the Bread of the human mind (Christ the Incarnate Truth) the proper characteristics of the human soul are preserved; its faculties elevated; and its purpose fulfilled, as it reaches the status of union with God, a status of experiential knowledge of God's energies, through which this union is achieved.

Later on, Pseudo-Dionysios reduces the Eucharist to a mere symbol or "the union of the intellect with God and Christ" (Meyendorff, *Byzantine Theology*, p. 28). One can ask the question if there is continuity between Saint Basil's doctrine on "Christ, Bread of the human mind," and that of Pseudo-Dionysios. The answer is that there is no continuity between the two. When Saint Basil speaks of Christ as the "Bread of the human mind," it is just another way for him to speak of Christ as the Incarnate Truth. This "Bread" and this "Truth" are means of union and communion with God, not, as tor Pseudo-Dionysios, a mere symbol of this union.

[119] *In Psalmum XLV,* 6; PG 29:445 B. Quote from 1 Cor 2.16.

[120] *De Spiritu Sancto,* 30,79; PG 32:217BC.

[121] *Letter* 233,l; PG 32:865AC.

[122] *Letter* 233,1; PG 32:865A. Cf. *De Spiritu Sancto,* 1,2; PG 32:69AB.

[123] *In Sanctum Baptisma,* 1: PG 31:424C.

[124] *De Spiritu Sancto,* 29,75; PG 32:209AB. Cf. ibid., 15,35; PG 32:132A.

[125] *De iudicio Dei,* 1; PG 31:653AC. Cf. *Moralia,* 80,9; PG 31:864A; and *Regulae brevius,* 1; PG 31:1081A.

[126] *De Spiritu Sancto,* 24,56; PG 32:172C.

[127] *Adversus Eunomium,* 3,6; PG 29:668C.

[128] Ibid., 3, 5; PG 29:665BC.

[129] In the Septuagint, the title for this Psalm is: "Song for the Beloved One" (ᾠδὶ ὑπὲρ τοῦ ἀγαπητοῦ). The Hebrew title is: "Love Song." Basil comments on the Greek title: the Beloved One is Christ.

[130] *In Psalmum XLIV.* 2; PG 29:392AB-C. Quote from Eph 4:22, and Col 3:10. As stated above, in Saint Basil's terms "ἐπίγνωσις" stands for "true knowledge," which is an "affective" and "moral" knowledge, offered by God to those who are worthy of His intimacy.

[131] See *In Psalmum XLIV,* 2; PG 29:389BC. See also ibid., 1-2; PG 29:388A-89A; and *In Psalmum LIX,* 2; PG 29:464B. On the theme of mystical marriage of the soul with Christ the Bridegroom see also *Dicta tempore famis,* 8; PG 31:325D-28A, quoted above.

[132] *In Psalmum XLIV,* 2; PG 29:389B.

[133] *De iudicio Dei,* 6; PG 31:688AB. Cf. *Regulae fusius,* 260; PG 31:1256BC; ibid., 114; PG 31:1160B; and ibid., 269; PG 31:1268C. Quote from 2 Cor l0.4-5.

[134] *Regulae fusius*, 269; PG 31:1268BC (quotations from Gal 5;19-21; Rom 8.7; and 2 Cor 10.4-5). Cf. ibid., 20; PG 31:1096D-97A; *De iudicio Dei*, 3; PG 31:656C-57B; *In Psalmum XXVIII*, 5; PG 29:293D-97A; and *In Psalmum XLV*, 3; PG 29:421A.

[135] *De iudicio Dei*, 6; PG 31:668B.

[136] *Regulae fusius*, 224; PG 31:1232A.

[137] *De Spiritu Sancto*, 15,35; PG 32:129D; See also *In Sanctum Baptisma*, 2 PG 31:428A.

[138] *Letter* 2,2; PG 32:224C-25A; ed. Courtonne, p. 6, lines 1-12. See also: *Regulae fusius*, 5,1; PG 31:920C-21A, ibid., 8,2; PG 31:937C; *Regulae brevius* 218; PG 31:1228A; *In Psalmum XXXIII*, 1; PG 29:353BC; ibid., 3; PG 29:357B, *In Psalmum XLV*, 8; PG 29:428C-29A; and *In Psalmum XLVIII*, 11; PG 29:457B.

[139] See *In ebriosos*, 6; PG 31:456B. See also: *In illud, attende*, 8, PG 31:216C *In Psalmum XXXIII*, 3; PG 29:357AC. *In Psalmum XLV*, 8, PG 29:428C; *In Psalmum XLVIII*, 11; PG 29:460A; and *De Spiritu Sancto*, 22,53; PG 32:168AC.

[140] *De Spiritu Sancto*, 22,53; PG 32:168C. Cf. *De fide*, 2; PG 31:681A; *Letter* 2,2; PG 32:225AC; ed. Courtonne, pp. 6-7, lines 21-46. Cf, also *In principium Proverbiorum*, 4; PG 31:393B; and *In illud, attende*, 7; PG 31:216B. An indirect reference is made to Mt 5.8

[141] *Regulae brevius*, 21; PG 31:1097B. See also ibid., 32, PG 31:1104C; ibid., 45; PG 31:1112A; and *In Psalmum XXXIII*, 1; PG 29:353BC.

[142] *Letter* l59,1; PG 32:620B. Cf. *Regulae fusius*, Prooemium; PG 31:896B.

[143] *Regulae fusius*, Prooemium; PG 31:896B-D. See also ibid., 2, 1-3, PG 31:908B-16C; and *In Psalmum XLV*, 7; PG 29:428A.

[144] *De Spiritu Sancto*, 30,78; PG 32:217C. Cf. ibid., 8,17; PG 32:97B; *In Psalmum XXIII*, 4; PG 29:360BC; *In Psalmum XL V*, 5; PG 29:424C; *In ebriosos*, 1, PG 31:445A; *In Principium Proverbiorum*, 14; PG 31:416AB; and *Regulae brevius*, 248; PG 31:1248C-49A.

[145] *Homilia de fide*, 3; PG 31:169B; see also ibid., 3; PG 31:472A; *In illud, attende*, 6; PG 31:213A; and *De Spiritu Sancto*, 22,53; PG 32:168C.

[146] *In Psalmum XLV*, 8; PG 29:429B.

[147] *De Spiritu Sancto*, 15,35; PG 32:128C. See also: ibid., 8, 18; PG 32:100B (quotation from Eph 2.18); and *Contra Sabellianos*, 2; PG 31:601C.

[148] *De Spiritu Sancto*, 8,18; PG 32:100C.

[149] Ibid., 26, 61; PG 32:180C. Cf. *De ieiunio*, 1. 9; PG 31:180C.

[150] *De Spiritu Sancto*, 26,64; PG 32:185BC. See also: *Letter* 38, 4 PG 32:329C; *Letter* 226,3; PG 32:849A; *Adversus Eunomium*, 1,17; PG 29:552B, ibid. 1,18: PG 29:553A; and ibid., 1,26; PG 29:569BC. Cf. *Letter* 38,8; PG 32:340AC; *Contra Sabellianos*, 2; PG 31:601C; ibid., 4; PG 31:608C, *De Spiritu Sancto*, 8,18 PG 32:100C; ibid., 8,19: PG 32:101C; ibid., 8,21; PG 32:105BC; and ibid., 9,23; PG 32:109B.

[151] *De Spiritu Sancto*, 18,47; PG 32:153B.

[152] "Ἐπὶ τὸν Θεὸν καταφεύγει, μόνην εἶναι ἡγούμενος ἀνάπαυσιν τὴν ἐν αὐτῷ διαμονήν" *In Psalmum XXXIII*, 6; PG 29:416C.

[153] *In Psalmum XXXIII*, 6; PG 29:365A. See also ibid., 7; PG 29:368C, and *In Psalmum XIV*, 4; PG 29:421BC.

[154] "ἡ ... οὐσία αὐτοῦ μένει ἀπρόσιτος." *Letter* 234, 1; PG 32:869B.

[155] "αἱ ... ἐνέργειαι αὐτοῦ πρὸς ἡμᾶς καταβαίνουσιν." *Letter* 234,1; PG 32:869AB.

Three

Applications of the Theme "Eikon Theou" (Image of God) According to Saint Basil the Great[1]

The theme of the image of God finds various applications in the theology of Saint Basil the Great. Among these applications are those in the domain of Trinitarian theology, angelology, anthropology, Christology, ecclesiology, and finally, eschatology. As a small contribution to the understanding of the theology of this great Cappadocian father, the present study intends to briefly discuss each of these applications.

TRINITARIAN DOCTRINE
Among the various applications of the theme of the image of God, those made in the field of "Theology" are particularly important. Saint Basil establishes the divinity of the Son of God by using the scriptural theme of the image.

The Son, Image of the Invisible
Against Arianism, which attacked the divinity of the Son of God, Basil affirms the Son's divinity by using the theme of the image of God. The Son is the living image of the Invisible God. This means that the Son, as an image of God, has the same essence as God. Because He is the perfect image of the Father, he reflects not only the "magnificent attributes" of the essence of the Father, but also the very essence itself. Thus, the Son fully reflects both the essence and energies of God the Father.[2] Nevertheless,

49

although the essence and energies of the Son are identical to those of the Father, the persons of the Father and of the Son are by no means identical. Each person possesses his unique personal properties, "*propria personarum.*" In this way the identity of essence and energies does not exclude the diversity of persons between the Father and the Son: the "*propria personarum*" (ἰδιαζόντως ἐπιθεωρούμενα)[3] are not reflected in the image of God. The paradox of similarity and dissimilarity between image and its archetype is kept, even in the most perfect expression of this image, the image of God in His Son.[4]

The Spirit of God: Image of the Son?

The fifth book of *Against Eunomius,* employs the theme of image in defending the divinity of the Holy Spirit: "As Christ is the image of God…so the Spirit is the image of the Son,"[5] also, "the Spirit is the visible and natural image of God and of the Lord."[6] However, this work is rejected as inauthentic and is attributed to Didymos the Blind.

In his authentic works, Saint Basil does not develop the idea of the Holy Spirit as the image of God. There are two reasons for this: the first is methodological; the second is theological. Insofar as methodology is concerned, Basil always establishes his doctrine on the basis of Holy Scripture. Reasonings are accepted to elaborate a doctrine only if the doctrine is basically found in Holy Scripture. Yet, nowhere in the Scripture is the Spirit said to be the "image of God" or the "image of the Son." For this reason Basil does not draw upon the theme of image in his justification of the divinity of the Spirit.

Moreover, from a theological perspective, the idea of the Spirit as the "image of God" or as the "image of Christ" violates the scriptural doctrine of "monarchy" in the divinity[7] advocated by Basil. According to the doctrine of monarchy, the Father has an absolute supremacy in the All-Holy Trinity. He is the source and the principle in the life of the Blessed Trinity: "The natural goodness, the innate holiness, the royal dignity, passes from the Father through the Only Begotten to the Spirit."[8] According to this doctrine, if an "image passes" to the Spirit through the Son, it must be the image of God the Father. Yet, Saint Basil does not call the Spirit the image of God the Father. The Spirit is called the "spiritual light" which enlightens man and shows him the Image of the Invisible God: Christ, through Whom man contemplates the light of the paternal Archetype.[9]

ANGELOLOGY

Are the angels created in the image of God? Saint Basil does not give an explicit answer to this question. There is only one text in the *Hexæmeron* which refers to the image of God and the angels. In this instance, he refutes the Philonian doctrine of the "image of angels."[10] According to this doctrine, God creates man with the assistance of the angels[11] and is addressing the angels when He says: "Let us make man according to our image and likeness." Basil states that the Son of God, not the angels, is the one to whom God addressed the words of Genesis 1:26. The Son of God, not the angels, is the "living image" of God, identical with the fatherly Archetype. However, he does not state whether the angels themselves are made in the image of God.

Nevertheless, the concept of the creation of the angels themselves in the image of God is implied in Saint Basil's theology. The same constitutive elements of the image are found in the angels and in man: Basil speaks frequently of the reason and the freedom of the angels; he speaks of their knowledge and love of God, of their perfection, their holiness, and their communion in the Holy Spirit. They are established in the Good through the use of their free will; they are "stable" in their choice for God, even though they are of "unstable" nature, as is man.[12] For Saint Basil, the angels are superior to man, setting an example for him to follow: "Man, who pursues perfection, elevates himself to the dignity of angels;"[13] he does this because he is created in the image of God, thus being virtuous like the angels.[14] If man, although he is inferior to the angels, has the potential of being assimilated with God because of the image of God in him, the angels, who have the same and even superior prerogatives than man, should also be created in the image of God. This, although the creation of the angels in the image of God is not explicitly stated – probably either because it is not scriptural, or because the opportunity or need of making such a statement did not arise – nevertheless, this doctrine is in continuity with the theology of Saint Basil.

ANTHROPOLOGY

Saint Basil uses the theme of the image of God mostly in the domain of anthropology, where he makes multiple applications of it.

Saint Basil sees the creation of man in the image of God as an expression of God's love towards man. Man is particularly favored among God's creation, elevated by God to the special dignity of being created in His image. This dignity distinguishes man from the rest of creation: man is the only one to be created in the image of God.[15]

What in man reflects the image of God? Where in man's dual nature, both material and spiritual, is the image of God to be found? Saint Basil excludes the body from the image of God. Unlike his brother Gregory of Nyssa,[16] Basil believes that man's body cannot reflect God, because God is bodiless.[17] Only the human soul is created in the image of God. The soul possesses whatever there is which makes man God-like. Thus man is led to knowledge of God through his soul, through that which within him is Godlike; in this way he gains knowledge of "the Like by the like." In knowing the soul as "bodiless and invisible," man knows God, bodiless and invisible.[18]

More specifically, Saint Basil notes the special attributes of man which characterize the image of God within him. Man's reason (λογικὸν) and his freedom of will (αὐτεξούσιον) are seen by him as the main faculties of the human soul which reflect the image of God in man. They make man God-like; furthermore, it is through their good use that man progresses in likeness with God.[19] Our "affectivity," which is principally our faculty of love, is also included in the image of God in us. God has implanted in us the seeds of our force of loving the Creator. Man is called to cultivate these seeds, to know and love God, to unite himself with Him – to resemble Him.[20] Furthermore, the power that man has over creation is included as a consequence of man's creation in the image of God: the "royal faculty" (ἡγεμονικὸν) is given to man so that he might master the creation.[21] Moreover, the human soul is crowned with immortality, which is part of the image of God in man.[22]

What exactly does Saint Basil understand when he speaks of "image of God" in reference to the hypostases of the Holy Trinity? Is man created "in the image of the Trinity," as Saint Augustine would say in the West?

The question seems legitimate, since Saint Basil cites the same attributes which St. Augustine notes as the elements of the image of God in man: reason, will, and love.[23] Yet, Saint Basil does not make the same use of these elements. For Augustine, these elements are equivalent to the *propria personarum* of the Father, the Son and the Holy Spirit; thus reason is ascribed to the Father, will to the Son, and love to the Holy Spirit. On the contrary, for Saint Basil these faculties of the soul reflect the common attributes (κοινῶς ἐπιθεωρούμενα) of the divine substance, distinct from the substance itself and common to the three hypostases of the Holy Trinity. The *propria personarum* are not reflected in the image of God in man.[24]

For Saint Basil, man is not called the "image of the Father," or the "image of the Son," or the "image of the Holy Spirit." Only the Son of God is called the image of the Father, the "Image of the Invisible God." What man is in relation to the hypostases in the Trinity, is that he is "in the image of God" (the Father), which the Son imprints in us, being our "creative cause," and the Spirit leads to perfection, being our "perfecting cause." It is only the Father who, being our "primordial cause," is the source of the "image of God" in us. The other two persons do not have their image in us as persons.

As for the "nature" of this image, the image of God in us is the reflection in us of divine attributes, such as: immortality, reason, freedom, will, love, perfection and holiness, otherwise called the energies of God, common to the three persons of the Holy Trinity.[25]

As one can see, this interpretation of the image of God in us in Saint Basil's theology has nothing in common with the Augustinian view of man as an "image of the Trinity."[26] R. Leys supports this conclusion when speaking of the theology of Basil's brother, Saint Gregory of Nyssa; indeed he finds no place for the view of man created in the image of the Trinity in Saint Gregory as in any Eastern Father.[27] Saint Basil is no exception.

SPECIAL PROBLEMS

Image and Likeness

One of the special problems concerning the image of God in man is the distinction between "image" and "likeness." This distinction, considered by some scholars as a philosophical one, has its beginning in Origen.[28] It is greatly developed in the homilies *On the Human Structure*, attributed to Saint Basil.[29]

Following Origen, in the first homily *On the Human Structure*, Basil establishes the distinction between "image" and "likeness" as a distinction between the Aristotelian terms δύναμις (power) and ἐνέργεια (energy, action):

> The reasonable and spiritual part of my being, in which I am created in the image of God, is a power. The action consists in the accomplishment of virtue, in achieving good in my activity, and reaching the likeness of God through my best [Christian] behavior.
>
> Thus, since my creation, I have received in my nature what makes me to be in the image of God: this is the origin and the roots of the good in me. The likeness of God comes to me through my actions, my labors to achieve the good, my virtuous life. This is why my Creator has not attributed to me the likeness of God at my creation. For it is written in the Gospel: 'Become (γίνεσθε) perfect, as our heavenly Father is perfect.'[30]

Fr. E. Stephanou is correct in seeing in this text the fulfillment of the promise given by Saint Basil in his last homily, *On Hexæmeron*. Saint Basil says: "In what has man the image of God and how does he participate in His likeness? This is what we are going to discuss in what follows, if God allows."[31] This plan is followed by the homilies *On the Human Structure:*

The end of the ninth homily gives the division of the next homily planned by Basil: 'Ἐν τίνι οὖν ἔχει τὸ κατ' εἰκόνα Θεοῦ ὁ ἄνθρωπος καὶ πῶς μεταλαμβάνει τοῦ καθ' ὁμοίωσιν.' The originality of the answer is already contained in the way the question is posed by the Saint: to be κατ' εἰκόνα of God is a matter of nature (ἔχει), whereas to be καθ' ὁμοίωσιν of God is a matter of personal effort and of freedom of will (μεταλαμβάνει). Now, the *Ia De Structura* is entirely concerned with responding to this clear division. The author summarizes his answer in the following nice sentence, quoted by Saint Maximos in his *Loci Communes*. 'Ὥστε τὸ κατ' εἰκόνα μὲν ἔχεις ἐκ τοῦ λογικός εἶναι, καθ' ὁμοίωσιν δὲ γένῃ ἐκ τοῦ χρηστότητα ἀναλαβεῖν.' (*Ia De Structura*, 21; PG 30:33A). I confess that the author of *De Hominis Structura* has captured and realized the original plan of Saint Basil well, based on an idea both nice and new.[32]

The same E. Stephanou[33] finds an interesting parallel doctrine in the homily *On Psalm 48*. In this text, the image of God in man is seen as the great natural privilege of man: man is "precious in his natural construction" (τὸ τίμιον ἐν τῇ φυσικῇ κατασκευῇ ἔχων) because of the image of God in him, which distinguishes him from the rest of creation.[34] On the basis of this image, man was called to become God-like: "Man was elevated above the whole creation; no creature but he is called the image of God in the highest. Yet, man did not realize his dignity: he stopped following God and resembling the Creator. On the contrary, he enslaved himself to his passions; he compared himself with the unreasonable animals; he became their equal."[35] S. Giet[36] finds a similar text in the book *On the Holy Spirit,* where Basil sees the purpose of man's creation as "resemblance with God, as much as this is possible for the human nature."[37] In the life of grace, through the operation of the Holy Spirit, man "abides in God, resembles God," and achieves the "ultimate desirable:" "he becomes God."[38] One thing is clear from these texts, that man has to *become* God-like, whereas he is created in the image of God, which makes him more precious than any other creature. The distinction between image and likeness is implied in these texts.

Other texts speak in the same sense. Thus, in the homily, *On Observing Yourself,* we read:

> You are a man, the only living being to be created by the hands of God Himself, Creator of the universe. Just think about it: is this privilege not enough to fill your heart with joy and confidence? Made in the image of Him who created you, you can elevate yourself to the dignity of angels, through your virtuous life. You are endowed with an intelligent soul, so that you know God, reason on the nature of beings, and collect the agreeable fruits of science. All animals on earth are subject to your authority.... These are your advantages as a human; but there is one of a superior order: God became man for you, the Holy Spirit poured out his grace; the dominion of death has been destroyed; the hope of resurrection has been given, divine precepts perfect your life; the observance of the commandments gives you the power to come closer to God; the Kingdom of Heaven and the crowns of justice are reserved for those who do not avoid the labors inherent in the practice of virtue.[39]

The same ideas are present in this text, as in the previous texts: the image of God in man is seen as the great natural privilege of man, imprinted in his reasonable soul. On the basis of this image, man has power over the whole creation. Departing from this image, man is able to journey towards God, and to achieve a dignity equal to that of the angels. In the life of grace, man receives extra help from God to achieve the purpose given to him at his creation: to become God-like, to unite himself with God, to participate in His glory.

The image of God in man as a reality given at his creation and the likeness of God as a reality to be fulfilled seem to be quite distinct in Saint Basil's thought. Yet, there is at least one important text from the *Great Rules* which seems to identify the two: it is the text of the "hymn of the benefits" that God bestowed upon man. The first of these benefits is that "God created man in His image and likeness" (κατ᾽ εἰκόνα Θεοῦ καὶ ὁμοίωσιν ποιήσας τὸν ἄνθρωπον ὁ Θεός).[40] This text dates from the early years of Saint Basil. It is possible that at this time Basil followed the biblical manner of speaking, according to which "image" and "likeness" are synonyms. It is possible that there is evolution in Saint Basil's thought: he introduces a distinction between two synonyms in order to present the Christian doctrine of a dynamic "image" of God in man, leading to likeness with God.

In the years of maturity of theological thought, man's creation in the image of God means, for Basil, that man is endowed with reason, capable of knowing God. The likeness of God is achieved through knowledge of God.[41] Image and likeness are distinguished as "power" and "action," the faculty of knowing and the activity of this faculty – that is, the knowledge and the love of God.[42]

Another related way of distinguishing between image and likeness in Saint Basil's thought is distinguishing between being and becoming, present in the minds of many of the Eastern Fathers.[43] The "image" is given at the beginning, but it has to be fully realized at the end of the process. "Image" is "likeness," or "similarity" with God. Yet, the "image" has to become fully the "likeness." Man has to realize the potential likeness with God, already present in the image. He has to become more and more what he already is: the image of God, that is, God-like. The power of knowing God, in which man has the image of God, can be used to know God, and thus, to be God-like through "assimilation" with Him in His energies.[44] The image of God in man, his reason and freedom of choice, is made perfect through activity, that is, through deployment of the potential which is in it. Without this activity the image remains static, unachieved, unfulfilled. It only realizes itself when it fully becomes the likeness of God.

In the last analysis, we can say that in Saint Basil's theology, the image is seen on an "ontological" level, as a matter of "nature." Likeness is seen on an ethical level, as a purpose to achieve. From this point of view, the distinction between image and likeness is not only a theoretical one, it is also very practical: it deals with the destiny of man himself. To achieve likeness with God on the basis of the image of God in man is to achieve the purpose for which man is created. To fail in this enterprise is to fail in achieving man's ultimate destiny.

Image and Gender

In Saint Basil's doctrine, the body is not directly involved with the image of God. The image is imprinted in the human soul, reflected by the superior faculties of the human spirit: intelligence and freedom of will. In this male and female are absolutely equal. Man and woman are equally created in the image of God, and they are equally called to resemble God. Saint Basil puts these words on the lips of Julitta the Martyr: "We are made of the same dough as men. Like them we are made in the image of God. The female sex is equally (ὁμοτίμως) as capable of virtue as is the male sex. Are not we then related to men in everything?"[45] "There is only one virtue both for man and woman," says Basil, "because there is only one creation of equal dignity for both." Consequently, "there is only one kind of reward for both… Those who have the same nature, have also the same activity. Those who are doing the same work receive an identical reward."[46]

Thus, male and female are equally created in the image of God. They are equally called to likeness with God. They receive the same rewards when they accomplish their common task.

Image and Evil

Through the image of God in man, the latter is called to know and to love God. Adam is called to "abide close to God" (πρόσεδρος Θεοῦ), and to "unite himself to God through love." Not to know God and not to be in union with Him through love, is to lose "life according to nature." To lose life according to nature is to "corrupt the soul made in the image of God," and to resemble the senseless beasts. This depravation of the human nature is called evil. Evil has no "ontological" existence. It is a "loss of the good." However, evil has a veritable psychological existence, with painful consequences in the ontological domain. The foundation of evil is not in God, for God created everything "good, even very good." The foundation of evil is in human freedom: "The source and the principle of evil are in us, in our free will." Two kinds of evil are distinguishable, according to Saint Basil: "evil according to its nature," that is, moral evil; and "evil according to our senses," that is, physical evil. The latter is often used by God to serve the good, and to fight the veritable evil, which is moral evil. This moral evil is the only evil deserving of its name: "Sin is the real evil, the only one to deserve this name." This evil "depends on our will, for we have the power to give in to the vice, or to abstain from it."[47]

Image and Grace

The work of divine economy consists of restoring the faculties of knowledge and love of the human soul, so as to orient them anew toward their true object: God. This is what restoration of the fallen image means; this is the work of Christ, man's "deliverance from death," that death which is a consequence of his sin, that is, his estrangement from God, his source of true life.

The "blessed end" of human life is the "knowledge of God."[48] This knowledge introduces man to God's familiarity. God offers Himself to man as an Object of Knowledge. This knowledge is not only intellectual, but also experiential. It "assimilates" man with God, it makes man God-like.[49] Reason, which reflects the image of God, is granted to man to that end.[50]

Adam failed to achieve this goal. The "fall" resulted from this failure: the tarnishing of the image of God in man, his comparison and resemblance not with God but with the senseless beasts, and separation from God, which is equal to death.[51] Christ liberates man from death, renews life in man, and restores the fallen image. The Spirit gives to this image its original beauty. Departing from this restored image, enlightened by the Holy Spirit to see the image of the invisible God in His Son, man is led to the knowledge of God, his "blessed end." In this knowledge man is united with God; man is transformed by Him; he resembles Him; he arrives to divine filiation, to "divine dignity," to "theosis," and he becomes "god."[52]

The above represents the theology of Saint Basil concerning the image in relation to the divine economy of the two persons of the Trinity, the Incarnate Logos and the Holy Spirit. Although we cannot expect Saint Basil to answer questions which were not raised until later, it does seem perfectly legitimate to look for clues which might indicate how he might have responded.

Questions which we may consider include the following: Is there a distinction between "nature" and "supernature" in Saint Basil's theology? Where is the image to be found if we accept this distinction? How can we explain the possibility of grace for man? Is there anything comparable to the doctrine of "created grace" of the Latin middle ages?

Basil speaks of "nature" many times in his writings. One meaning of "nature" according to Basil is that which can be distinguished from "grace": the Son of God is "similar" to God "by nature" (ἐκ φύσεως), whereas man is similar to God "by grace" (ἐκ τῆς χάριτος).[53] Man is an adopted son of God through grace; the Son of God is the Son by nature. Perfection, holiness, and deification, are the result of grace, which is communicated to man in the Holy Spirit, the "source of sanctification" and of all the gifts which He distributes to man. These gifts, given to man "by grace," exist in the Spirit "by nature."[54]

It is clear that "nature" here means the concrete reality, the ontological substratum of a person. "Nature" is opposed to whatever is not this ontological substratum, whatever − in the case of the human person − comes "from outside."[55] Thus, in Saint Basil's thought, in the case of man who enters in terms of communion with God, there is a distinction between "nature" and "grace," the latter coming "from outside" of human reality. The basis for the distinction between "nature" and "supernature" is certainly to be found in this distinction between "nature" and "grace."

What is the relation between nature and grace? Saint Basil is always in the context of Eastern Christianity, in which grace does not come to be "added" to nature. Grace assumes, restores, transforms and transfigures the nature; it does this not by being added exteriorly, but by working from the inside. Several things support this view: the distinction between essence and energies in God, used to explain the life in divine grace; the inhabitation of man by the Holy Trinity, through the energies of God; and the image of iron in the fire used to explain the deification of created nature in the Holy Spirit.[56]

The image of God in man is the great natural prerogative of man. It is part of the human nature such as is created by God. It is imprinted by the creator Logos in the human nature. Grace renders to this image its original beauty; moreover, grace strengthens and transfigures this image, making it conform more with God. Grace gives man more potentialities to realize his destiny of perfection and *theosis*, achieved by special assistance from the perfecting and deifying cause, the Holy Spirit. Man in the life of grace "participates in the resemblance" of God.[57]

In Saint Basil's theology there is nothing similar to the Augustinian and scholastic doctrine of "original justice" as an "added gift." The image is imprinted in the very nature of Adam. The relative perfection which Adam could achieve depended upon his use of the potential hidden within him in the image of God. The loss of this relative perfection through the fall, the loss of the orientation of the image towards its transcendent Archetype, hurt the image of God in man, thus hurting the human nature: separated from God, Adam found himself in unauthentic existence, equal to death. The decay and fall of man was more than the loss of an "added gift."

The superiority of grace over the image is seen in the way in which God granted His grace to man: through the incarnation of His Son, and the "distribution" of His Holy Spirit. When the Son of God became man, He liberated man from death, renewed life in him, and redeemed him through His precious blood. This is what constitutes man's value, man's dignity: man is bought with the precious blood of God. Moreover, Christ bestows upon him a "divine dignity," including everything that accompanies it. Christ gave man the power to "become God," through His Holy Spirit Whom He sent to him.[58]

What in the human nature explains the receptivity of divine

grace? Is there an intermediate reality between God and man which enables man to be capable of being united with God? Is there anything comparable to the "created grace" of scholastic theology?

It would be presumptuous to ask this kind of question in relation to Saint Basil's theology, or to the theology of any Greek Father. In the Christian East the doctrine of uncreated divine energies explains the mystery of communion between God and man in the life of grace.[59] The idea of "created grace" is completely foreign to the theology of Eastern Christianity.

Yet, there is an expression in Saint Basil's book, *On the Holy Spirit,* which, in the minds of some, could suggest a kind of "created grace."[60] Saint Basil speaks of the Holy Spirit as the "form" of our soul.[61] Is this not a doctrine similar to that of "created grace"?

Benoit Pruche, recent editor of the text of *On the Holy Spirit,* makes the following comments:

> In this text of Saint Basil, one cannot see 'an intermediary creature,' or a 'grace' coming from the Spirit without being the Spirit Himself, but which would become after reception the 'reality' of the recipient. What one can and should see there is the Holy Spirit in person, as He offers Himself directly in participation in order to make the soul spiritual through an immediate communion with Him. It is at this point that one can truly call Him the 'formal cause' of our sanctification.[62]

Saint Basil, and with him the whole theological tradition of the East, which finds its best expression in the theology of Saint Gregory Palamas (fourteenth century), tries to find out what in God explains the possibility of divine grace, or life in communion with Him.[63] Saint Basil does not try to explain what in the created nature justifies its union with the Uncreated Nature. This is what the Christian West tries to do with the concept of "created grace."[64] As for Saint Basil, he is satisfied with the statement that in the case of grace the Holy Spirit, "inaccessible by nature," becomes "communicable by goodness."[65]

If one wishes to push for an answer to the question of what on the human side explains the possibility of grace, this answer, according to Saint Basil's thought, would not be found in an "added gift," but rather in the image of God in man. This image, the "particle of grace"[66] which God put in man at his creation and which is ultimately the presence of God in man,[67] gives man regenerated in Christ the possibility to "renew himself in knowledge according to the image of his Creator," to resemble God, and to "become god" (by grace).

One final remark pertaining to the distinction between "nature" and "supernature," and "image" and "grace" in Saint Basil's thought must be made: there is no understanding whatsoever for Saint Basil or any of the Greek Fathers of an "independent nature."[68] Human nature, created in the image of God, is intrinsically dependent on God as the basis of its very being. The only way in which the image is able to keep its full potential is to continue to be the link between God and man, between the Archetype and the image. When the image deteriorates, man loses his life "according to nature." The restored image in Christ and the resemblance with God through virtuous life on the basis of the image of God in man, the likeness with God and the life of *theosis*, these constitute true human life, the "life according to nature."[69]

Image and Glory

When properly used, the dynamism of the image leads to resemblance with God. This resemblance, which is an assimilation with God, makes man a participant of the divine nature inasmuch as man is able to participate in it. The divine nature in which man participates is called the energies of God[70] or, according to another favored expression of Saint Basil, the "goods of life eternal." Among these energies or goods is that of divine glory, which surrounds the divine essence.

Saint Basil says: "Had man kept the glory in which he was first elevated by God, his exaltation would have been real, and not imaginary! Man would have been glorified by the power of God in the Highest, and adorned with His wisdom; man would have rejoiced in the goods of life eternal."[71]

Adam was elevated in this glory through his creation in the

image and likeness of God. He had the power to stay in it through the exercise of love. However, his failure to do so resulted in a loss of the divine glory.

> But, having renounced the glory that he had from God, he desired another one, that he could not reach, and he lost that which he could gain. His unique resource, the only way to heal his evil, is to return to the dignity from which he fell; it is to be motivated by humble feelings, not to imagine a vain structure of glory that he finds in himself, but to search for his glory in God. Thus he will correct his mistake; he will heal his illness; and he will return to the divine precept from which he ran away.[72]

The grace of Christ gives man the possibility of this "return" to the dignity from which he has fallen. Saint Basil says:

> In what can man really glorify himself? What makes him great? God says: 'Let him who wants to glorify himself... put his glory in knowing me and acknowledging that I am the Lord!' Man's grandeur, his glory and dignity consist in knowing what is really great, to attach himself to it, and to seek his glory in the Lord of glory. The Apostle says: 'Let him who glorifies himself, be glorified in the Lord. Jesus the Christ is given to us to be our wisdom, our justification, our sanctification, our redemption, according to what has been written: Let him who glorifies himself be glorified only in the Lord.' The veritable and perfect way of being glorious in God is not to boast about our righteousness, but to acknowledge that when left on our own means, we are deprived of veritable righteousness: we are justified only by faith in Jesus the Christ. Saint Paul glorifies himself in the disdain for his own righteousness, and in the attitude of seeking justification from faith in Jesus the Christ, and which comes from God through faith. In this justification he knows Christ, participates in His sufferings and experiences the power of His resurrection: he becomes confirmed with His death and does everything possible to reach the blessed

resurrection of the dead. There it is where all pride disappears. O man, to you nothing is left in which you can boast. All of your glory and hope consist in mortifying everything which is in you, so that you seek for the life that you enjoy in Jesus the Christ. Of this life, we now experience the foretaste, living by the goodness and the grace of God, 'For it is God who operates in us the will and the energy according to His good pleasure.' It is God who, through His Spirit, reveals to us His own wisdom, which He had predestined for our glory.[73]

God wants man "to be worthy of being glorified."[74] This is why He gave man His Son, His wisdom, to make His abode among him through His "God-bearing flesh," through Christ whose human nature was made glorious by being inhabited by the divinity. Through His Christ, God sent His Spirit to impart in man the glorious humanity of Christ. In the Light of the Holy Spirit, man becomes "spiritual" and a "Spirit-bearer."

> [Man is] transformed in a certain way to become something more brilliant, through His glory.... This is what it means 'to be transformed by the glory of the Spirit in one's own glory!' [Man thus becomes glorious], not in a stingy or feeble way, but in a way commensurate to the capability of the being enlightened by the Spirit.[75]

Of this glory, St. Basil concludes, man has now received the "earnest," but he expects the fulfillment in the age to come.

CHRISTOLOGY AND ECCLESIOLOGY

Basil is especially interested in "theology," that is, the Trinitarian doctrine. He has to defend the divinity of the Word and of the Holy Spirit against his enemies: the Arians and Pneumatomachs. It is only towards the end of his life (about 376) that Saint Basil begins to articulate the doctrine of the Church concerning the incarnation of the Word. Basil responds to the Christological heresy of Apollinarios of Laodicea, which adds itself to the still persistent Trinitarian heresies. Against Apollinarios, who diminishes the human nature of Christ by negating the existence of a reasonable soul in it, Basil states that Christ "was not a soulless flesh, but a divinity using a flesh with soul."[76]

The Apollinarian heresy marks the beginning of the dispute on the dogma of Incarnation, as we can see it in several of Saint Basil's letters, dating from the end of his life.[77] In all of these letters, Basil defends the reality of the human nature in Christ. If Christ had not assumed a true human nature, the entire work of divine economy would have been negated in its foundation. Death, which dominated human nature, could not have been overcome without its contact with a concrete human nature united with the divinity. Sin could not have been abolished without the righteousness of the God-man Jesus.[78]

What is interesting in these texts, with respect to the image of God in man, is that the human nature, made in the image of God, was healed from sin and death through its assumption by the Logos. In the restoration of the human nature by Christ, the restoration of the image of God in man is certainly included. The image is the great natural prerogative of man. Yet, the theme of the restoration of the image is not very much developed by Basil; it is left up to other Fathers in the Christian tradition of the East to do this kind of work.

The great concern of Saint Basil until the end of his life is the defense of the Trinitarian dogma. In his *Hexæmeron*, the last work of his life, Basil seems satisfied with simply alluding to the Christological heresy.[79] In the theological and apologetical works of Saint Basil, we cannot expect complete doctrinal presentations in the domain of Christology since the need for it does not arise during Saint Basil's lifetime.

Although the Christological doctrine with its anthropological implications is not greatly discussed in the great theological and apologetic works of Saint Basil, we can nevertheless find elements of this doctrine in his irenic works. In his commentaries on the Psalms, Saint Basil presents us with several elements of his Christological doctrine which have anthropological implications.

While meditating upon various verses of the Psalms, Saint Basil presents the doctrine of the Incarnation of the Logos and the redemption of man in a positive fashion. He speaks of the *kenosis* of the Son of God, who, "being rich by nature – for everything that belongs to the Father belongs to Him as well – became poor for us, to enrich us by His poverty." The Son of God emptied Himself, taking up the condition of a slave, so that "from His fullness we all receive, grace upon grace." Christ became man's peace and reconciliation with God: He "in His person created the two-in-one new man, who, through His blood shed on the cross, reconciled every being in Him, both on earth and in heaven."[80]

On other occasions, Basil speaks of the following themes: the "God-bearing flesh, vestment of the divinity," through which God came among men;[81] the "redemption by the blood of the Only-begotten;"[82] the "God-bearing flesh" sanctified through its union with God; the flesh as the "residence" of God, through which He manifested Himself to us, and through which God resides in the midst of His city, the Church.[83] Basil tells us of "the God-Man, Jesus the Christ, the only one capable of giving Himself up and offering Himself to God as a ransom for all of us."[84] Ultimately, Basil develops the theme of Christ the Beloved One, the Bridegroom of the soul in particular, and of the Church in general.[85]

In all of these texts, as in the apologetic texts, Basil is interested more in the Only-begotten Son of God than in the Incarnate Logos. The human nature of Christ is seen in relation to the redemptive work of the Logos. The anthropological implications of the Logos becoming flesh remain undeveloped. The fate of the image of God in the human nature of Christ is not discussed here, either. Yet, the doctrine is implied in statements such as: "The Son of God humiliated Himself to raise us up and became poor to enrich us." Christ accomplished all of this in His own humanity; the first fruits of man's own regenerated humanity are in Him. His "God-bearing flesh" through which God manifests Himself to man and in which He resides in the midst of His city, the Church, is the instrument of man's redemption. In this humanity of the Logos, the restoration of human nature as a whole takes place. Human nature cannot be understood without its great "natural prerogative," the image of God in it.

Is the Church as a whole in the image of God? The Church is not only the body of Christ, but His spouse, too. For Saint Basil, as for Saint Paul, the body of Christ is constituted by the totality of its members. This totality, the Church, is also called the spouse of Christ. Saint Basil applies this last name both to the Church and to the individual soul. Just as for the Church, Basil asks for the same kind of ornaments for the individual soul, worthy of the Spouse, and "worthy of him who is created in the image of God," that is, man.[86] It is implied that the Church as a whole reflects the same qualities which we find in the individual soul, and which make the latter to be "in the image of God." Yet, there is no explicit statement made about the Church being "in the image of God." In Saint Basil's doctrine, ecclesiology is as greatly undeveloped as is Christology.

Eschatology

What happens to the image of God in man at the end of time? The image of God contains a dynamism that cannot be exhausted. Under the guidance of the Holy Spirit, this dynamism leads man to resemblance with God, to *theosis*, and divine filiation. What happens to this dynamism at the coming again of the Lord?

There is at least one text in Saint Basil's writings which gives us a hint about the last things, as far as human fate is concerned. The image of God is not mentioned in the text; yet, the doctrine of the image is implied in the text, in relation to the dynamism which is in it and the life of holiness which results from it. The text reads as follows:

> [The psalmist] describes the future time in comparison with actual conditions. On earth, he says, I am surrounded with the labors of death; in heaven, my soul is delivered from death. On earth, my eyes pour tears because of suffering; in heaven, there are no more tears to darken the pupils of the eyes of those who rejoice in the union of the vision of the divine glory. 'For God will wipe all tears from all faces.' On earth, the dangers of failures are multiple; this is why it is written: 'Whoever flatters himself about being upright, let

him be careful not to fall.' In heaven, the feet are stable; life is without change; there is no more danger of falling into sin. There are no more revolts of the flesh, no collaboration of a woman in sin. There is no longer man and woman in the resurrection. There is only one and unique life, the life of those who please their Master and reside in the land of the living. This world is mortal: it is the place of those who die. The nature of visible things is composite; now, whatever is composite is by nature perishable. Man being in the world and being part of the world by necessity participates in the nature of the universe...

But there, where there is no longer change, neither of the body nor of the soul – for there is no further deviation of thought, or change of opinion, as there are no more circumstances which can jeopardize the stability and tranquillity of our thought – there is the land of those who really live and who are always identical with themselves. It is in this land that we will be as agreeable as possible to God, as the prophet promises: for no more external things will be able to take us away from our purpose, the true service of God, identical to the service of angels.[87]

At the end of time, the dynamism which God put in the image of God in man will achieve on the one hand, the maximum of its deployment, becoming resemblance to God; on the other hand, it will be stabilized because it will achieve its purpose, a true service of God, identical to that of the angels. There will be no further opportunity for another fall – estrangement from God, with "death as the wages of sin" – there will be the life of those who live in God, who resemble God; there will be the life of "gods by grace," the life of those who "live the veritable life in Jesus the Christ, to whom belong glory and power in the ages of ages. Amen."[88]

ENDNOTES

[1] This study originally appeared as part of my thesis "La dialectique de l'image de Dieu chez Saint Basile le Grand," submitted to the School of Theology of

the University of Louvain in partial fulfillment of the requirements "pro gradu Doctoris in Sacra Theologia." It has been revised, especially with regard to the notes. I am deeply appreciative of the good suggestions of my thesis director, the late Monsignor Gerard Philips, under whose guidance this work was written.

[2] Among the many passages which we find in Saint Basil's works in reference to this doctrine, see: *Adversus Eunomium,* 1,18, PG 29:552C; ibid.; 1,20; PG 29:556C; ibid., 1, 23; PG 29:564A; ibid., 1, 27; PG 29:572A; ibid., 2, 16; PG 29:604C-605A; ibid.,2, 17; PG 29:605B; ibid., 2, 31; PG 29:645B. Cf. *Contra Sabellianos,* 2; PG 31:604BC, *De Spiritu Sancto,* 8, 21; PG 32:105AB; *Homilia de fide,* 2; PG 31:465C468B; *Letter* 105; PG 32:513A; *Letter* 226, 3; PG 32:849A; *Letter* 236, 1; PG 32 :877 AB; and *Liturgy,* ed. F. E. Brightman, in *Liturgies Eastern and Western, Being the Texts Original or Translated of the Principal Liturgies of the Church* (Oxford, 1896), p. 322, lines 28-30; and p. 402, lines 18-19.

[3] See *Letter* 28, 6; PG 32:336C; ed. Courtonne, 6; p. 89, line 7; ibid., 4; PG 32:332A; ed. Courtonne, 4; p. 85, lines 40-42; *Adversus Eunomium,* 2, 28; PG 29:637B; ibid., 1,14; PG 29:545A; ibid., 2,4; PG 29:577C; ibid., 1, 7; PG 29:524D.

[4] See my thesis *La dialectique de l'image de Dieu chez Saint Basile le Grand,* University of Louvain, 1964, pp. 50-62.

[5] "Εἰκὼν μὲν Θεοῦ Χριστός,... εἰκὼν δὲ Υἱοῦ τὸ Πνεῦμα." *Adversus Eunomium,* 5; PG 29:724C.

[6] "Ὅτι εἰκὼν ἀληθὴς καὶ φυσικὴ Θεοῦ καὶ Κυρίου τὸ Πνεῦμα." Ibid., 5; PG 29:725B.

[7] "Τὸ εὐσεβὲς δόγμα τῆς μοναρχίας." *De Spiritu Sancto,* 18, 47; PG 32:153BC.

[8] Ibid., 18, 47; PG 32:153B.

[9] Ibid., 18, 47; PG 32:153AB.

[10] *In Hexæmeron,* 9, 6; PG 29:205AC; ed. Giet, pp. 516-18.

[11] Philo the Jew, *De opificio mundi,* 24, 14-15; ed. Cohn, 25.

[12] *Adversus Eunomium,* 3, 2; PG 29:660AC; ibid., 3, 4; PG 29:661BC; *De Spiritu Sancto,* 16, 38; PG 32:136A-140B; *In Hexæmeron,* 1, 5; PG 29:13A; ed. Giet, pp. 104-106, ibid., 2; 4; PG 29:40C-41A; ed. Giet, pp. 162-164; ibid., 3, 9: PG 29:73D-76A: ed. Giet. p. 236.

[13] *In Hexæmeron,* 9, 6; PG 29:205BC; ed. Giet, p. 518.

[14] *In illud, attende tibi ipsi,* 6; PG 31:212B.

[15] *Regulæ fusius tractatæ,* 2, 3; PG 31:913B; *In Psalmum XLVIII,* 8; PG 29:449BD; and *In illud, attende tibi ipsi* 6; PG 31:212BC.

[16] Roger Leys, *L'image de Dieu chez Saint Grégoire de Nysse* (Brussels, 1951), pp. 64-65. Even for Gregory, though, priority is given to the human soul, created in the image of God. For Gregory, the body participates in the nobility of the soul, being the instrument through which the soul-in-the-image-of-God expresses itself (ibid.).

[17] *In illud, attende,* 7; PG 31:216A.

[18] Ibid., 3; PG 31:204A; also ibid., 7; PG 31:261A.

[19] *Regulæ fusius,* 2, 2; PG 31:913B; *In Psalmum XLVIII,* 8; PG 29:419C; *In illud, attende,* 3; PG 31:204A; ibid., 6; PG 31:212BC; ibid., 7; PG 31:216B; and

Quod Deus non est auctor malorum, 6; PG 31: 344B.

[20] *Regulæ fusius*, 2,1; PG 31:908B-914A.

[21] *Regulæ fusius*, 2, 3; PG 31:913B; *In illud, attende*, 6; PG 31:212BC; and *In Hexæmeron*, 9, 5; PG 29:201C; ed. Giet, p. 508.

[22] *In illud, attende*, 3; PG 31:204AC; and *Ad adolescentes*, 8; PG 31:588C; ed. Boulenger, 10; p. 60, lines 21-22.

[23] For the doctrine of Saint Augustine see J. Heijke, "St. Augustine's Comments on '*Imago Dei*,' An Anthology from All his Works Exclusive of the *De Trinitate*,"in *Classical Folia*, Supplement 111 (1960), pp. 14, 16, 20, 37-38, 49-50, 51-52, 66, 67, 68, 72-75, 77, and 87-88. Also, excerpts from the *De Trinitate* in English translation referring to the same doctrine are found in Henry Bettenson, *The Later Christian Fathers* (London, 1970), pp. 229-236. See also Gerald McCool, "The Ambrosian Origin of St. Augustine's Theology of the Image of God in Man," in *Theological Studies*, 20.1 (1959), pp. 62-81. Cf. Vladimir Lossky, *The Mystical Theology of the Eastern Church* (Cambridge, England, 1968), p. 81.

[24] These "propria personarum" or hypostatic idioms (properties) are different in Saint Basil and Augustine. For Saint Basil, these idioms are "fatherhood" (or the "pious dogma of monarchy") for God the Father, "generation" for the Son, and "procession" for the Holy Spirit. See *Letter* 38, 4; PG 32: 329A-352A; ed. Courtonne, pp. 84-84, lines 1-50; cf. *Contra Sabellianos*, 6; PG 31:612BC, and *Letter* 105; PG 32: 513AB. See also my article "Image as 'Sign' ' (Semeion) of God: Knowledge of God through the Image according to Saint Basil," in *The Greek Orthodox Theological Review*, 21:1 (1976), p. 35.

[25] See my article *Image as 'Sign,'* p. 35, note 55. Cf. Lossky, *The Mystical Theology*, pp. 79-80 and 115.

[26] One might be tempted to see a kind of "image of the Son" or "image of the Spirit" in such expressions as "conformity with the image of the Son of God," or "put on Christ," or "spiritualization," or "conformity with the Spirit." In reality, this "image of the Son of God" is identical with the "image of the Father." Both of them indicate the common "magnificent attributes" or energies of God, fully shared together with the substance by the three hypostases of the Holy Trinity. This is the image that God put in us at our creation. As for the expressions "put on Christ" and "become spiritual," they refer to the restoration of the image in the life of grace. They indicate participation in the "magnificent attributes" of the Holy Trinity, which descend to us from the Father through the Son in the Holy Spirit.

[27] Leys, *L'image de Dieu*, pp. 93-97.

[28] Erik Peterson, "L'immagine di Dio in S. Ireneo," in *La Scuola Cattolica*, 69.1 (1941), pp. 50-51: In chapter 6 of his book *Against the Heresies*, Saint Irenæos makes a distinction between "image," as being similarity with God, found in our body, and "likeness," as being resemblance with God, the result of the work of the Holy Spirit in us. Peterson makes the following remark: "The distinction between the image and the likeness of God in man (which we find) in this chapter of Saint Irenæos is important, because in a sense it anticipates the future doctrine of the Church" (ibid.). Cf. Gustaf Wingren, *Man and the Incarnation, A Study in the Biblical Theology of Irenæos*, translation Ross Mackenzie (Philadephia,

Great Britain, 1959), pp. 14-26, 90-100, 147-59, 201-213. See also Henri Crouzel, *Théologie de l'image de Dieu chez Origène (Paris,* 1956), pp. 32, and 217-45. We read on page 217: "The distinction between 'image,' which is given at the beginning, and the 'likeness,' which is the purpose of human life – [a distinction] which we have found in Platonic philosophers, in Irenæos, and in Clement [of Alexandria] – also occupies an important place in the doctrine of Origen on the image."

[29] From my study of these homilies I would agree with Stanislas Giet that the ideas in them are those of Saint Basil, even if in their present form the homilies do not seem to be Basilian. They are probably the work of some stenographer who took notes while Saint Basil was lecturing on the subject. The study of the doctrine of the image in the undoubtedly authentic works of Saint Basil confirms this view. Cf. Stanislas Giet, "Saint Basile a-t-il donné suite à l'Hexaémeron?" in *Recherches de Science Religieuse* (1946), p. 520, note 3.

[30] *De hominis structura,* 1.20; PG 30:32CD.

[31] *In Hexæmeron,* 9.6; PG 29:208A; ed. Giet, p. 520.

[32] Elpide Stéphanou, "Le sixième jour de l'Hexaémeron de Saint Basile," in *Echos d'Orient,* 168 (1932), p. 391.

[33] Ibid.

[34] *InPsalmum XLVIII,* 3; PG 29 449BD.

[35] Ibid.

[36] Giet, *Saint Basile a-t-il donné suite,* p. 520, note 3.

[37] *De Spiritu Sancto,* 1. 2; PG 32:109C

[38] Ibid., 9.23;PG 32 109C.

[39] *In illud, attende, 6;* PG 31:913B.

[40] *Regulæ fusius,* 2. 3; PG 31:913B.

[41] *De Spiritu Sancto,* 1.2; PG 32:69B: "There is no likeness [of God] without knowledge" (ὁμοίωσις δὲ οὐκ ἄνευ γνώσεως).

[42] *Letter* 233, 1; PG 32:364C865C: Reason, which bears in it the of the creator, is oriented towards the knowledge of God; this knows with God." Cf. my article *Image as 'Sign,'* p. 25.

[43] See for example the doctrine of Saint Irenæos, in Peterson, *L'imagine di Dio,* p. 52; the doctrine of Origen, in Crouzel, *Théologie de l' image,* pp. 217-222; doctrine of Saint Athanasios, in Regis Bernard, *"L'image de Dieu d'après Athanase* (Paris, 1952), pp. 130-35; the doctrine of Saint Gregory of Nyssa, in Leys, *"L'image de Dieu,"* pp. 116-119; and the doctrine which preceeds him, in Walter Surghardt, *The Image of God in Man according to Cyril of Alexandria* (Woodstock, Maryland, 1957), pp. 1-11. Cf. Jean Giblet, *L'Homme, image de Dieu dans les commendaires litteraux de Philon d'Alexandrie* (Louvain, 1949), pp. 97, 114; Vladimir Lossky, *In the Image and the Likeness of God* (st. Vladimir's Seminary Press, 1974), pp. 138-39; and Timothy Ware, *The Orthodox Church* (Middlesex, England, 1964). pp. 224-26.

[44] *Letter* 233, 1; PG 32:865A. See also *De hominis structura,* 1.20; PG 30:32BC.

[45] *In martyrem Iulittam,* 7; PG 31:241A.

[46] *In Psalmum* 1.3: PG 29:216D-217A.

[47] *Quod Deus,* passim; PG 31:329A-353A. See also *In Hexæmeron* 2.4-5; PG 29:36B-40B; ed. Giet, pp. 152-62.

[48] *De Spiritu Sancto,* 8.18; PG 32:100C. See also *Letter* 233, 2; PG 32:868B.

[49] See my article *Image as 'Sign,'* p. 40ff.

[50] *Letter* 233. 1-2; PG 32:864C-868B.

[51] *Regulæ fusius,* 2.3; PG 31:931BC; *In Psalmum XLVIII,* 8; PG 29:449D-452A; and *Quod Deus,* 6-8; PG 31:344A-348B.

[52] *Regulæ fusius,* 2.34; PG 31:913C-916A; *De Spiritu Sancto,* 9. 23; PG 32:109AC; and *Homilia de fide,* 3; PG 31: 468C-472A; Cf. *De Spiritu Sancto,* 15.36; PG 32:132B; cf. also my article *Image as 'Sign,'* pp. 52-53.

[53] *In Hexæmeron,* 9.6; PG 29:208B; ed Giet, pp 520-22

[54] *De Spiritu Sancto,* 8.19; PG 32:100D; ibid., 15.35; PG 32:132AB; ibid., 9.22; PG 32:108C; *Letter* 105: PG 32:513B; and *Liturgy,* ed. Brightman, p. 323, line 9; p. 402, line 24. The whole thrust of Saint Basil's argument in the book *On the Holy Spirit* is to prove that the Spirit, Who is the "Source of Sanctification," cannot be of the same nature with those whom He sanctifies. The fact that the Spirit is the source of the divine life which He communicates to us is the proof that the Spirit is divine. Thus, the Spirit is of the same value with the Father and the Son, and, together with them, worthy of the same honors (ὁμότιμον).

[55] It is understood that for the divine persons of the Son of God and of the Holy Spirit "nature" contains "grace." The distinction between nature and grace applies to the human reality only. In the theological tradition of the East – according to the terminology that Saint Basil himself was using – there is a clear distinction between "essence" and "energies" in God; that is, a distinction between the nature of God as transcendent, unreachable, incommunicable (essence), and the nature of God as immanent, descending towards us, reachable, communicable to us (energies). God is unknown in His essence, yet known in His energies (*Letter* 234, 1; PG 32: 689AB. Cf. my article *Image as 'Sign,'* p. 36). Grace is nothing else than these energies of God, which reach man. See Lossky, *The Mystical Theology,* p. 87.

[56] This image is applied to the angels in *Adversus Eunomium,* 3.2; PG 29: 660AB, also *De Spiritu Sancto,* 26.63; PG 32:184AC.

[57] *In Psalmum XLVIII,* 8; PG 29:449B; *Letter* 283,1; PG 82:865A. Cf. *De Spiritu Sancto,* 1.2; PG 32:69AB.

[58] *Regulæ fusius,* 2.3-4; PG 31:913B-916C; *In Psalmum XLVIII,* 8 PG 29:449B-452B; and *In illud, attende,* 6; PG 31:213A.

[59] See Charles Moeller and Gerald Philips, *Grace et Oecuménisme* (Chevetogne, 1957), pp. 12-21.

[60] Actually, there is such an interpretation of Saint Basil's doctrine, found in E. Scholle, *Die Lehre des hl. Basilius von der Gnade* (Friburg in Brisgau, 1881), passim.

[61] *De Spiritu Sancto,* 26.61; PG 32:180BC

[62] Benoit Pruche, "Basile de Césarée, Traité du Saint-Esprit," in *Sources Chrétiennes,* 17 (Paris. 1947), p. 73; cf. ibid., pp. 225-226, in footnote.

[63] Philips, *Grâce,* p. 19.

[64] Philips, ibid., pp. 22-41.

[65] *De Spiritu Sancto,* 9.22; PG 32:108C.

[66] *In Psalmum XLVIII,* 8; PG 29:449BD. See also *Dicta tempore famis et siccitatis,* 5; PG 31;317AB.

74 In the Image of God

67 See my thesis *La dialectique*, pp. 297-347; see also my article *Image as 'Sign,'* pp. 19-20.

68 John Meyendorff, *Byzantine Theology* (New York, 1974), p. 138. Cf. Lossky, *The Mystical Theology*, pp. 126-27.

69 *Quod Deus, passim;* PG 31; 329 A-353A.

70 *Letter* 234, 1; PG 32; 689AB. See also my article *Image as 'Sign,'* p. 36.

71 *De humilitate*, 1; PG 31:525AB.

72 Ibid., PG 31:525B.

73 Ibid., 3; PG 31:529B-532A.

74 *In Psalmum XXIX* 7; PG 29:304AB.

75 *De Spiritu Sancto*, 15.23; PG 32:109BC; ibid., 21.52; PG 32:165BC; and ibid ., 15. 36; PG 32:132B.

76 "Οὐχὶ σὰρξ ἦν ἄψυχος, ἀλλὰ θεότης σαρκὶ ἐμψύχῳ κεχρημένη." *Letter* 234, 1; PG 32:877C.

77 *Letter* 250, 8; PG 32:965C; *Letter* 251; PG 32:963B-972D; *Letter* 252; PG 32:973A-976A; *Letter* 253, 4; PG 32:980BD; and *Letter* 255, 2; PG 32:984B-988C. All these letters were written during the year 377.

78 See especially *Letter* 251; PG 32:971AC, and *Letter* 252, 1-2; PG 32; 973AC.

79 *In Hexæmeron*, 9.6; PG 29:205C; ed. Giet, p. 518. Saint Basil alludes to the heresy of Apollinarios of Laodicea, calling it a "new circumcision."

80 *In Psalmum XXXIII*, 5; PG 29:361BD.

81 *In Psalmum LIX*, 4; PG 29:468AB.

82 Ibid., 3; PG 29:465A.

83 *In Psalmum XLV*, 4-5; PG 29:424AD.

84 *In Psalmum XLVIII*, 4; PG 29:440BC; cf. ibid., 4; PG 29:44lAC.

85 *In Psalmum XLIV*, passim; PG 29:389C-413D.

86 Ibid., 9; PG 29:409BC; ibid., 10; PG 29:409B, and ibid., 11; PG 29:412AC.

87 *In Psalmum CXIV*, 5; PG 29:492B-493C.

88 Ibid., 5; PG 29:493C.

Four

Some Preliminary Notions of "Baptismal Ecclesiology": Baptism and Eucharist, Constitutive of the Church as Communion[1]

In a recent article "The Local Churches and Catholicity," John Erickson indicated the need for a "baptismal ecclesiology," as both a completion and a corrective of the shortcomings of "eucharistic ecclesiology."[2] "The Church is a eucharistic organism," he says, "but only because the Church is a baptismal organism." The author continues:

> Modern ecclesiology, like modern church practice, has tended to ignore the significance of baptism. Emphasis has been on eucharistic fellowship, with relatively little concern for the preconditions for this fellowship. Baptism, to be sure, is acknowledged as necessary. But for most of us in the West, at least, baptism is something that happens in infancy, of little continuing significance in life save that it qualifies one sooner or later for the Eucharist. Early Christians had a deeper understanding of its meaning and of its significance for the Church.[3]

The author supports this same position in a more recent paper, presented in the context of the dialogue of Orthodox and Roman Catholic Bishops in the United States.[4]

In this last paper, the author rightly states that the statements of our consultation on *Apostolicity as God's Gift* and *Primacy and Conciliarity*, emphasis has been given "on baptism as foundational for church life."[5] The author continues: "Early Christians, – but also many third world and Eastern European Christians today –

75

had a much deeper understanding of baptism's meaning and significance for the Church, for ecclesiology. ...Our prevailing eucharistic ecclesiology must be corrected by a baptismal ecclesiology."[6]

The author quotes the two Consultation statements, and concludes:

> I believe that rediscovery of the ecclesiological significance of baptism could have some dramatic – though possibly unsettling – consequences for Orthodox/ Catholic theological dialogue, both International and North American, and also for your work in this Joint Committee of Orthodox and Catholic Bishops. If you Catholics accept us as truly baptized, if we Orthodox accept you as truly baptized and not just as acceptable by "oikonomia," then what does this say about our mutual responsibility for building up and strengthening our baptismal faith...? ... Perhaps, if we begin with a stronger sense of our common baptismal identity, we will find fewer areas – whether relating to marriage or to primacy – in which our traditions are not easily harmonized.[7]

In the spirit of our dialogue, which intends to discuss "some preliminary notions on 'baptismal ecclesiology'," I would like to present for discussion the following items: a review of some modern studies on the Sacraments (or "Mysteries" of Christian Initiation; a brief presentation of these sacraments, mostly from an Orthodox point of view; the relationship between Christ and the Holy Spirit in theology and liturgy; the interrelatedness of Baptism and Eucharist as sacraments of communion and constitutive of the life of the Church; a review of some questions regarding "baptismal ecclesiology" as relating to "eucharistic" and "communion ecclesiologies"; and draw some conclusions pertaining to "baptismal ecclesiology."

I. MODERN STUDIES PERTAINING
TO THE SACRAMENTS OF INITIATION

There is a variety of recent studies pertaining to the sacraments of initiation, both from an Orthodox and from a Roman Catholic perspective. There is no reason here to be exhaustive. We select just a few of them, as an example of contemporary scholarship.

From an Orthodox point of view, one of the major contributions to liturgical theology and the three sacraments of initiation (the Sacraments of Baptism, Chrismation, and Eucharist) is Fr. Alexander Schmemann's book *Of Water and the Spirit*.[8]

The book is a commentary on the service of initiation as it is presently conducted in the Orthodox Church. As he goes along with his commentary, the author finds the opportunity to discuss historical, theological, structural, liturgical, and pietal issues pertaining to the sacraments of Christian initiation as experienced in the life, practice, tradition, and liturgical piety of the Orthodox Church.

In the introduction, entitled "To Rediscover Baptism," the author indicates that during the "golden age" of Christian liturgy, "the sacrament of baptism was performed on the paschal night as an organic part of the great annual celebration of Easter." Baptism was an integral part of the paschal liturgy. Baptism was a paschal celebration, and Pascha was a baptismal celebration.

Fr. Schmemann deplores the absence of appreciation of baptism in the life of the Orthodox Christian today; absence from the *leitourgia* (the public worship of the worshipping community) of the Orthodox Church, as baptism is not usually connected with the celebration of the Holy Eucharist; and absence from the piety of the Church, as baptism does not celebrate the paschal mystery of the triumph of new life in the Risen Christ. "The foundation is still here with us," he says. "Baptism is performed. But it has ceased to be comprehended as the door leading into a new life and as the power to fight for this new life's preservation and growth in us."

The author deplores the reduction of baptism from the paschal celebration of new life by the community, to a private rite of incorporation into the Church. Baptism has ceased to be "the very heart of the Church's liturgy and piety."

Academic theology has reduced the rich patristic baptismal theology to two points regarding baptism: the removal of the "original sin," and the conferring of a kind of grace to begin one's Christian life. "But baptism as the sacrament of regeneration, as re-creation, as the personal Pascha and the personal Pentecost of man, as the integration into the *laos*, the people of God, as the 'passage' from old into a new life, and finally as an epiphany of the kingdom of God: all these meanings which made baptism so central and so essential to early Christian piety and experience are virtually ignored, and this precisely because they do not fit into the legalistic framework adopted from the West."

The author deplores that western questions like that of the "validity" of the sacraments in general and Baptism in particular have become the main questions of "this type of theology," disconnected from the liturgical piety and life of the Church as a worshipping community. Fr. Schmemann says:

> If the 'validity' of the sacrament requires nothing but a valid priest and a minimum of water, if furthermore, nothing but 'validity' is important, why not reduce the sacrament to these essential prerequisites? Why not have water and oil blessed in advance in order to save our precious time? Why bother with archaic rubrics which prescribe that 'all the candles be lighted' and the priest 'be vested in white vestments'? Why involve the parish, the congregation, the people of God in all this? Thus today it takes some fifteen minutes to perform in a dark corner of a church, with one 'psaltist' giving the responses, an act in which the Fathers saw and acclaimed the greatest solemnity of the Church: a mystery 'which fills with joy the angels and the archangels and all the powers from above and the earthly creatures,' a mystery for which the Church prepared herself by forty days of fasting and which constituted the very essence of her paschal joy. A decadent liturgy supported by a decadent theology and leading to a decadent piety: such is the sad situation in which we find ourselves today and which must be corrected if we love the Church and want her to become again the power which transforms the life of man.

Fr. Schmemann concludes that "we must rediscover baptism – its meaning, its power, its true *validity*." The purpose of his essay is precisely to help in that rediscovery, "or, rather, to enumerate preliminary conditions for it, for the real rediscovery must take place each time the Church celebrates this great mystery and makes all of us its participants and witnesses."

As a liturgical theologian, Fr. Schmemann intends to bridge the gap between academic theology, liturgy and piety of the Church. He has certainly succeeded in doing this in his essay. It is worth quoting the conclusion of his introduction, where Fr. Schmemann summarizes his views on liturgical theology, on the importance of Baptism (and, by extension, initiation sacraments), the imparting of new, resurrected life by it, the connectedness between Baptism and Pascha, and the meaning of this connection, which is the cause of the joy which fills our Christian lives. He says:

> To understand liturgy from inside, to discover and experience that 'epiphany' of God, world and life which the liturgy contains and communicates, to relate this vision and this power to our own existence, to all our problems: such is the purpose of liturgical theology. Of all this, baptism is truly the beginning, the foundation, and the key. The whole life of the Church is rooted in the new life which shone forth from the grave on the first day of the new creation. It is this new life that is given in baptism and is fulfilled in the Church. We began this introduction with the mention of the initial liturgical connection between Pascha and baptism. This whole study is indeed nothing else but an attempt to explain the meaning of this connection and to communicate, inasmuch as it is possible for our poor human words, the joy with which it fills our Christian life.[9]

In the five chapters which follow, Fr. Schmemann discusses the preparation for Baptism, Baptism itself as the Mystery of Water, the Sacrament of the Holy Spirit (Chrismation, Consignation, or Confirmation), the entrance into the Kingdom (baptismal procession and Eucharist), and the rituals of churching.

In "Preparation for Baptism" (Chapter 1), Fr. Schmemann discusses the meaning for this preparation both on behalf of the person to be baptized (pre-baptismal catechesis for adults), and the worshipping community, whose faith and life is also edified by Baptism.

Lent was traditionally the time of preparation of the catechumens, leading to Easter, which was the fulfillment of this preparation, through the celebration of new life in the baptismal/paschal celebration.

The author calls the Church itself preparation and fulfillment, as it prepares for, but also celebrates the presence, here and now, of the kingdom of God, whose life we celebrate in the baptismal/paschal mystery.

Regarding infant Baptism, the author rejects the need for an (intellectual) understanding in order for the Baptism to be possible and/or "valid"/fruitful. Later, he says that what makes Baptism possible and fruitful is the understanding and faith not of the baptized person, whether adult or infant; it is the "faith of Christ" Himself, which is the faith of the Church.[10]

Fr. Schmemann reviews the ritual of the catechumenate, which includes the exorcisms, the renunciation of Satan, and the pledge of allegiance to Christ.

In discussing the exorcisms, he discusses evil represented by the devil. Evil is not the absence of good, he says. It is a "negative presence," which opposes the will of God. That "presence" is not fictitious: it has a "person" behind it, being that of the devil and his fallen angels.

Christ came to annihilate the power of the devil through his death and resurrection. Together with Christ, and joined to Him, we fight the devil and his pomp (pride, *pompa diaboli*). Denouncing him and rejecting him by breathing and spitting upon him, we make the firm commitment to fight against him throughout our Christian life.

In declaring our allegiance to Christ, we recognize him as "King and God." What makes the difference between us and the devil in acknowledging Christ, is that the devil may recognize Him as God, but not as *King*.

The ritual of catechism concludes with the proclamation of the faith, as contained in the Nicene-Constantinopolitan Creed (adjusted from plural to singular for baptismal purposes).[11]

The chapter concludes with the final prayer of the catechumenate ritual: "Call Thy servant to Thy holy Illumination; and grant unto him the grace of Thy holy Baptism. Put off from him the old man and renew him unto life everlasting. And fill him with the power of Thy Holy Spirit, in unity of Thy Christ, that he may be no more a child of the body, but a child of Thy kingdom."

Chapter Two discusses "Baptism." A community celebration of the paschal mystery, Baptism is a *passage* into God's kingdom, which renews the whole church in its commitment to the life of the kingdom.

In the baptismal mystery, the *mystery of the water* has three dimensions: the *cosmic* one, in which creation (the water exorcised) is renewed and re-created (Baptism as new creation); the *ecclesiological* one, in which Baptism purifies, regenerates, and renews the new members of the Church through the Holy Spirit (Baptism as sacrament of the Church); and the *eschatological* one, in which Baptism makes the church a partaker of the new life of the kingdom of God, resurrected life in Christ (Baptism as sacrament of the kingdom).

As the author reviews the blessing of the water, he remarks that Baptism begins with the eucharistic blessing of the kingdom. This indicates the connectedness between Baptism and Eucharist. The same can be said of the Sacrament of Holy Matrimony, as both Baptism and Matrimony not only were [are] normally "celebrated in the context of the eucharistic gathering of the Church," but also "the Eucharist was [is] their self-evident 'end' and fulfillment."

In the *petitions* before the great blessing of the water, some of the elements of Baptism are revealed: the water is sanctified by the Spirit; it "contains" the "grace of redemption," and the blessing brought to the Jordan by Christ; it "contains" the "purifying operation of the super-essential Trinity," manifested in the Jordan River at Christ's Baptism; in the water, the descent of the Holy Spirit grants "illumination by the light and understanding of piety"; the water becomes "effectual unto averting of every snare of the enemies, both visible and invisible"; it makes the baptized "worthy of the Kingdom incorruptible," a "child of the light and an heir of good eternal things"; a "member and a partaker of the death and Resurrection of Christ our God," which is one of the major themes connected with Baptism in the Greek patristic tradition. Finally, the baptismal water is for the baptized "a laver of regeneration, unto remission of sins, and a garment of incorruption."[12]

The prayer which *the priest offers on behalf of himself* is quoted and commented upon; the priest prays for his own unworthiness, asking God not to take it into account, so that the sacrament may not be affected by it; there is no magic in the sacraments, and no magic with Baptism, Fr. Schmemann acknowledges; also, "validity" is not enough, if there is no fulfillment of the sacrament, a fulfillment which involves not only the baptized, but the entire church as well. Baptism is a process, which involves the entire Christian community, Fr. Schmemann concludes. As the whole community takes part in the preparation for Baptism, the whole community is also responsible for the eternal salvation of the newly baptized.[13]

The *consecration of the water* follows. Its parts are quoted and analyzed: It is a *eucharistic prayer*, similar to that of the Holy Eucharist: preface, *anamnesis* (remembrance) of the saving events of salvation history, and God's self-disclosure; the last one here is the manifestation (*epiphany*) of the Holy Trinity in the Jordan River, the hallowing of its streams by the Holy Spirit, and the restoration of matter (water) to its original status of creation as a means for man to have communion with God.

The *epiclesis* (invocation) of the Holy Spirit and the *consecration* of the water follows. Through this consecration, the water is restored and fulfilled as a means of communion with God. "The holy water in Baptism, the bread and wine in the Eucharist, stand for, i.e., *represent* the whole creation, but creation as it will be at the *end*, when it will be consummated in God, when He will fill all things with Himself."

Consecrated matter is not an *end* in itself; it is a means of communion with Him whose *epiphany* and *presence* this matter is. This is why the Orthodox do not venerate the eucharistic gifts outside the Eucharistic Liturgy; the hallowed water becomes a means of transformation and regeneration, new birth and new creation for the baptized. The consecratory prayer concludes:

> Wherefore, O Lord, manifest Thyself in this water, and grant that he who is baptized therein may be transformed; that he may put away from him the old man, which is corrupt through the lusts of the flesh, and that he may be clothed with the new man, and renewed after the image of Him who created him: that being buried after the pattern of Thy death, in baptism, he may, in like manner, be a partaker of Thy Resurrection; and having preserved the gift of the Holy Spirit, and increased the measure of grace committed unto him, he may receive the prize of his high calling, and be numbered with the first-born whose names are written in heaven, in Thee, our God and Lord Jesus Christ. For unto Thee are due glory, dominion, honor, and worship, together with Thy Father who is from everlasting and Thine All-Holy and Good and Life-Giving Spirit, now and ever, and unto ages of ages. Amen.[14]

The blessing of the *Oil of Gladness* and the anointing with it follows. Fr. Schmemann makes a few comments on the significance of oil, which is traditionally used as medicine, as a "natural source of light" (thus becoming a symbol of joy), and as a symbol of peace and reconciliation.

The pre-baptismal anointment of both the water and the body of the catechumen is the symbol of joyful life, the gift of the Holy Spirit.[15]

As oil is applied to the entire body of and the senses of the catechumen, the entire man (soul and body) is restored and re-created in Baptism, being fully restored in wholesomeness.

The next section, on "'Form' and 'Essence,'" is actually a question regarding the various theological understandings of Baptism. Baptism is the "self-evident beginning and foundation of Christian life," Fr. Schmemann says. However, "the explanations and interpretations of this fundamental act began at a rather early date to differ from one another."

Fr. Schmemann is stricken by the "inability of modern or post-patristic theology to explain the relationship between Baptism and death and Resurrection of Christ." He sees a shift in academic theology, interpreting Baptism only as removal of the "original sin" and the bestowing of a kind of "grace."

However, Baptism should always be understood in terms of *death and resurrection*, not as images, but as reality. The author finally discusses the question of "form" and "essence": baptism is the "likeness" of Christ's death and resurrection. This "likeness" is what theologians call "form," and this "form" reveals the "essence," which is *participation in* and *epiphany of* the death and resurrection of Christ.

With regard to "form," the "validity" of the sacrament is discussed, to say that the "validity" of the sacrament "does not depend on the question of 'form'."[16]

The next section deals with the actual meaning of "Likeness of Christ's Death and Resurrection," to indicate that *likeness* is actual *participation* in Christ's death and risen life.

The author discusses Christ's *voluntary* suffering and death; Christ's *desire* for this death, for the sake of the "life of the world"; the "spiritual meaning" of death, a death accepted by Christ in order to annihilate "death by death."

The author discusses the inability of modern man to understand death in any other way but biological. With Christ's death and Resurrection, there is no change in biological death. However, biological death is not the *whole* of death. The real death is death as a *spiritual reality*, that is man's *separation from life*. This life is *God's life*.

This *spiritual death* is not opposed to the soul's "immortality," but it is opposed to *life*, true life in God. The *whole* death is the result of *sin*. It is from this death that Christ's death frees us. For there is no real (spiritual) death in Christ's (physical) death; this is why Christ passes from death into life. In Christ, "death is no more."

Thus, dying in Christ's likeness means dying unto sin, in order to be liberated from sin and be resurrected into life in Christ and through Christ's death and Resurrection.[17]

The last section in the chapter is "Baptism." In order for Baptism to be *fulfilled*, there should be the *desire* for it. What does this mean in terms of *infant* Baptism? Actually, not very much!

The efficacy of Baptism does not depend upon our personal faith (either as an adult or youngster) but *on the faith of Christ*, expressed and adhered to by the Church. *Personal faith* is good for *conversion* of an unbeliever, as it is good for infant Baptism, when expressed by the godparent or the child's parents. However, what constitutes the Baptism is not personal faith, but the faith of Christ: "as many of us as have been baptized in Christ, have put on Christ." It is He who acts in us.

Regarding infants, the Church admits them to Baptism, because they belong to her from birth: they are the children of Christian parents. Their *churching* indicates their belonging to the Church, even before Baptism. The Church baptizes them, knowing that their parents' faith is a guarantee as to their Christian upbringing. However, the Church does not do the same with the children of unbelievers, or members of other non-Christian faiths.

The last item in this section is the actual Baptism (immersion) of the catechumen, baptized in the name of the Holy Trinity by triple immersion and emersion.

The "baptismal grace" given at Baptism is the gift of Christ, the gift of Christ's death and Resurrection, as a personalized reality. It is the foretaste of risen life in Christ and through Christ.

One more important element in this section is a quotation from St. Gregory of Nyssa, according to whom "this [baptismal] water truly" is "for us both tomb and mother." "Tomb" indicates participation in Christ's death and Resurrection. "Mother" indicates the "new birth," "birth from on high," "of water and the Spirit," which are the indications of Christian Baptism in the books of the New Testament.[18]

Chapter Three of the book is dedicated to "The Sacrament of the Holy Spirit." What is meant by this is certainly not that the Spirit is given through the Baptism of water (this would be the case for the Syriac tradition, or that of St. John Chrysostom in his *Catecheses*). Here the Sacrament of the Holy Spirit is the second sacrament, that of *Chrismation* (or Confirmation).

The chapter begins with the bestowal of the *White Garment*, also called *shining garment*, *royal robe*, and *garment of immortality*. The garment symbolizes the "spiritual purity and righteousness for which each Christian must strive in his life." It is a symbol of the newness of life, the glorious life of resurrection, the life of the kingdom. It reminds us of the white garments of Christ on Mount Tabor at His Transfiguration, as well as the apparitions to the disciples of the glorious, Risen Lord.[19]

The next section speaks of *The Seal of the Gift of the Holy Spirit*. The ritual of Chrismation, which follows that of Baptism, is both an *integral part* of the baptismal celebration, thus of Baptism, but also *distinct* from and the *fulfillment* of Baptism.

What is given this time is not Christ *per se*, but the Holy Spirit, who anoints Christ and makes Christ who He is: the Anointed of God, anointed by God's Holy Spirit. It is the same Spirit, Who anoints Christ, Who also anoints the Christians at Baptism (see St. Irenaeos: *Chrisma, Christus, Christiani*).

In receiving the "Spirit of adoption," at Baptism, we become an extension of Christ-the-Anointed-of-God and adoptive sons in the Son of God. What we receive through the Sacrament of the Holy Spirit is not the gifts of the Spirit, but the Spirit Himself.[20]

The following sections speak of the "three offices" given to the baptized on the basis of his/her Chrismation with Holy Chrism: In the same way oil was used in the Old Testament to anoint kings, priests, and prophets, so the Christian at Baptism (which includes Confirmation) are anointed kings, priests, and prophets.

A *king* is someone vested with *authority* and *power*. So it is with man at Baptism. Being appointed king of creation by God, and having failed his mission, he is now restored to his authority and power to bring creation under God's dominion. This kingship is restored through Christ's death upon the cross. It is given to man through Baptism (participation in Christ's death) and Confirmation (Chrismation), which anoints him with the same anointment of Christ: His Holy Spirit.[21]

A *priest* is someone who mediates salvation and sanctification for man and the world. Christ is the High Priest. However, one of the gifts that comes from the Spirit's anointment is that the baptized is an extension of Christ as priest. St. Peter calls this priesthood of all believers (all baptized) a "royal priesthood." It is the context in which "institutional," or "ordained" priesthood finds its meaning, fullness, and fulfillment. It is man's responsibility to mediate salvation and sanctification for the world, thus bringing it to *communion* with God.

Fallen man refuses to be this priest for God's creation. In today's society, he becomes the *consumer* of the world instead of receiving the world eucharistically and offering it back to communion with God.

Christ restores this priesthood by accepting it. The Church is the extension of this priesthood. In the context of the royal priesthood, institutional priesthood, which is Christ's personal priesthood, receives a new meaning: that of being "set apart" and representing Christ, entrusted by Him with the continuation of His ministry in a unique way.[22]

A *prophet* is someone who hears the voice of God, and represents the will of God in the midst of his fellowmen. Man was called to be God's prophet. Man's fall took him away from this office. False prophets and pseudo-prophecy is the result. Christ restores the gift of prophecy by becoming God's prophet par excellence. The gift of Christ's prophecy is extended to the baptized. This gift goes together with sobriety, inner-wholeness and integrity, discernment, and understanding. It does not agree with irrationality.[23]

The final section of this chapter is "The Holy Spirit." As it is true that the Holy Spirit give us Christ, so it is true that Christ gives us the Holy Spirit, as in a continuous Pentecost. Baptism fulfilled in confirmation (chrismation) is thus our personalized Pentecost and the gift of the Holy Spirit Himself.

St. Seraphim of Sarov sees as the goal of Christian life "the acquisition of the Holy Spirit." For St. Paul, the kingdom of God is "righteousness, and peace, and joy in the Holy Spirit" (Rom. 14:17).

Some people have difficulty understanding the Holy Spirit, considering Him as a "divine It." The reason is that these people attempt to have intellectual knowledge of the Spirit; they want to know things *about* the Spirit instead of knowing Him (the Paraclete) by experiencing His presence in the life of the Church. And yet his presence in us is the fulfillment of true happiness.

The Spirit communicates to us the abundant life of the kingdom. He makes us the Body of Christ. And yet his person is not revealed to us, as He is the only one of the three persons in God not to have his icon (image) in another person.

His presence in us is known through the abundance of the "fruits of the spirit."[24]

Chapter Four deals with "The Entrance into the Kingdom." Baptism and confirmation are that entrance into the life of the kingdom, present in Christ and the Spirit who communicate it to the Church as the *inaugurated* kingdom.

Section one speaks of the importance of the baptismal procession following baptism and confirmation, and before the readings. Now, the procession is a circular one around the baptismal font. This is the remnant of the actual procession from the *baptisterion*, where the first two sacraments of initiation were celebrated, to the main church of the paschal/eucharistic celebration. The baptismal procession and the paschal procession were only one.

The event into which the two sacraments lead is the new reality of God's inaugurated kingdom, an event celebrated at Pascha. The Eucharist, to which the two sacraments lead, is also a celebration of this same paschal event and the new reality of God's inaugurated kingdom.

Fr. Schmemann notices that Baptism is a paschal celebration, and pascha is a baptismal celebration. Traditionally, Baptism was celebrated at the paschal vigil, after a long catechumenate throughout Lent. The readings of the Epistle and the Gospel at the Vespers of Holy Saturday (now the Vesperal "first" pascal Divine Liturgy celebrated on Holy Saturday morning, or in Jerusalem, following the ceremony and miracle of the new resurrection light Holy Saturday afternoon) are identical with those read at the celebration of Baptism, and vice-versa.

Another linkage between baptismal and paschal celebration is the closed (royal) door before the procession: this door opens following the procession and before the readings. Traditionally, the baptismal/paschal procession led to the main door of the church, which was closed up to the point of the procession.

When the two celebrations (baptismal and paschal) are still connected, their order is the traditional one: vigil, Baptism, procession, and Eucharist.

As Pascha is both an end and a new beginning, so is Baptism: it is the end of the lengthy preparation leading toward it, throughout Lent; and it is a new beginning, an eschatological celebration of the kingdom already present, even if it is not yet fully so.[25]

The next section deals with the relationship between two of the initiation sacraments, "Baptism and Eucharist."[26] *Baptism* is the sacrament of *regeneration*, whereas the *Eucharist* is the sacrament of the Church, that is, "the sacrament which fulfills the Church as the presence and the gift in 'this world' of the kingdom of God."

Let us quote the author with regard to interrelatedness and interdependence of the three sacraments of Christian initiation, Baptism, Chrismation, and Eucharist:

> In the early tradition, baptism, chrismation and Eucharist 'belong together,' form one liturgical sequence and 'ordo,' because each sacrament within it is fulfilled in the other in such a way that it is impossible fully to understand the meaning of one in separation and isolation from the other two. If chrismation, as we have tried to show, fulfills baptism, Eucharist is the fulfillment of Chrismation. Fulfillment here means not 'validity,' each sacrament being 'valid' in its own right, but the spiritual, dynamic and existential correlation of these sacraments in the *new life* received from Christ. In baptism we are born again of Water and the Spirit, and it is this birth which makes us *open* to the gift of the Holy Spirit, to our personal Pentecost. And finally, it is the gift of the Holy Spirit that 'opens' to us access to the Church, to Christ's table in His kingdom. We are baptized so that we may receive the Holy Spirit;

we receive the Holy Spirit so that we may become living members of the Body of Christ, growing within
the Church into the fullness of Christ's stature.[27]

The next section speaks of the "Rites of the Eighth Day:" they
are the washing off of the Holy Chrism and the tonsure, which are
now performed at the end of the baptismal celebration, but which
traditionally were celebrated later, "on the eighth day."

A post-baptismal catechesis, called *mystagogia*, took place during Bright Week. The seven days of the week symbolize the world
of creation, whereas the eighth day is the day of the kingdom,
inaugurated with Christ's resurrection and the descent of the Holy
Spirit on Pentecost. The *eighth day* is actually a day beyond time
and beyond the created world: it is the day of the new creation,
during which we are no longer *in statu viae*, but *in statu patriae*,
the ecclesiological time of the kingdom.

Of course, there is a constant tension between these antinomic
realities: history and eschatology, old and new, world and kingdom, already and not yet, vertical and horizontal.[28]

The "Washing off the Holy Chrism" and "The Tonsure" are the
last sections in this chapter. The washing off of the Chrism done
for practical purposes, receives a symbolic meaning as well, indicating the neophyte's readiness to now fight the devil and serve
the kingdom. The original laying on of hands (originally done by
the bishop and now by the priest) indicates the commission given
to the newly baptized to join in the fight against evil powers and
work for the expansion of the kingdom. The challenge with which
the neophyte is faced is that of *martyria* (witness).

The *tonsure* is a rite known to the Old Testament, as well. It
signifies both offering one's life to God, sacrifice, and dedication.

The prayer leading to the tonsure is an opportunity of thanks-
giving to God for the beauty of man's creation, even the fall.

The baptismal rite in its entirety, including Chrismation and
the Eucharist, is the passage for the neophyte into God's Holy
Kingdom. "It is when the baptismal liturgy is accomplished that
Baptism begins to work with us."[29]

Chapter Five deals with "The churching" of a child, a rite performed on the fortieth day after the child's birth. It is a rite of purification for the mother, and of a preliminary incorporation (registration) of the child in the church.

The rite is in continuity with Old Testament practices. However, together with the continuity with the old order of things, there is a fulfillment of these things and a new attitude which accompanies the fulfillment, that of freedom.

In discussing the rites of the first day of birth, which indicate that a kind of *forgiveness* is given to the mother, the author tries to explain that forgiveness as a help for healing and wholesomeness for the mother: "What can the Church offer her except forgiveness, which is always the passage into life redeemed by Christ?"

The rite of the naming of the child with a Christian name on the eighth day after the child's birth is presented and discussed. The naming is a kind of commitment on behalf of the parents that the child will be brought up in the Christian faith.

The actual rite of the churching concludes the chapter. It is a rite which benefits the mother, who now is restored to community life and the reception of the holy sacraments, especially the Eucharist.

The churching prayer benefits the child, who is now being prepared for Baptism "in due time."[30]

In the conclusion[31] the author wants to make certain that no one misunderstands his study as an effort to restore the past. On the other hand, he supports continuity with this past, guided by God's Holy Spirit, who is always the same Spirit, as Christ is "the same yesterday, and today, and forever" (Heb. 13:8).

It is imperative for the Church to keep its tradition, continuity in life and practice in a changing world, which, however, is the same in terms of its hostility toward the Gospel of Christ. The Church cannot be identified with this fallen world.

The Orthodox should regain and recover the *mind* and the *experience* of the Church "which is the only source of a truly Orthodox worldview and of a truly Christian life. And this source, always living and life-giving, is precisely baptism ... as that essential act by which the Church always reveals her own faith, her 'experience' of man and the world, of creation, fall and redemption, of Christ and the Holy Spirit, of the new life of the new creation, as indeed the source of the whole life of the Church and of the Christian life of each one of us."

For the experience and life of the Church to become *baptismal* again, it is necessary to rediscover the true meaning and power of baptism, as the sacrament of the water and the Spirit. This can only be achieved through *education*, which has always been understood "as the indivisible unity of *teaching, liturgical experience,* and *spiritual effort.*" The author comments on each of these three tools of pertinent Christian education for renewal of our theology, liturgy, and spirituality on the basis of the sacraments of Christian initiation. He concludes:

> Obviously none of these 'recoveries' – the theological, the liturgical, the spiritual – can be instantaneous, the fruit of merely external reforms and 'adjustments.' We need much patient study, much pastoral concern, and much love. And above all we need a deepening of our Church consciousness, of the very mind of the Church, truly a thirst and hunger for 'living water.' But I am absolutely convinced that such recovery is not only desirable and possible, but that indeed only in it, only by a common 'rediscovery' of the true meaning of Baptism, of its fullness, beauty, power and joy, can we again make our faith 'the victory that overcomes the world' (1 Jn. 5:4). It is this conviction that I wished to confess, however inadequately, in this study.[32]

From a Roman Catholic point of view, in the recent publications of the *Rite of Baptism for Children*[33] and *Rite of Christian Initiation of Adults* (henceforth R.C.I.A.)[34] pertinent information is given in the introductions, as well as in the commentaries, of the various rituals. There is a welcome change in the Roman Catholic practice which is very encouraging in terms of rapprochement between the two practices, Eastern and Western.

From the point of view of the abundant scholarly studies on Christian initiation, some of the articles with which I have consulted are the articles in *Made, Not Born,*[35] in which the following important articles are included: "Christian Initiation: Tactics and Strategy" by Aidan Kavanagh, O.S.B; "Christian Initiation in the New Testament" by Reginald H. Fuller; "Development of Christian Catechumenate" by Robert M. Grant; "Dissolution of the Rite of Initiation" by Nathan D. Mitchell; "Christian Initiation: The Reformation Period" by Leonel L. Mitchell; "Christian Initiation, Post-Reformation to the Present Era" by Daniel B. Stevick; "Christian Initiation of Adults: The Rites" by Aidan Kavanagh, O.S.B.; "Christian Initiation: The State of the Question" by Ralph A. Keifer; and, "Hope for the Future: A Summary" by Robert W. Hovda. Reference to some of this literature will be made in my presentation.

Besides these studies, some of which were published as far back as 1974, there are some more recent articles on the same subject with which I have consulted. They are, in chronological order: "The Postconciliar Infant Baptism Debate in the American Catholic Church" by Paul F. X. Covino;[36] "Infant Baptism Reconsidered" by Mark Searle;[37] and "Recent Research on Christian Initiation" by Georg Kretschmar.[38]

Most of these studies encourage the development in the western practice to consider the restoration of the Christian initiation rites as one celebration for the adults (see R.C.I.A.); they support the interconnectedness-interdependence of the three initiation sacraments; they see infant Baptism in a new light, not only encouraging that the practice should continue, especially when the parents are Christians; but also that there is room for confirmation and Eucharist to be given to the infants and children, as part of a unified and continuous Christian initiation, just as with the adults.

The reasons advanced (by at least one of the authors) in defending a unified Christian initiation for children are similar with those advanced by Fr. Schmemann: the recovered "public and ecclesial dimension of the sacraments," which enables us "to recognize that sacraments, when properly celebrated, are meant to redound to the benefit not only of the recipient but of the whole ecclesial community."[39]

The same author advances the argument from contemporary "data of the human sciences concerning the child-in-relationship" not known before, and the fact that even adults are not fully "intellectually" informed of what is involved in the sacraments, that is God's gift more than our doing. For all these reasons, the author concludes: "far from barring children from the font, the chrism, and the altar, the Church should welcome their participation in these sacraments as a reminder both of the catholicity of the Church and the fact that, no matter how informed or committed we might be as adults, when we take part in the sacramental liturgies of the Church we are taking part in more than we know."[40]

Also, another important finding in these studies is the Jewish precedent of the Spirit being imparted *before* Baptism according to the Syrian (especially Syriac) sequence.[41]

This finding not only confirms the Jewish roots of Christian faith and practice, but also allows us to see the close interrelationship of the first two sacraments, those of the "water" and the (gift of the) "Spirit," Baptism and confirmation.

These recent studies also establish that the "disintegration of the primitive rite of initiation" is the doing of the western Middle Ages, and express the desire for the correction of this practice. Georg Kretschmar says: "The unity of water-baptism, imposition of hands [chrismation] and first communion which that expression [regarding disintegration] assumed to be the norm did undeniably fall asunder in the West in the Middle Ages. It was by contrast preserved in the Orthodox and other oriental rites, a point now clearly and forcefully emphasized by theologians of those churches."[42]

On the basis of these readings, let me now attempt a brief synthesis regarding the three sacraments of initiation and their interrelatedness and interdependence.

II. THE SACRAMENTS OF INITIATION AS
SACRAMENTS OF CHURCH COMMUNION

What the three sacraments of initiation have in common is that all three of them are a paschal/pentecostal celebration, having their origin in Christ and the Spirit, the *Uhr Sakrament*. All three of them, interrelated and interdependent, impart the paschal/pentecostal mystery of new life in Christ and the Spirit, the life of the kingdom inaugurated by the paschal mystery of the restoration/re-creation of the human nature by the Risen Christ, imparted by the Spirit in the continuous Pentecost of the Church.

The ultimate purpose of all three initiation sacraments is communion with God, participation in the life of the kingdom inaugurated by Christ and the Spirit, and the life of *theosis* (transfigured life in God) made available by them. More specifically, each of the three initiation sacraments contributes to the restoration of communion with God and impartation of the paschal/pentecostal mystery and the new life of the kingdom as follows:

The *Sacrament of Baptism*, of *Water and the Spirit*, is the "sacrament of regeneration," of the renewal of creation of a "new birth," necessary so that the "old," or biological birth, accompanied by "original," or "ancestral" sin may be counteracted and discontinued.

St. Gregory of Nyssa is right in seeing Baptism as both "womb and tomb." It is a "womb," in that it is the sacrament of "new birth," birth all over again, or "birth from on high." Adoption to sonship is the gift of the Spirit, the "Spirit of adoption." The gift of "adoption to sonship" is given by the Spirit at Baptism, as Baptism imparts "the grace of the Jordan River," the grace of the Baptism of Christ, in Whom and through Whom we are adoptive sons (sons by grace). The Syrian (Syriac) tradition should be thanked for this contribution. St. John Chrysostom is a representative of this tradition when he speaks of Baptism as the gift of both Christ and the Spirit, without reference to another, second initiation sacrament which in the Jerusalem tradition imparts the Spirit: the sacrament of Chrismation.

Another important dimension of Baptism is expressed in the epistle to the Romans: participation in the paschal mystery, the death and resurrection of Jesus Christ. The triple immersion-emersion of Baptism is the symbol (which makes present what it symbolizes) of Christ's death and Resurrection. We are really participants in Christ's death, and we really enjoy the life of resurrection, the new life in Christ's inaugurated kingdom, stemming from our Baptism. The Christian baptism is also our *tomb* in terms of burying our "old," sinful man, so that we may walk in the newness of life, the risen life in Christ.

Thus, Baptism is our new, personalized Pascha, for Christ Himself is given to us at Baptism through the operation of the Holy Spirit. At this point, a text by Methodios (of Olympos) in his *Symposium* is very revealing. The text says:

> Now I think the Church is here said *to bring forth a man child* (cf. Rev 12:5) simply because the enlightened spiritually receive the features, and image, and manliness of Christ; the likeness of the Word is stamped upon and is begotten within them by perfect knowledge and faith, and thus Christ is spiritually begotten in each one. And so it is that the Church is with child and in labor until Christ is formed and born within us, so that each of the saints by sharing in Christ is born again as Christ.
>
> This is the meaning of the passage in Scripture which says: Touch you not my anointed; and do no evil to my prophets: (Ps. 104:15); those who are baptized in Christ become, so to speak, other Christs by a communication of the Spirit, and here it is the Church that effects this transformation into a clear image of the Word. Thus the Word of truth must be stamped and imprinted upon the souls of those who are born again.[43]

Christians (which means "anointed ones") are anointed by the Spirit at baptism, becoming "other Christs by a communication of the Spirit," St. Methodios says. There is no specification how this "anointment of the Spirit" takes place.

In another proof text by St. Ephrem the Syrian, this "anointment of the Spirit" happens through the pre-baptismal unction of by the baptismal oil. St. Ephrem says: "The oil is the dear friend of the Holy Spirit; it serves him, following him like a disciple. With it the Spirit signed priests and anointed kings; for with the oil the Holy Spirit imprints his mark on his sheep. Like a signet ring whose impression is left on the wax, so the hidden seal of the Spirit is imprinted by oil on the bodies of those who are anointed in

Baptism; thus they are marked in the baptismal mystery."[44]

Later in the text St. Ephrem specifies: "The priesthood ministers to this womb [Baptism] as it gives birth; anointing precedes it, the Holy Spirit hovers [Gen. 1:2] over its streams ..."[45] The anointment does not follow, as in the Jerusalem tradition, but precedes Baptism. And the Holy Spirit is given in that "kaleidoscopic view" of Baptism. The Spirit is given in the oil ointment, but He also "hovers over its [the Baptism's] streams."

Of course, in the Jerusalem tradition the sequence is different: Jesus is "confirmed" as the beloved Son of the Father following His Baptism in the Jordan river; and the Spirit, who "confirms the truth" of the voice of the Father calling Jesus His beloved Son, appears "in the likeness of a dove" following Jesus' Baptism. The same sequence is to be kept at the Baptism of Christians, the anointed ones in the Anointed of God, Christ, whose extension they become by the anointment of the Spirit at Baptism.

Fr. Schmemann is absolutely right when he sees the two sacraments, Baptism and Confirmation, as interdependent and interrelated. Chrismation is, more than anything else, the *fulfillment* of Baptism; it is part of Baptism (in the East there is no distinct celebration of confirmation apart from the baptismal celebration), but also distinct as the seal of the gift of the Holy Spirit imparted on the occasion of Baptism.

As the Paschal mystery is fulfilled in the mystery of Pentecost; as Christ, the Anointed of God, and the Risen Lord of the Christian faith, is made present in the life of the Church through the descent of the Spirit in a continuous Pentecost, so in Baptism, "Christ is formed and born within us" (St. Methodios quoted above) in the womb of the Church, Baptism, through the operation of the Holy Spirit.

Chrismation (Confirmation) is the fulfillment of Baptism, and our personalized Pentecost. During this Pentecost, and according to His promise, Christ, given to us at baptism by the Holy Spirit, sends us personally the gift of the Holy Spirit, to lead us to fulfillment in Christ, anoints us with the same gifts with which He anoints Christ, and gives us the "panoply" (armor) of the Spirit, so that we may "fight the good fight" against evil and its pseudo-power, the devil and his pride (pomp) that we denounced and rejected at Baptism.[46]

Fr. Schmemann is right when he identifies the gift given at Baptism (and "Confirmation") not as the many "gifts" of the Spirit (in plural), but the Spirit Himself. The text read at the application of Holy Chrismation is that of *dorea*, a *free gift*.[47]

Since this sacrament is a free gift, the gift of the Spirit, one does not need to be fully cognizant of the importance of the gift (such knowledge is supposed to be that of the "adults"; this is why after the disintegration of the initiation ceremony in the West and after Confirmation was separated from Baptism, Confirmation began to be considered as an "adult sacrament"). Infants and children are as entitled to receiving the gift as are adults. On this point, Aidan Kavanagh asks: "If age is a serious obstacle to confirmation, why then is age not a serious obstacle to receiving baptism? Theological discussion will have to cope with this anomaly."[48]

One of the common traditions between East and West is that this "second sacrament" of Christian initiation involves the bishop directly. In the West, the laying on of hands by the bishop is normally indispensable. In the East, the priest who celebrates the Baptism is authorized by the bishop to represent him. As a sign of this authorization, the bishop is the only one to consecrate and provide the Holy Chrism.[49]

Both baptismal rites, Eastern and Western, include a kind of commission by the bishop (or, in his absence, the priest in the bishop's name) through a laying on of hands upon the neophyte. Thus, the neophyte, who through Baptism and Chrismation is anointed by God's Holy Spirit to be a "king, priest and prophet," receives the authorization and the assignment by the head of the Christian community to exercise his (her) ministry within and on behalf of the community. After he (she) receives the gift of the Spirit, he (she) is now sent to witness as a present day apostle living a present day Pentecost.

Finally, the third sacrament of initiation is that of the *Holy Eucharist*. The other two sacraments find their *fulfillment* in the

Eucharist, the "Sacrament of the Church." As St. Ephrem says in his *Hymns*: "Once this womb [Baptism] has given birth, the altar suckles and nurtures them: her [the Church's] children eat straight away, not milk, but perfect bread [the Eucharistic Bread, of course!]."[50]

The neophyte, a newborn baby, is already ready not just for milk, but for that "perfect Bread" of the Eucharist, the "Bread of Life" for both children and adults. Introduced into the life of the kingdom, the newness of life of the paschal mystery which is the center of the life of the Church as the inaugurated kingdom, the neophyte is ready to fully partake of this life; the life which is a gift, and which sustains everyone, old and young alike, to everlasting life, the goal of our creation.

In Fr. Schmemann's words, according to the Church fathers and the tradition of the entire Church, East and West, the Holy Eucharist is "the 'focus'," the source and the fulfillment of the entire – and not merely the "liturgical" life of the Church, the "sacrament of the Church's self-manifestation and edification."[51]

The Spirit descends "upon the community and upon the gifts" not only to consecrate the gifts and change them to be truly the Body and Blood of Christ, but also to consecrate the worshipping community, the Church, and make it the living Eucharist, the living Body of Christ. The purpose of the consecration of the gifts is not for them to be "venerated," but consumed, so that "Holy Gifts" may be given "unto the holy," and so that the many may be gathered together, as the One Bread, the One Body of Christ, the "real presence" of the resurrected, transfigured life in Christ the Risen Lord.

The Eucharist, being, together with Baptism, the celebration of the paschal mystery, and the celebration with Chrismation of Pentecost, the "birthday of the Church," is the "sacrament of the Church" in so many ways. It is the glorious and risen body of Christ; Christ made present through the Spirit; the new life of the kingdom inaugurated, manifested in the Pentecost continually present in the life of the church; the kingdom inaugurated and the *eschaton* anticipated. It is the sacrament joining together history and eschatology, vertical and horizontal, living and dead, poor and rich, male and female, rulers and subjects, clergy and laity, created and uncreated existence, into one communion of love. In this Eucharist is the sacrament of the Church.[52]

All three sacraments of initiation are the sacraments which constitute and build up communion in the life of the Church. It is the communion of eternal life, the life of the kingdom, the life of God destined to us, and made available to us by the Father through the event of His Christ in the Spirit.

All three sacraments of initiation are events of faith in the life of the Church. They manifest the church realities of which they are called to be the epiphany. The one main reality which all these sacraments manifest, is the reality of the eternal life of God in which man is called to participate and which our Christian One God, a trinity of hypostases, offers in communion to man and the entire creation.

Thus, insofar as these sacraments put us in communion with the life of the Holy Trinity, all three of them are sacraments of communion. Let us now pause for a moment to ponder the role that the three divine persons play with regard to these communion sacraments of Christian initiation.

III. The Sacraments From the Trinity

John Zizioulas rightly states that being in general is communion. For being to really be, it has to be relational. Thus is true being, the being of God, shared by a trinity of hypostases. Shared by three divine hypostases, God's being is relational par excellence.

Now, God creates beings out of non-pre-existing matter; he creates spiritual entities, as well, and calls them into being through relations with the three persons of the Trinity, and with one another. Man has a very special place amongst the other creatures: being created as a psycho-physical unity, he not only has received the call to be God's image, reflecting personhood and its gifts, the highest of which is love; but he also receives the challenge to bring God's creation into full communion with God, as the keeper and guide of God's creation in its movement toward God.

Unfortunately, Adam fails to achieve his call. Thus, the coming of a "new Adam" is imperative. Not only does Christ, the new Adam, restore creation to its original beauty; but He also achieves the goal of man's creation, which is eternal life in God.

The Father is the author and origin of eternal life for His creation. He creates by His two hands, the Son and the Spirit. He creates through the Son, and perfects His creation through the Spirit.

Following man's failure to keep his life in communion with God, God sends His Son to restore life for the world: "He came so that we may have life, and have it abundantly" (Jn. 10:10). Through His incarnation, His becoming flesh, He restores humanity into life in communion with God. The Spirit of God makes Christ the Anointed of God; He works with Christ throughout His life making of His event, the event of salvation and deification, participation in the life of God.

Christ is risen from the dead through the power of God, His own power, but also the power of the Holy Spirit. There is absolute "synergy" of the three divine hypostases as they accomplish their work, be it the work of creation, or of its restoration through Christ's "economy," the plan of salvation executed by Christ, in the power of His Holy Spirit.

The Spirit gives the Anointed of God, Christ the Savior to the world and man; and Christ, on Pentecost, shares his anointing (see St. Irenaeos: *Chrisma, Christus, Christiani*) with human persons.

The Spirit, source of life for us, source of new life in Christ and the gift of sanctification, forms Christ in us and bestows on us His life. This is done in the sacramental life of the Church, and especially the three sacraments of Christian initiation, which incorporate us into new life in Christ and the Spirit, through the power and operation of Christ and the Spirit.[53]

If the life of the Trinity is communion; and if this communion is extended to us through the sacramental life of the Church, and especially the Eucharist, we realize the importance of the life of the Church as communion for all, both for Christians, whether by themselves or in dialogue among themselves, and also for the world for the life of which Christ sacrificed His own life.

Let us now spend a few moments to discuss sacraments, the initiation sacraments, and especially the two basic sacraments, which, according to John Chrysostom, came out of the open side of Christ which the soldier pierced with a spear: the sacraments of "blood" and "water," Eucharist and Baptism.

IV. Baptism and Eucharist as Constitutive of the Church as Communion

The importance for the building up of Church communion of Baptism, which together with Eucharist are part of Christian initiation and constitute the major and basic sacraments of the Church, cannot be overestimated and overemphasized.

Professor Erickson, quoted at the beginning of this essay, gives us enough clues with regard to this. But so does John Zizioulas, and so do most of the authors quoted to this point.

Fr. Schmemann has a classical statement with regard to Baptism and Eucharist as builders of the Church, as community and communion. After establishing that the goal of the Eucharist is building communion with God and among the worshipping community as *ecclesia*, that is a eucharistic gathering, he says:

> Clearly only such understanding and experience of the Eucharist reveals it as the self-evident and necessary fulfillment of baptism. Baptism, we are told, *integrates* us into the Church. But if the Church's ultimate being and essence are revealed in and through the Eucharist, if Eucharist is truly *the sacrament of the Church* and not only one of the Church's sacraments, then of necessity to enter the Church is to enter the Eucharist, then Eucharist is indeed the fulfillment of baptism. And the best way to understand this is to follow the newly baptized as they now *enter* the church in procession, join the body of the believers and together with them begin their participation in the eucharistic celebration.[54]

John Zizioulas, in his introduction to *Being As Communion*, emphatically states: "The being of each human person is given to him (her); consequently, the human person is not able to force himself absolutely from his 'nature' or from his 'substance' [essence], from what biological laws dictate to him [her], without bringing about his annihilation....The demand of the person for absolute freedom involves a 'new birth,' a birth 'from on high,' a baptism."[55] Is there a better foundation of Baptism as creating Church communion? This communion is not possible without a "new birth" that only baptism provides.

The same author returns to the doctrine of Baptism when he wants to find a concrete way of applying the "historical Christ," Christ who became history, to the concrete life of the Church seen as communion. He says:

> Christ's existence is applied to our historical existence not *in abstracto* or individualistically, but in and through a community. This community is formed from out of ordinary existence, through a radical conversion from individuals to personhood in baptism. As death and resurrection in Christ, baptism signifies the decisive passing of our existence from the 'truth' of individualized being into the truth of personal being. The resurrectional aspect of baptism is therefore nothing other than *incorporation into the community*. The existential truth arising from baptism is simply the truth of personhood, the truth of communion. A new birth is required for this, simply because birth by normal procreation, as stated in the previous chapter, is for created beings a cause of individualization and is thus a birth of beings destined to death. Eternal life needs the new birth of baptism as a 'birth in the Spirit,' just as Christ's own birth was 'in the Spirit,' so that each baptized person can himself become 'Christ,' his existence being one of communion and hence of true life.[56]

Zizioulas discusses the possibility of the priority of the work of the Spirit over Christ's and vice versa, on the basis of the Syrian

(Syriac) testimony of a priority of the work of the Spirit as Confirmation comes before Baptism. Zizioulas dismisses the importance of this priority, choosing for *simultaneity* of the two: "… there is … evidence suggesting that baptism itself was inconceivable in the early Church without the giving of the Spirit, which leads to the conclusion that the two rites were united in one synthesis both liturgically and theologically, regardless of the priority of any of the two aspects over the other."[57]

In another context, Zizioulas calls baptism "ordination of the laity." Both this "ordination" and that of the bishop have to be placed in the context of the Eucharist, the celebration of the kingdom, where history and eschatology meet. The sacraments, including those of initiation, are "iconic" in their character, as all of the ecclesial institutions. All these institutions, as signs of the presence of the kingdom, exist epicletically, that is they depend on the Holy Spirit and the prayer of the community.[58]

In discussing culture and Church, Zizioulas states that the Church may at times be critical of culture: "This is indicated by the fact that the Eucharist is preceded by baptism. The world cannot become Church without some kind of purification."[59]

As he discusses the local church constituted by its ministries, the author does not only discuss episcopacy as a constitutive ministry of the church as a eucharistic assembly, he also adds the ministries of the *laos Theou* (people of God), which is "an indispensable form of local church structure." There is here certainly a hint to "lay ordination" through Baptism, of which he spoke in the same context in the previous pages.[60]

In discussing the orders of the church, which are constitutive of its ecclesial being, the author says (in footnote): "The idea that the 'layman' is not a 'non-ordained' person but one who through baptism and chrismation belongs to his own order in the Church is fundamental in the correct understanding of the eucharistic synaxis and its ecclesiological implications."[61]

Finally, as the author discusses the responsibility of the Church not only to be an epiphany of the *eschaton*, but also to lead the world to God in a constant tension between history and eschatology, faith and culture, horizontal and vertical dimensions of the life of the Church, he emphatically states: "There is a constant interrelation between the Church and the world, the world being God's creation and never ceasing to belong to Him and the Church being the community which through the descent of the Holy Spirit transcends in herself the world and offers it to God in the eucharist." He continues in the footnote: "This transcendence which is possible only 'in the Spirit' presupposes a baptismal purification of man and his world and in this sense it is important to bear in mind the 'paschal' character of the Eucharist ... and the intimate relationship between baptism and Eucharist."[62]

It is a pity that the author never got a chance to exploit this "intimate relationship" between Baptism and Eucharist. I am certain that from the few hints he gives us, he would have important and interesting things to say.

The last author I would like to present regarding the constitutive character of the initiation sacraments with regard to church communion is Aidan Kavanagh. As he discusses Christian initiation in terms of tactics and strategy, he tries to find a "mutually profitable relationship" between the "converting individual" [person] and the church community to heal the trauma caused to the "individual" as a result of "the Church's insensitivity to crisis." The author offers communion as this "mutually profitable relationship": the kind of communion which is "the ultimate purpose of the whole initiatory process," and especially the Eucharist. He calls Baptism the beginning of Eucharist, and Eucharist the sustainer of Baptism. In his own words:

> This mutually profitable relationship is, on a sustained basis, what I conceive communion to be. Establishing such communion is the ultimate purpose of the whole initiatory process. Sustaining such communion beyond its initiatory phase is the ultimate purpose of the whole of Church order, the heart of which is the sacramental economy centering especially on the Eucharist. One might say, in sacramental terms, that baptism and all it presupposes is the way the Eucharist begins, and that

the Eucharist and all it causes is the way baptism is sustained. *Sacramenta significando efficiunt gratiam quam significant.* Sacraments by signifying cause the grace they signify.[63]

In this same context see the importance of *Lumen Gentium* (number 3) regarding the basic sacraments of Baptism and Eucharist in the life of the Church:

> The Church – that is, the kingdom of Christ – already present in mystery, grows visibly through the power of God in the world. The origin and growth of the Church are symbolized by the blood and water which flowed from the open side of the crucified Jesus (cf. Jn. 19:34), and are foretold in the words of the Lord referring to his death on the cross: 'And I, if I be lifted up from the earth, will draw all men to myself' (Jn 12:32). As often as the sacrifice of the cross by which 'Christ our Pascha is sacrificed' (1 Cor 5:7) is celebrated on the altar, the work of our redemption is carried out. Likewise, in the sacrament of the eucharistic bread, the unity of believers, who form one body in Christ (cf. 1 Cor 10:17), is both expressed and brought about. All men are called to this union with Christ, who is the light of the world, from whom we go forth, through whom we live, and towards whom our whole life is directed.[64]

Baptism and Eucharist are constitutive of the life of the Church as communion, however, in a complementary, non-antagonistic manner. Not only Baptism and Confirmation, but the rest of the sacraments as well find their fulfillment in the Eucharist, the sacrament of the Church. No wonder that communion, which is the goal of and the result of all the sacraments, but especially the Eucharist, is taken as synonymous to Church; and no wonder that communion ecclesiology is here to stay. In the classification of sacraments as initiatory, healing, and community service oriented, the Eucharist makes all three lists. It is not just another sacrament as a means of "grace," but the very heart and center of the whole life of the Church. No one of the other sacraments can be called "the sacrament of the Church" to the same degree as the Eucharist.

Baptism is the foundational sacrament, the one which incorporates into the church, the "sacrament of regeneration." But incorporation into and the beginning of the new life of the kingdom through a new birth cannot define or express the life itself of the church. The Holy Eucharist can.

In the light of these remarks, let us now see the shortcomings of eucharistic ecclesiology, and appreciate some of the correctives that can be offered from the point of view of an ecclesiology which is inspired by Baptism.

V. "Eucharistic" versus "Baptismal" Ecclesiology

In the two articles of John Erickson[65] quoted at the beginning of this presentation, some criticism is rightly addressed to a one-sided "eucharistic ecclesiology" of the late Fr. Nicholas Afanasieff. To say that "where there is the Eucharist celebrated, there is the Church" needs qualifications.

John Zizioulas, the "painstakingly balanced," brought about many corrections to Fr. Afansieff's statement. The major one is the simultaneity of "local" and "catholic" Church. In excluding "all pyramidal structures" from his eucharistic ecclesiology, Zizioulas does not exclude a hierarchy among the local churches (dioceses) of a given area, the existence of the Synod (or Synods) and councils; but also, along with the idea of "collegiality" goes that of the primacy of a major bishop in a given area. That "primacy," based on Apostolic Canon 34, presupposes collegiality and is interdependent with it.

Zizioulas deplores the "rupture" in Orthodox (eucharistic) ecclesiology, which occurs when the dioceses of the second century became so difficult to handle that they were broken down into parishes, headed by presbyters. This presbyteral system of church structure makes all ministries, including those of the bishop and the deacon, unnecessary. A healing of this system is needed: it is the creation of small dioceses, where the bishop can be the pastor, knowing his flock; where he may be the "eucharistic bishop" presiding over the one Eucharist of his diocese; and he may restore his "presbyters" around him.

With John Erickson I would agree that things may be a little bit more complicated than that. I would concur that "return to a second century situation" as described in the letters of St. Ignatios of Antioch may be romantic and anachronistic. I concur that eucharistic ecclesiology may only allow for a weak primacy (or primacies). I concur that overemphasis on the eschatological dimension of the Church, as found in the Eucharist, may bring about triumphalism and irresponsibility in dealing with the "historical" and horizontal aspects and dimensions of the life of the church. Yes, the Church is already "*in statu patriae*," as the kingdom of God is inaugurated in Christ and the Spirit, in the life of the Church.

But, at the same time, the church is also "*in statu viae*" and lives in history. Its responsibility is to bring the event of Christ into the midst of human history and heal the human miseries through the healing power of Christ. The Church's responsibility is to make certain that the "great commission" finds its realization "in our lifetime." How is all of this going to happen?

Professor Erickson proposes some remedies. More, stronger, and more efficient "communion structures" are needed, including stronger, permanent "primacies" of bishops which would not alternate, but continue as special ministries in the life of the Church.

Communication(s), networking, and connectivity, are some more remedies. All these suggestions are welcome. But can we ultimately speak of "baptismal ecclesiology," on an equal footing with "eucharistic ecclesiology"? Can you equate the beginning and birth of a new life of the neophyte with the life of a grown up, the "mature soldier" of Christ, who is constantly fed by the Bread of Life in the Holy Eucharist?

Triumphalism is always a danger. But it can be easily overcome, if we are aware of it, and if we stress the historical dimension of the life of the Church simultaneously with the eschatological; if we take the historical Christ as seriously as his eschatological kingdom already present in the Spirit but not yet fully here.

Yes, "baptismal ecclesiology" may be a complement and a corrective to "eucharistic ecclesiology." However, "communion ecclesiology," which is behind both of them and constitutes their goal, is here to stay: it is the only ecclesiology which can help Christians achieve the well desired rapprochement, in the name of Christ the common Lord.[66]

From what we have discussed in this paper, one of the major contributions of "baptismal ecclesiology" may be the baptismal anointment of Holy Chrismation, giving us the "seal of the gift" of the Holy Spirit, and bestowing upon every faithful the royal, priestly, and prophetic office. We can seek new applications of these offices in the life of the Church, under the supervision of the bishop.

VI. CONCLUSIONS

Let us now draw some conclusions from these notes on perspectives of "baptismal ecclesiology":

1. It is imperative for our theology and church life to rediscover the baptismal piety of the Church, namely, the paschal experience of Baptism and the pentecostal experience of Chrismation.

2. Both of our traditions should take advantage of the findings of contemporary scholarship with regard to sacraments in general and initiation sacraments in particular, if we want to enhance our church life and mission and enrich our academic theology with the findings of liturgical scholarship.

3. Let us understand that what makes the sacraments what they are – epiphanies of the new reality of the kingdom and new life in Christ and the Spirit – is the faith of Christ, as lived and experienced in the Church. Then, questions like that of the "infant Baptism" and imparting the three sacraments of initiation in an uninterrupted celebration can easily be answered to the positive.

4. Let us realize the interdependence and interrelatedness of the sacraments of initiation, and realize that Baptism and Chrismation find their fulfillment in the Eucharist.

5. Let us realize that the "gift of the Spirit" given at Baptism is not the "gifts" of the Spirit, but the person of the Spirit Himself, which is our anointment as He is Christ's.

6. Let us utilize the "baptismal offices" and ministries – those of king, priest and prophet – and make concrete applications in the

use of these baptism-based ministries for the building up of the Body of Christ and the advancement of the cause of God's inaugurated kingdom.

7. We must realize that the life of the blessed All-Holy Trinity is communion; that the Church is invited to be part of this communion, and that Christ and the Holy Spirit play a key role in imparting this communion. The Holy Spirit makes Christ what He is (the Anointed of God), and Christ sends upon us the Holy Spirit as in a continuous Pentecost.

8. We must realize that Christ and the Spirit play a *simultaneous* role in the effectuation of the sacraments, especially Baptism and Chrismation (see especially Syriac tradition).

9. We must realize that communion is the ultimate goal and the result of all the sacraments and that all the sacraments augment communion with Christ, and the community whose life they impact.

10. We must realize that the "historical Jesus," that is Jesus made history, is imparted to humankind through the sacraments, and especially the Eucharist; and that all antinomies and dichotomies (local-universal, horizontal-vertical, historical-eschatological, already-not yet) are overcome in the eucharistic celebration.

11. We must realize that "eucharistic ecclesiology" needs correctives of its triumphalism and naiveté, and that new communion structures, besides strengthening the old ones, are much needed for today's church.

12. Some of these structures are communication structures, networking and connectivity. It is up to the local and regional churches to use their creative imagination in securing these structures.

13. A stronger primacy is needed to go along with collegiality; that is, stronger than a triumphalistic eucharistic ecclesiology would allow. Permanent primatial structures are provided by Church history. They should be utilized for the benefit of a united Church mission in today's world. If a "pyramidal structure" is not favored by "eucharistic ecclesiology," probably a "truncated cone" primatial structure will be favored by a communion ecclesiology (the head of the pyramid will be occupied by Christ Himself, leading

the kingdom to the Father, Who is above all).

14. Finally, "baptismal ecclesiology" which is meant only to correct and complement "eucharistic ecclesiology" cannot replace "communion ecclesiology." "Communion ecclesiology" is here to stay as the only hope for rapprochement among today's separated Christians.

ENDNOTES

[1] Paper presented to the Orthodox - Roman Catholic Theological Consultation of North America.

[2] John H. Erickson, *The Local Churches and Catholicity: An Orthodox Perspective*, in *The Jurist* 52 (1992) 490-508.

[3] Ibid., p. 505.

[4] John H. Erickson, *American Orthodox-Roman Catholic Dialogue on Synodality and Primacy in the Church: The State of the Question*, given in Pittsburgh, October 4-6, 1994, as a response to a paper by Fr. Brian Daley presented to the Joint Committee of Orthodox and Roman Catholic Bishops.

[5] Erickson, *Synodality and Primacy*, p. 6.

[6] Ibid., p. 6.

[7] Ibid., p. 7.

[8] Alexander Schmemann, *Of Water and the Spirit* (Crestwood, NY: St Vladimir's Seminary Press, 1974).

[9] Ibid., pp. 7-13.

[10] Ibid., pp. 16-8.

[11] Ibid., pp. 19-35.

[12] Ibid., pp. 37-43.

[13] Ibid., pp. 44-5.

[14] Ibid., pp. 45-51.

[15] Ibid., pp. 51-3.

[16] Ibid., pp. 53-60.

[17] Ibid., pp. 60-6.

[18] Ibid., pp. 66-70.

[19] Ibid., pp. 71-5.

[20] Ibid., pp. 75-81.

[21] Ibid., pp. 81-94.

[22] Ibid., pp. 94-9.

[23] Ibid., pp. 99-103.

[24] Ibid., pp. 107-8.

[25] Ibid., pp. 109-15.

[26] Ibid., pp. 115-21.

[27] Ibid., p. 116.

[28] Ibid., pp. 121-4.

[29] Ibid., pp. 124-9.

[30] Ibid., pp. 131-47.

[31] Ibid., pp. 149-54.

[32] Ibid., p. 154.

[33] *Rite of Baptism for Children* (Washington, D.C.: United States Catholic Conference, 1969).

[34] *Rite of Christian Initiation of Adults*, Study Edition (New York: Catholic Book Publishing Co., 1980).

[35] *Made, Not Born, New Perspectives on Christian Initiation and the Catechumente* (The Murphy Center for Liturgical Research, Notre Dame, IN: University of Notre Dame Press, 1980).

[36] *Worship* 56 (1982) 24-260.

[37] In Mark Searle, ed., *Attractive Futures for Worship*, vol. 2: *Baptism and Confirmation* (Collegeville: Liturgical Press, 1987) 15-54.

[38] In *Studia Liturgica* 12 (1977) 87-106; reprinted in *Living Water, Sealing Spirit*, by Maxwell Johnson, ed. (Collegeville: Pueblo, 1995).

[39] Mark Searle, *Alternative Futures, Infant Baptism Reconsidered*, p. 405.

[40] Ibid., pp. 408-9.

[41] Georg Kretschmar, *Recent Research on Christian Initiation*, p. 30: "Thus, the Syrian sequence: impartation of the [Holy] Spirit – immersion finds its most convincing analogy in the regulation of the Qumran community that purification by Spirit was a prerequisite of cultic lustrations (IQS 3, 4ff.)."

[42] Ibid., p. 12.

[43] Methodios, *Symposium*, quoted in Thomas Halton, *The Church: Messages of the Fathers of the Church*, vol. 4; (Wilmington: Michael Glazier, 1985), pp. 54-55.

[44] St. Ephrem, *Hymns on Virginity*, Hymn 7:6, quoted in Thomas M. Finn, *Early Christian Baptism and the Catechumenate: Western and Eastern Syria*, "Message of the Fathers" vol. 5; (Collegeville: Michael Glazier, 1992), 20 and 155.

[45] Ibid., Hymn 7:8, p. 155.

[46] It is significant that one of the Greek Fathers, St. Cyril of Jerusalem in his *Catechisms*, characterizes Holy Chrismation as the sacrament which gives the Christian the strength to fight his spiritual fight (*"roboratur ad pugnam"*).

[47] Note that R.C.I.A. uses the same expression: "N., be sealed with the gift (*donatio*) of the Holy Spirit"; 235, p. 163.

[48] A. Kavanagh, *Christian Initiation for Adults: The Rite*, p. 128.

[49] Note that recently in the West the bishop may extend the same authorization to the priest; R.C.I.A., n. 232, p. 161.

[50] Ephrem, *Hymn* 7:8, p. 155.

[51] Schmemann, *Of Water*, p. 117.

[52] See Schmemann, *Of Water*, pp. 116-21. It is important to notice the strong language that *The Constitution on the Sacred Liturgy* of the II Vatican Council uses regarding the centrality of the Eucharist in the entire life of the Church. Number two (2) says: "For it is the liturgy through which, especially in the divine sacrifice of the Eucharist, 'the work of our redemption is accomplished,' and it is through the liturgy, especially, that the faithful are enabled to express in their lives and manifest to others the mystery of Christ and the real nature of the true Church. The Church is essentially both human and divine, visible but

endowed with invisible realities, zealous in action and dedicated to contemplation, present in the world, but as a pilgrim, so constituted that in her the human is directed toward and subordinated to the divine, the visible to the invisible, action to contemplation, and this present world to that city yet to come, the object of our quest. The liturgy daily builds up those who are in the Church making them a holy temple of the Lord, a dwelling-place for God in the Spirit."

And number ten (10) even more emphatically states: "Nevertheless the liturgy is the summit toward which the activity of the Church is directed; it is also the fount from which all her power flows. For the goal of apostolic endeavor is that all who are made sons of God by faith and baptism should come together to praise God in the midst of his Church, to take part in the Sacrifice and to eat the Lord's supper." *Sacrosanctum Concilium*, in *Vatican Council II: The Conciliar and Post-Conciliar Documents*, ed. Austin P. Flannery, O.P. (Collegeville: Liturgical Press, 1984), pp. 1 and 6.

[53] See J. Zizioulas, *Being as Communion* (Crestwood, NY: St. Vladimir's Seminary Press, 1985), especially chapters 2 and 3, pp. 110-142. Also, D. Staniloae, *Theology and the Church* (Crestwood, NY: St. Vladimir's Seminary Press, 1980), especially chapter 1, pp. 11-44.

[54] Schmemann, *Of Water*, pp. 117-8.

[55] Zizioulas, *Being As Communion*, p. 19.

[56] Ibid., p. 113.

[57] Ibid., pp. 128-9.

[58] Ibid., pp. 137-8.

[59] Ibid., p. 254.

[60] Ibid., pp. 256-7.

[61] Ibid., p. 153, n. 52.

[62] Ibid., pp. 162-3.

[63] Aidan Kavanagh, *Christian Initiation: Tactics and Strategy*, pp. 3-4.

[64] *Lumen Gentium* no 3; in *Vatican Council II: the Conciliar and Post-Conciliar Documents*, p. 351. One can realize how far the second Vatican Council has come in comparison with Vatican I, *First Draft of the Constitution of the Church of Christ*, where the church is seen in a very static and juridical way as the "true, perfect, spiritual and supernatural society"; chapter 2, in John Neuer, S.J., and Henrich Roos, S.J., *The Teaching of the Catholic Church*, ed. Karl Rahner, S.J. (New York: Paulist Press, 1962) pp. 213-214.

[65] Erickson, *Local Churches*, especially pp. 498-508; and *Synodality and Primacy*, especially pp. 4-7.

[66] An important article on *Communion Ecclesiology* by Paul Avis is included in Blackwell's *Encyclopedia of Modern Christian Thought*, ed. Alister E. McGrith, (London: Basil Blackwell, 1994), pp. 133-4.

Five

The Theology and Experience of Salvation[1]

Preliminary Remarks

The title of this presentation can be somewhat misleading: it can be understood as separating theology from experience, or even opposing the two. Actually, according to the best tradition of the Orthodox Church, there is no way that we can separate theology from experience or experience from theology. *Lex orandi* is always *lex credendi,* and *lex credendi* is always *lex supplicandi;* the law of prayer is the law of faith and vice versa. The great tradition of the East is well known for its harmony between doctrine and piety, which is evident in the hymnology and the liturgy of the Church.

Theology for Orthodoxy is always an experiential theology. In the words of an Eastern Orthodox theologian of the last century, Philaret of Moscow, theology is "the word regarding God, from God, in the presence of God, for the glory of God." It is the reflection of our minds on the divinely revealed truth and the proclamation of this doctrine of faith for the glory of God. Yet, this proclamation is but meaningless, empty words if it does not reflect our Christian life and experience, if it does not reflect the personal experience in our lives of the truths we are proclaiming. A theologian whose theology is purely theoretical and not at all experiential is not a true theologian.

Accordingly, we cannot separate our experience of salvation from our theology of salvation and vice versa. Therefore, we must present the mystery of our salvation in Christ not only as it developed in theological reflection, but also as it is experienced in the history and life of the Orthodox Church.

INTRODUCTION

When we speak of salvation in our Christian tradition, we speak of the central event of our holy history *(Heilsgeschichte)* which is hidden in God in eternity, made known to us in Christ, and made constantly present to us in the life of the Christian Church through the Holy Spirit of God. Our salvation can be approached either from a positive or from a negative point of view. The negative dimension of salvation is that of liberation from danger; in the Orthodox tradition we understand this to be liberation from the state of unauthentic life, that state of decay into which created nature has fallen. When approached in this negative fashion, salvation has also been called redemption and justification. However, we can also approach salvation from a positive point of view. The positive dimension is that of sanctification or deification. This deification is life in communion with God, life in the grace of God. As understood by the Eastern tradition, the grace of God is the life of God which is communicated to us, i.e., His uncreated energies.[2]

The statement pertaining to man's salvation which we find in many of the Greek Fathers is that "The Son of God became what we are so that we might become what He is: He became flesh so that we might become gods by grace."[3] The truth of this statement becomes evident when we consider the two divine economies – the economy of the Son and the economy of the Holy Spirit – the involvement of these two persons of the Holy Trinity in the work of our salvation. Christ's saving mystery and event is central to our salvation; yet, it must be conditioned by the Spirit event. The mystery of the descent of the Holy Spirit and His personal involvement with our salvation history on Pentecost is also an important event which seals the work of Christ and applies the event of salvation in Christ to each of us personally. I will divide this presentation into three parts: (1) the presuppositions of our salvation, (2) salvation in Christ and in the Spirit, and (3) salvation as experienced in the sacramental life and practice of the Eastern Orthodox Church.

PRESUPPOSITIONS OF OUR SALVATION

In the Epistle to the Hebrews we read the following statement:

> For it was fitting that he, for whom and by whom all things exist, in bringing many sons to glory, should make the pioneer of their salvation perfect through suffering. For he who sanctifies and those who are sanctified have all one origin. That is why he is not ashamed to call them brethren, saying, 'I will proclaim thy name to my brethren, in the midst of the congregation I will praise thee.' And again, 'I will put my trust in him.' And again, 'Here am I, and the children God has given me.' Since therefore the children share in flesh and blood, he himself likewise partook of the same nature, that through death he might destroy him who has the power of death, that is, the devil, and deliver all those who through fear of death were subject to lifelong bondage (Heb 2:10-15).

In this text we see that God calls us to His glory and that He bestows upon us His salvation through its pioneer, our Lord Jesus Christ, Who is of one origin with us in His humanity. He partakes of our flesh and blood: He does this so that through His own death He might destroy death and him who had power over death, the devil. In this way Christ delivers all those who, through fear of death, were subject to a lifelong bondage to sin, corruption, and death.

To understand the saving work of Christ, let's look more closely at the theology evident in the above pericope from the Epistle to the Hebrews. Man is created by God through His Son (the Creative Logos) for the glory of God – that is, in order for man to participate in the glory of God. The Greek fathers use the term *theosis* to express this reality of "sharing in the divine nature" (2 Pet. 1:4). Man is created in the image of God with the potential of becoming like God. Man can obtain one of the most characteristic properties of God, that of immortality. Man is created for immortality, for eternal life with God. Man as a whole, body and soul, is called to this life of immortality in communion with the Immortal One, the only one immortal by nature. Man too can become immortal by grace, by participating in the divine energies of God.[4]

Yet, man's venture is well known, as described in the first chapters of the book of Genesis. Man could become a "god by grace," as much and as far as he was in communion with God. Instead, he tried to become a "god without God." This was his failing: he tried to find life outside of the source of life, God. What he found instead when he abandoned life was death.

Man's real nature is created to be dependent upon the grace of God. However, when man rejected God, this ceased to be true. As a result, man's own nature became deteriorated. This state of decay is called by the Greek fathers the darkening of the image of God in man. What this darkening entails is that man's "natural" powers, his reason and freedom, are weakened: man cannot think right anymore; his freedom becomes a freedom of choice between good and evil, (γνωμικόν θέλημα) with a propensity towards evil.[5] The law of the flesh takes over in man. Through man's sin, division is introduced within nature in general and within human nature as well. As described by Saint Maximos the Confessor, the distinctions within nature became real oppositions instead of being overcome by Adam: men are opposed to women and thus they become a threat to each other; earthly paradise is opposed to oecumene; heaven is opposed to earth; visible creature is opposed to invisible; and created nature is opposed to uncreated nature.[6] The harmony that God created in nature as it came out of His hands was lost.

The state of separation from God in which Adam puts himself has as a result the decay of Adam's own nature: death – spiritual first, then physical, and finally eternal and eschatological – is the wage of Adam's sin. The cause of Adam's rejection of God is pride. It is the same kind of pride which led Satan to his revolt against God. Man identified with Satan in identifying his will with the devil's. The devil also tried to become a "god without God." This led Adam under the devil's dominion. Man's freedom was changed to slavery to death and to the master of death. Death is this lie, invented by the devil, this parasite which enters God's creation, invented by the created will. Man cannot liberate himself from this state of slavery. Only the God-Man can liberate him. This is the work of Christ: to eliminate all obstacles[7] separating man from God in order for man to go back to his Creator, to reach the purpose of his creation – *theosis*, life in God, participation in the glory of God.

SALVATION IN CHRIST AND THE HOLY SPIRIT

Through His incarnation and His life in the flesh, the God-Man destroys one by one all obstacles that separate man from God. He not only allows man to return to his original state of innocence, but above and beyond this, He achieves the purpose of man's creation: *theosis*, sharing in the divine nature (2 Pet 1:4) and life in communion with God, even life in abundance (Jn 10:10).

Christ, the Incarnate Word of God, destroys the obstacle of nature through His incarnation: He restores man to being, to his true state of being in communion with God. In the incarnate Logos the human nature which the creative Logos creates and assumes is united with the divinity from the very beginning of its existence. This humanity does not have an independent existence since it does not have a human person; it is the humanity of God, of the Word of God who became flesh.

Christ destroys the obstacle of sin through His cross, thereby restoring man to well-being. Christ does not only wash away our sin by the cross; He does not only give up His life "as a ransom for many" (Mk 10:45, Mt 20:28). He does not only become the sacrificial lamb which "carries away the sin of the world" (Jn 1:29). But above all, Christ offers His own blood to replace the poisoned blood of the old man, the man of the fallen nature. He offers His blood in order to effect a kind of "blood transfusion," to "wash away the poison of the serpent" (Troparion of Great Vespers, Feast of the Exaltation of the Cross). By doing this Christ revivifies the dry bones of Adam, whose skull, according to a pious tradition, was found under the cross of the Lord on Golgotha (the "Place of the Skull").

The way in which the Christian East understands the sacrifice on the cross is very different from the legalistic understanding of

Anselm, which states that God's offended justice had to be satisfied. God's "immense justice" does not need to be "satisfied" by an "immense sacrifice of an immense person," as Anselm would have it. God sends His Son to die for us so that we might live; He does this out of love, not in order to satisfy His offended justice. This legalistic view of the sacrifice on the cross was rejected quite early by Saint Gregory the Theologian:

> But if the price is paid to the Father, why should that be done? It is not the Father who has held us as His captives. Moreover, why should the blood of His only Son be acceptable to the Father, who did not wish to accept Isaac, when Abraham offered Him his son as a burnt-offering, but replace the human sacrifice with the sacrifice of a ram?[8]

God only tolerates the death of His Son in His flesh, a death which the Son willingly accepts, although He is immortal even in His human nature since He is the Only One to be without sin, the cause of death.

Through His descent into Hades, Christ ties up the strong man and takes away his vessels (Mk 3:27). He destroys the devil and his power; He offers freedom to captives, liberating those serving the lifelong bondage of sin and death under the devil, the master of death and corruption. Christ destroys death by death. With His Resurrection, Christ restores humanity to eternal being. A new life beyond death and corruption is bestowed upon humanity by the Lord. Out of the grave comes life – the life of a spiritualized human existence which is that of the Risen Lord's humanity. The cross continues to be a scandal for the Jews and a foolishness for the Greeks, especially since the cross is the door to the Resurrection. Resurrection for the Greeks would mean a prolongation of the soul's captivity in the prison of the body; for this reason they make fun of Saint Paul who preaches the Lord's Resurrection to them (Acts 17:23). Yet, for us Christians, the Resurrection faith is essential to our belief and Christian hope (1 Cor 15:17). The process of the fallen nature's restoration in Christ does not stop with the cross. The Resurrection and Ascension into heaven are the apex of this restoration: our human nature achieves *theosis* and the glory to which it is destined; Christ, one of us, is sitting at the right hand in the glory of God the Father.

The Spirit of God comes to apply the work of our salvation and deification in Christ – a work already realized in our human nature – to each human person individually.[9] The Spirit comes to seal the work of Christ and also to lead it to perfection. Pentecost applies and seals Pascha. The Spirit event conditions the Christ event and is also necessary for our salvation.

The two "events" – the economy of the Son of God and the event of the Holy Spirit – are interdependent. They presuppose each other. Thus, the Spirit comes not only in the name of Christ, but also as a free agent: "He is sent to apply our salvation in Christ, but He also acts on His own authority" (ἀποστέλλεται μὲν οἰκονομικῶς, ἐνεργεῖ δὲ αὐτεξουσίως).[10]

When the work of the Holy Spirit is thus seen in relation to the work of Christ, the possibility of sacramental determinism is excluded.[11] If, however, Augustine's view of the Spirit as an "agent of the Son" were true, then this sacramental determinism could not be avoided. If this were so, once a person were baptized the grace of Christ would work automatically in him even without his consent. If grace were "sacramentally determined" and automatic, salvation would be accomplished without or even against the will of the human agent, without real "synergy," the cooperation that man offers to God in subordination to the divine will.

THE EXPERIENCE OF SALVATION IN CHRIST AND THE HOLY SPIRIT
    IN THE SACRAMENTAL LIFE AND PRACTICE OF THE CHURCH

It is through this "cooperation" that takes place between human freedom and God's grace in the Holy Spirit that salvation and *theosis* take place.

Faith is necessary in order for man to accept the workings of the grace of the Holy Spirit in him so that the deifying energies, the very life of God Himself, "energize" and make man alive. This faith is operating through love: there is no way we can oppose faith and works as two separate means through which we can obtain salvation. Works are the fruits of saving faith as much and as far as this faith "operates through love."[12]

This saving faith, a gift of the Spirit, both leads to the sacraments and is nourished and strengthened by them. Sacraments are signs or "symbols"[13] of the saving grace, the uncreated energy and life of God. The main sacraments are baptism and Eucharist, both of which "come out of the open side of the Lord."[14] Blood and water thus symbolize baptism and Eucharist.

Baptism is the sacrament of rebirth and regeneration. It is the restoration of the image of God in us, the restoration of the new humanity and newness of life in Christ. Baptism is each Christian's personal Pascha; in our baptism through a triple immersion and ascension from the water we become partakers of the Lord's death and Resurrection (Rom 6:3-11). This sacrament of our Christian initiation is not completed unless sealed by the "seal of the gift of the Holy Spirit," the Sacrament of Confirmation (βεβαίωσις) or "Chrismation" *(chrisma,* anointment). In this sacrament, which is combined with the Sacrament of Baptism, the newly baptized not only becomes a partaker of Christ's new, risen humanity, but he also becomes anointed with the same Spirit of God which anoints Christ's humanity. Christ is anointed with the Holy Spirit of God (Lk 4:18-19; Is 61:1-2). We are also anointed by this same Spirit at our Chrismation.[15]

Eucharist is the sacrament of our Christian growth. It is the supper of the Lord, as celebrated at the Last Supper and as completed by the last events in Christ's earthly life: His sacrificial death and Resurrection. The Risen Lord comes to us in the Eucharist in a mysterious way which is known only by Him. Following His order, "we do this in remembrance of Him" (Lk 22:19). Yet, this "remembrance" or "memory" is not a mere "memorial" in the modern sense of the word: it is a "memorial" according to the Jewish usage during the Lord's time which understood memorial to be the present actualization and participation in a past event. In this way the Lord's Supper is the present continuation and actualization of Christ's mystery.

The eucharistic elements participate in a sacramental double reality; through the action of the Holy Spirit, the bread and wine double as the Lord's Body and Blood, "becoming" the sacramental Body and Blood of the Lord in a mysterious way. The mystery is experienced only through faith. If we ask for a theological explanation, the doctrine of the energies of God can offer us an approximation in understanding the mysterious presence of the Lord in the consecrated species of bread and wine: the same energies which are present in the Lord's glorious Body are present in these elements, making them an extension of the Lord's physical body which sits at the right hand in the glory of God the Father. In receiving this sacramental Body, our lives become extensions of the newness of life which is in the Lord.

Worship is not attributed to the consecrated elements since the purpose of their consecration is the sanctification of the faithful through communion of the Lord's Body and Blood.

Orthodoxy speaks of other sacraments which involve the same type of "double reality," thus becoming "means of grace" for us. The number seven is a symbolic number which indicates the perfection of grace. Actually there are many more sacraments, such as the "word of God" which calls us to the newness of life in Christ. Among the traditional sacraments is the sacrament of forgiveness of sins (penance) which is based on the Lord's explicit order that the disciples forgive sins (Jn 20:22-23). The sacrament of the priesthood, or the laying on of hands for the installation of the Apostles' successors, guarantees the continuity of apostolic leadership in the Church without repeating personal infallibility, which is unrepeatable in the apostolic office. The Sacrament of Unction for the sick is based on the order given by Saint James to pray over the sick, anointing them with oil (Jas 5:14). Marriage is the sacrament which reflects the union that exists between Christ and the Church (Eph 5:32) and is given for the sake of the *theosis* of men and women and the expansion of God's kingdom. Besides these sacraments, the Orthodox Tradition also counts as sacraments the taking of monastic vows, the funeral service, and the blessing of water. In all of these sacraments the one grace of God – the one life of God communicated to human beings – takes up various shapes and manifestations as it gives life to us, a "life in abundance" (Jn 10:10).

As Christians, this sacramental grace nourishes our activities and permeates our whole lives as we strive to overcome sin and aspire to achieve *theosis* and "share in the life of God" (2 Pet 1:4). The abundance of the gifts of the Holy Spirit are bestowed upon us Christians, who prove ourselves to be "charismatics" when we become aware of the presence of these gifts in us. The highest gift is love (1 Cor 13:13). Love, poured into our hearts through the Spirit of God (Rom 5:5), is the characteristic of Christians (Jn 13:35), the proper attitude of members of the kingdom of God. It is only through the practice of this unselfish love, an energy of God which comes to us from God, that we are in communion with God Himself and in communion with our brothers and sisters. It is through the practice of love that we achieve the purpose of our creation, salvation and *theosis*.

CONCLUSION

Orthodoxy believes that salvation is not so much a negative reality, as it is a positive one: salvation is not so much to be freed from the bondage of the devil and his dominion of sin, death, and corruption, as it is life in communion with God. Human beings who are not in communion with God are "less than human." God created man for His life. Man's failure to stay in this life of communion with God is reversed by God's initiative to save him through Christ and in the Holy Spirit. Through its sacramental life and fullness of messianic gifts imparted by the Holy Spirit, the Church becomes the "ark of salvation" and the "inaugurated" kingdom of God. The kingdom is in progression; it is expanding to contain the whole world. We are involved with this process, with this struggle against "principalities, powers, masters of darkness of this world" (Eph 6:12). With the grace of God we are working not only towards our personal salvation, but towards the salvation of the whole world. This is our responsibility too, since it is for the life of the whole world that the Lord gave up His life. Let us accept this challenge, "for the creation awaits with eager longing for the revealing of the sons of God: for the creation was subjected to futility, not of its own will but by the will of him who subjected it in hope; because the creation itself will be set free from its bondage to decay and obtain the glorious liberty of the children of God" (Rom 9:19-21).

ENDNOTES

[1] Published in *The Greek Orthodox Theological Review*, 22 (1977): 405-415.

[2] The great Tradition of the Orthodox Church distinguishes between essence and energies in the one reality of God. A prooftext of this distinction in the New Testament is 2 Pet 1:4, where Christians are said to "share in the divine nature." This sharing in the divine nature cannot be sharing in the essence of God, yet it is a real sharing in the divine reality. The divine reality which can be shared by man is called the energies of God in the theological language of the East.

[3] Vladimir Lossky, "Redemption and Deification" in *In the Image and Likeness of God* (Crestwood, NY: St. Vladimir's Seminary Press, 1974), p. 97.

[4] George Florovsky, "Immortality of the Soul" in *Creation and Redemption* (Belmont, Ma: Nordland Publishing Company, 1967), pp. 216-219.

[5] Vladimir Lossky, *The Mystical Theology of the Eastern Church* (Cambridge, 1968), p. 125.

[6] Lossky, *Mystical Theology*, pp. 109-110.

[7] Nicholas Cabasilas, *The Life in Christ*, 111; PC 150, quoted in Lossky, *Mystical Theology*, p. 136.

[8] Gregory Nazianzos, *Oratio 45*, 22; PG 36:653, quoted in Lossky, *In the Image and Likeness*, p. 102.

[9] Ibid., pp. 106-08.

[10] Saint Basil, *Sermon on Faith* (Sermon 15) 3; PG 31:172A; Cf. *On the Holy Spirit*, 16:37; PG 32:1-33C.

[11] Lossky, *In the Image and Likeness*, pp. 104-106.

[12] Rom 3:28; Gal 2:16; 3:11; 5:6; and Jas 2:24.

[13] Alexander Schmemann, "Sacrament and Symbol" in *For the Life of the World* (Crestwood, NY: St. Vladimir's Seminary Press, 1973), pp. 135-51. A "symbol," according to the original meaning of the word, is not a "sign" empty of reality as it finally came to mean in the West, a "symbol" (from συμβάλλω, to put together) joins together two different realities, one visible (a created reality) and the other invisible (uncreated grace). It finally is a double reality: one visible reality and one invisible reality which is hidden behind the visible one.

[14] Saint John Chrysostom, *On the Gospel of Saint John, Homily 85;* PG 59:463: "Out of it [the open side of the Lord] came water and blood: these two fountains did not spring haphazardly; but [they sprang up] because the Church is constituted out of these two [fountains]. As a matter of fact, those initiated are born again through water (δι' ὕδατος μὲν ἀναγεννώμενοι) and are nourished

through blood and flesh (δι' αἵματος δὲ καὶ σαρκὸς τρεφόμενοι). This is where sacraments take their origin (ἐντεῦθεν ἀρχὴν λαμβάνει τὰ μυστήρια)."

[15] See Saint Irenæos, *Adversus Hæreses,* 3:9:2, quoted in Henry Bettenson, *The Early Christian Fathers* (Oxford, 1969), p. 86: "He [the Word of God] took flesh; he was anointed by the Father with the Spirit and became Jesus Christ [i.e. the Anointed] as also Isaiah says, there shall spring forth a rod from the root of Jesse, and a flower shall come up from this root, and the Spirit of God shall rest upon him, the Spirit of wisdom and understanding...' [Is 11:14]; and again Isaiah, foretelling his anointing, and the end for which he was anointed, says, "The Spirit of God is upon me, wherefore he has anointed me, and sent me to preach good tidings to the lowly..." [Is 61:1-2] . Therefore the Spirit of God descended on him; the Spirit of him who through the prophets had promised that he would anoint him, in order that we might receive of the abundance of his unction and be saved." Also ibid., 3:18 :3 (sub fin.) quoted ibid., p. 88: "In the name of Christ ['the Anointed'] is implied the anointer, the anointed and the unction. The Father is the anointer; the Son, the anointed; the Holy Spirit the unction. As the Word declares through Isaiah: 'The Spirit of God is upon me, because he has anointed me' [Is 61:11]."

Six

Orthodox Soteriology[1]

INTRODUCTION

The doctrine of salvation (*soteria, yishoua*) holds a central place in the life of every religion, and especially that of Christianity. Christianity is the religion of salvation, a salvation in Christ and through Christ. One of the major names of Christ is that of Savior (*Yeshoua, Soter*). In Saint Matthew's Gospel, the angel tells Joseph: "You shall call his name Jesus (Savior), for he will save his people from their sins" (Mt 1:21). And Saint Paul tells the Jews in the book of Acts: "God has brought to Israel a Savior, Jesus, as he promised" (Acts 13:23). In his speech to his compatriots the day of Pentecost, Saint Peter told them with regard to Jesus: "And there is salvation in no one else, for there is no other name under heaven given among men by which we must be saved" (Acts 4:12).

For the Christian in general, and for the Orthodox Christian in particular, salvation can only be understood in terms of salvation in Christ "For Christ is the head of the church, the body of which he is Savior" (Eph 5:23).

THE ORTHODOX CONCEPT OF SALVATION

One of the texts quoted above understands salvation as "freedom from sin" (Mt 1:21), or as "God being with us" *(Immanuel;* 23). According to Saint Paul, "Christ Jesus came into the world to save sinners" (1 Tim 1:13). In the Gospels we read that "the Son came to seek and save the lost" (Lk 19:10), to heal the sick (5:31) and to call not the righteous, "but sinners to repentance" (5:32).

He came "not to condemn the world, but that the world might be saved through him" (Jn 3:17). Also, we read that "God so loved the world, that he gave his only Son, that whoever believes in him should not perish, but have eternal life" (Jn 3:16).

Saint Paul also tells us that through Christ, God "has delivered us from the dominion of darkness and transferred us to the kingdom of his beloved Son, in whom we have redemption, the forgiveness of sins" (Col 1:13-14). Saint John the Evangelist tells us that with the coming of Christ "we have passed out of death into life" (1 Jn 3:14), and Saint Paul speculates that "if Christ has not been raised, then our preaching is in vain, and our faith is in vain" (1 Cor 15:14).

Finally, the Nicene-Constantinopolitan Creed of the faith tells us that Christ "for us men and for our salvation came down from heaven, and was incarnate by the Holy Spirit and the Virgin Mary, and became man."[2]

To summarize the doctrine found in the texts just quoted, we would say that salvation in Christ is given to humankind through Christ's incarnation, his entire life and work, through his sufferings, his death, and his resurrection from the dead. Salvation in Christ is freedom from sin, from death, and from the powers of darkness, and healing of our human nature. Ultimately, salvation is restoration of life in communion with God.

In the light of this summary of doctrine. I would like to briefly examine the following points of Orthodox Christian soteriology: presuppositions of salvation in Christ; the person of the Savior; the work of the Savior; salvation as sanctification: the work of the Holy Spirit; the church as "ark of salvation" and "communion of saints"; and fulfillment of salvation in Christ: Orthodox eschatology.

PRESUPPOSITIONS OF SALVATION IN CHRIST:
MAN'S FALL AND ITS CONSEQUENCES

The book of Genesis tells us of the creation of man: "Then God said, 'Let us make man in our image, after our likeness'... So God created man in his own image, in the image of God he created him; male and female he created them" (1:26-27).

In commenting upon these texts, the Greek fathers speculate that the image of God in man is the "great natural prerogative" of man, which makes man distinct from the rest of creation. Let me quote myself, as I have already summarized the doctrine in some other article: according to the Greek fathers,

> man, created in God's image and likeness, has a very special place in God's creation, called to be God's proxy toward His creation.
>
> Man is created as a psycho-physical unity: God 'uses his hands' to create man, to show special care about man's creation. God takes dust from the earth, fashions man, and breathes into man's nostrils the 'breath of life', man's soul, of a spiritual nature. Man becomes, the link between the spiritual creation of God (angels) and the material one (earth), for he partakes of both. This is why 'man's mission will be to bring the creation into communion with God' (Saint Maximos the Confessor).
>
> Man is created in the image of God, with the specific call to become God-like. The fathers of the Church elaborate on this doctrine of Genesis. Man's being in the image of God means that man has a spiritual soul reflecting God (the Father) as a person. Man is capable of knowing God and being in communion with God. Man belongs to God, for being God's child and image makes him God's relative. Man's soul is endowed with God's energies and life: one of these energies is love. Love, coming from God, is also directed toward God, creating union and bringing communion with God.
>
> The fathers also make a *distinction* between the image of God in man, and his likeness to God: image is the *potential* given to man, through which he can obtain the life of *theosis* (communion with God). *Likeness* with God is the *actualization* of this potential; it is becoming more and more what one already is: becoming more and more God's image, more and more God-like. The distinction between *image* and *likeness* is, in other words,

the distinction between *being* and *becoming*.

Being in the image of God and called to likeness with God also means for man that God's immortality is reflected in man, insofar as man continues to be in communion with God through God's image in him, and that man is assigned God's creation, to be God's proxy in it, to have dominion over it and keep it in touch with the Creator.

Saint Maximos the Confessor gives this noble mission to man (to Adam, the first man): man has to overcome all kinds of *distinctions* within God's creation, before man brings God's creation back to God: man was called to overcome the distinction between *male* and *female*, *inhabited earth* and *paradise, heaven* and *earth, visible* and *invisible* creation, and, finally, the division between *created* and *uncreated* thus unifying God's creation with the Creator. Since man failed to achieve this union (*theosis*), the 'New Adam', Christ, took it upon Himself to fulfill this original call of the first man (Adam).[3]

In spite of man's call to achieve *theosis*, life in communion with God, "in God's likeness," the "first Adam" failed God and failed himself. This failure, which is the essence of what in the theological language is called "sin" (missing the mark, *hamartia, hatta*), together with death, which is the "wages of sin" (Rom 6:23), the general deterioration of the human nature because of its separation from the "Source of Life," God, and the submission of the fallen human nature to the "powers of darkness," Satan and his "angels," is the main presupposition of the saving and deifying work of Christ.

Let me quote my own summary of the doctrine:

> *Man's Fall and Its Consequences*
> "Unlike Saint Augustine's doctrine of 'original justice,' which attributes to the first man several excessive perfections, perfect knowledge of God and God's creation, for example, that make the fall impossible, the doctrine of the Greek Fathers of the image of God in man

as a potential to be actualized, allows the possibility of a deterioration, as well. Saint Irenaeos speaks of the first man (Adam) as an *infant* (*nepios*), who had to grow up to adulthood. Instead, man failed himself, by not 'passing the test' of maturity given to him by God.

In spite of God's prohibition, man chose to eat from the tree of knowledge of good and evil (Genesis). Being 'good by nature,' man had to also become 'good by choice'. Unfortunately, it did not happen that way. Following the 'snake's advice (the devil's, that is), man also tried to do what the fallen angels did: to 'become a god without God.' Man's imperfection and innocence, or, better, naivete, and his relative pride, cultivated by the 'accuser,' became the cause of man's fall from God's communion, due to his disobedience and rejection of God. Man put his purpose in himself, instead of putting it in God. Man's free will is responsible for his own decline.

The consequences of this revolt against God, which the West calls *original* and the East 'ancestral' (*propatorikon*) sin, are that man lost his original innocence; the image of God in him was tarnished, and even became distorted; man's reason was obscured, his will weakened, the desires and passions of the flesh grew wild; man suffered separation from God, the author and source of life. He put himself in an unauthentic kind of existence, close to death. The Fathers speak of 'spiritual death,' which is the cause of the physical one, and which may lead to the 'eschatological,' eternal death: for 'the wages of sin is death' (Rom 6:23).

The state of fall, of unauthentic life close to death, this status of 'spiritual death,' continues to be transmitted to all of man's progeniture, even those who are born of Christian parents. The personal guilt of the first man belongs to him exclusively. However, the results of his sin are transmitted to the entire human race. A personal commitment through an engagement of one's personal free will is required, in order for things to turn around. Christ, who requires this personal commitment, made this change possible through His coming and His work upon earth.

The Case of Mary, the Mother of God

Does the Mother of God, Virgin Mary, participate in the 'ancestral sin'? The question does not make much sense for the Orthodox, for it is obvious that Mary, being part of the common human race issued of the first man (Adam) automatically participates in the fallen status and in the 'spiritual death' introduced by the sin of the first man.

The fathers of the Church meditate on Luke 1:35, to conclude that Mary was purified by the Holy Spirit on the day of the Annunciation, in order for her to become the 'worthy Mother of God.' However, even after she gave birth to the Son of God, Mary was not exempted of less serious ('venial') sins. Saint John Chrysostom attributes to Mary the sin of vanity, in the context of the first miracle of Christ in Cana of Galilee.

Mary was also saved by her Son, for God is her Savior (Lk. 1:47) as well. It is unfortunate that the Roman Catholic Church promulgated the doctrine of the so-called 'Immaculate Conception' in 1854, which contradicts the traditional doctrine of the Church concerning Mary.[4]

SALVATION IN CHRIST – THE PERSON OF THE SAVIOR

According to the doctrine of the Church fathers, and that of the Church councils, man could not have saved himself from his sinful condition and liberate himself from a "fallen nature"; he could not have restored the "fallen image" on his own; he could not have freed himself from his sinful condition (separation from God's communion), and ultimately the status of death, in separation from life, which is God. Man could not have freed himself from the dynasty of the Evil One, under which he subjected himself through his fall. The only healing of this situation could have come from God himself.

This is why a *divine person* or *hypostasis,* that of the *Word of God,* had to be incarnate, to *become flesh* so that He could bring man back to God (Jn 1:14). Let me again quote myself:

The Divine Plan of Salvation
'Man failed God and failed himself through his revolt against God. However, God did not abandon him. God kept following man with His loving care and providence. God prepared man's salvation in the same eternal Logos of God, through whom we are created, so that even after our fall we may return to immortality' (Saint Athanasios).

The plan of God for man's salvation is called the plan of 'divine economy,' i.e. divine dispensation. God the Father conceives the plan, the Son executes it, the Holy Spirit fulfills it and leads it to perfection and finalization.

God the Father acts out of love for man, in sending His own Son for the salvation of the world (Jn. 3:16). When the time was ripe, after a series of purifications throughout the Old Testament that led to the Virgin Mary who could respond to God, accepting man's salvation on behalf of humankind, God sent forth His only-begotten Son, 'born of a woman, born under the law, to redeem those who were under the law, so that we might receive adoption to sonship' (Gal 4:4-5).

Christ's Incarnation and the Mystery of Salvation
Christ saved humankind through what He is, and through what He did for us. Beginning with Saint Irenaeos, the Greek Fathers continually reiterate the statement that the Incarnate Son of God 'became what we are (a human being) so that we may become what He is (gods by grace).' 'He became incarnate, so that we may be deified,' Saint Athanasios says. By assuming our human nature, the Incarnate Logos, a divine person, brought this humanity to the heights of God. Everything that Christ did throughout His earthly life

was based on the presupposition that humanity was already saved and deified, from the very moment of His conception in the womb of Mary, through the operation of the Holy Spirit.

Jesus the Christ, the God–Man

Anointed by the Holy Spirit of God since its conception, Christ's humanity is the humanity of the Messiah (the Anointed One) since the beginning of its existence.

Christ is at the same time the son of the Virgin, but also the natural Son of God, by His very nature. His humanity is a real humanity, with a body and soul, which suffered hunger and thirst, which suffered humiliation and the Cross. The Church condemned such heresies as that of the Docetists, who said that Christ's humanity was not real; Arios who taught that there was no soul in Jesus; and Apollinarios of Laodicea who taught that there was no reason in Jesus.

The Church also defended the divinity of Jesus against the Ebionites, who denied Christ's divinity; the Monarchian heresy which subordinated the Son to the Father; and Arianism, which also denied the divinity of the Logos of God. Against all these heretics the Church upheld the doctrine that Christ, a divine person, is 'true God of true God,' for He is the only begotten Son of God, not in a metaphorical, but a natural sense. He has the divine properties of omniscience and pre-existence in terms of God's creation. He is the only one without sin: He operates miracles through His divinity, accepts divine honor and worship due to the divinity, and accepts faith in Him.

Humanity and divinity are hypostatically united together: the two natures exist in the one person of the Word who became flesh, a divine person (or hypostasis). Christ exists 'in two natures,' without being of two natures; the two natures exist united together 'without confusion, without change, without division, without

separation.' (Council of Chalcedon). The first two ad-
verbs are addressed against the heresy of Eutyches and
the monophysites who confused the natures and the
last two against the Nestorians, who separated and divided humanity and divinity in Christ.

Consequently, Christ has two wills also and two op-
erations, one human and one divine; the two work
together 'to achieve man's salvation'; however, the human will and operation is always subjected to the divine
(Third Council of Constantinople, the Sixth Ecumenical, against Monothelitism).

The consequences of this hypostatic union of the two
natures in Christ are the 'coinherence' of human and
divine nature, the *communicatio idiomatum*, the natural
sonship of Christ's humanity, one worship of the two
natures in Christ, deification of Christ's human nature, Christ's double knowledge and power (however,
attributed to one person), Christ's absolute
unsinfulness, and the Mother of God being truly
Theotokos and Virgin before, during, and after she gave
birth to the only-begotten Son of God.[5]

As the fall of man was a catastrophe, a "cosmic event" with cata-
strophic consequences for the whole cosmos, so it was with the
Incarnation of the Word of God, the "Word-becoming-flesh," that
is a "cosmic event" which reversed the results of the previous one.
To quote Fr. John Meyendorff:

To affirm that God became man, and that His humanity possesses all the characteristics proper to human
nature, implies that the Incarnation is a cosmic event.
Man was created as the master of the cosmos and called
by the creator to draw all creation to God. His failure
to do so was a cosmic catastrophe, which could be re-
paired only by the creator Himself.

Moreover, the fact of the Incarnation implies that the
bond between God and man, which has been expressed
in the Biblical concept of 'image and likeness,' is un-
breakable. The restoration of creation is a 'new creation,'
but it does not establish a new pattern, so far as man is

concerned; it reinstates *man* in his original divine glory among creatures and in his original responsibility for the world. It reaffirms that man is truly man when he participates in the life of God; that he is not autonomous, either in relation to God, or in relation to the world; that true human life can never be 'secular.' In Jesus Christ, God and man are one; in Him, therefore, God becomes accessible not by superseding or eliminating the *humanum,* but by realizing and manifesting humanity in its purest and most authentic form.

The Christ-event is a cosmic event both because Christ is the Logos – and, therefore, in God the agent of creation – and because He is man, since man is a 'microcosm.' Man's sin plunges creation into death and decay, but man's restoration in Christ is a restoration of the cosmos to its original beauty.[6]

This restoration of creation in Christ, beginning with the restoration of the "fallen image" of God in man, became a reality through the person first, and then the work of the Savior, Jesus the Christ, the God-Man.

In his essay on the soteriological teaching of the Greek Fathers, Constantine Dratsellas says:

As far as the soteriology of the Fathers is concerned, I would like to lay stress and underline the following points:

1) The Fathers dealing with the theanthropic Person of the Incarnate Logos speak also at the same time of His saving work. They never separate Jesus Christ from His redemptive work. And as Emil Brunner says: 'Das Werk und Person des Erlosers sind eine unauflosliche Einheit,' (Brunner E., *Der Mittler,* Zurich 1947, p. 359). They always combine the being and the acting of God in the person and the work of the redeemer. This is very important for a correct understanding of patristic theology and for evaluating the patristic thought.

2) When the Fathers speak of the incarnation of the Logos they mean not only the birth of Christ and His assuming human flesh but the whole mystery of His

economy, and therefore, His birth, His life on earth, His work, His sufferings, His death, His resurrection. It is worth noticing that the Fathers always lay much stress on Christ's Resurrection which is the center of Christian faith and the affirmation of His birth, His life and His death, etc. And when they speak of His death, they see it in the light of His incarnation. They see the mystery of Christ as a whole. They never separate these two aspects of this mystery. They speak of the whole incarnate Logos and of His saving work, and they ascribe the Salvation of man to the whole Christ, to His whole saving work and not to one particular act of His life.

These conclusions lead us to a third one, which is that 3) the fathers never formulated any special theories on soteriology. They are inventions of modern theologians who form several theories and then try to find some of the fathers as supporters of their personal ideas. This leads to a dangerous misunderstanding of patristic theology."[7]

In the light of these statements, let us now discuss the saving work of Jesus the Savior, the incarnate Word of God who entered our human history, lived among us, taught us the truth of God, led us to salvation, suffered the cross and death for us, was resurrected on the third day for us and freed us from death and the One who has dominion over death, giving us everlasting life upon which death has no claim.

SALVATION IN CHRIST – THE WORK OF THE SAVIOR

Christ, the incarnate Word of God, is seen in the theology of the Greek fathers as the "New Adam."[8] As the first (old) Adam was the leader of humankind into disobedience, thus inventing sin (separation from God) and its consequence, death and deterioration of nature, so the second (new) Adam introduces obedience to God, and a life in constant communion with God for humankind. Christ, the creative Logos, created and assumed a new, perfect humanity, in constant union and communion with God, the humanity which exists only as "en-hypostasized" in the One (divine) hypostasis of the word-who-became-flesh.

The new (second) Adam thus becomes a "new model" for humankind, and the One who achieves *theosis* in the human nature, through His Incarnation (Saint Maximos the Confessor). Therefore, salvation, as life in communion with God, is already present in Christ's humanity, on the basis of the hypostatic union of human and divine natures in Christ.

What needs to be done, is for the other obstacles also to be abolished, so that humanity (and the entire cosmos in it) may be freed from the other consequences of the "ancestral sin," that is, sin, death, and submission to the devil. My summary of the Eastern Orthodox doctrine follows:

> *Jesus the Prophet, the Priest, and the King*
> Jesus had the following obstacles to overcome in order for Him to accomplish the work for which he came (*theosis*): the obstacle of nature, the obstacle of sin, the obstacle of death, and the dominion of the devil. The obstacle of nature was overcome with His incarnation; the obstacle of sin and death was overcome by the cross and the Resurrection of Jesus. The dominion of the devil was overcome by Christ's descent into Hades (Hell).
> According to Eusebius of Caesarea and the patristic tradition of the Church, the mission of Christ (continued by the Church) is threefold: prophet, priest, and king.
> As a prophet, Jesus taught humankind the truth of God, being Himself the incarnate Truth, the Way and Life. Christ's teaching is characterized by clarity and lucidity, simplicity and completeness. Christ is the teacher who backs His teaching with His life.
> As a priest, Christ offers Himself as a victim 'for the life of the world.' Through His sacrifice on the cross, Christ 'redeems us from the curse of the law, by his precious blood,' bestowing 'immortality upon human-

kind' (Troparion of the Crucifixion). The blood shed upon the cross washes away our sin; as it fell upon Adam's (man's) skull and dry bones (according to a pious tradition Adam's tomb lay under the place of crucifixion on Golgotha) they were made alive again; man's poisonous blood was replaced with the life-giving blood of God (Troparion of the Feast of the Exaltation of the Cross). Through Christ's death upon the Cross, man was restored to life.[9]

In the Acts of the Apostles, Saint Peter accuses his compatriots of "killing the author of life, whom God raised from the dead" (3:15). Saint Peter also tells them: "The God of our fathers raised Jesus whom you killed by hanging him on a tree. God exalted him at his right hand as leader and Savior, to give repentance to Israel and forgiveness of sins" (Acts 5:30-31). In commenting upon these passages, the Greek fathers speculate that "it was not possible for death and corruption to keep the author of life" (Saint Basil's Liturgy), and that Jesus, the New Adam, suffered death in His humanity, so that through the power of His divine hypostasis He may destroy death by enduring death and thus free humankind from death and corruption. "For suffering death upon the Cross, He destroyed death by death" (Byzantine Liturgy).

The "cosmic event" of death and corruption introduced to created nature by the first Adam, is counteracted by another "cosmic event," the death of a divine hypostasis upon the Cross. By enduring it in His humanity, by enduring separation between soul and body upon the Cross, the Incarnate Word of God overpowered death and the One who has dominion over death, the devil. The Greek fathers, following Saint Gregory of Nyssa, deployed the "fish-hook" interpretation of the death of Christ upon the Cross. According to this interpretation, the devil and the devil dominated Hades were self-deceived and defeated in trying to exercise dominion over Christ, for this was not possible. As the paschal sermon attributed to Saint John Chrysostom says: "Hades received a body, and encountered God; it received mortal dust, and met heaven face to face."

Byzantine theology does not elaborate on the Pauline doctrine of justification through the death of Christ, as we find it in Romans (5:16-11) and Galatians (3:13). To quote Fr. Meyendorff:

> [The Greek fathers] never develop the idea in the direction of an Anselmian theory of 'satisfaction.' The voluntary assumption of human mortality by the Logos was an act of God's 'condescension' by which He united to himself the whole humanity; for, as Gregory of Nazianzus wrote, 'what is not assumed is not healed, and what is united to God is saved': therefore, 'we needed a God made flesh and put to death in order that we could live again.'... The death of Christ is truly redemptive and 'life-giving' precisely because it is the death of the Son of God in the flesh... In the East, the Cross is envisaged not so much as the punishment of the just one, which 'satisfies' a transcendent Justice requiring a retribution for man's sins. As Georges Florovsky rightly puts it: 'the death on the Cross was effective, not as a death of an Innocent One, but as the death of the Incarnate Lord.' The point was not to satisfy a legal requirement, but to vanquish the frightful cosmic reality of death, which held humanity under its usurped control and pushed it into the vicious circle of sin and corruption.[10]

The cross of Christ is an expression of not only His priestly, but also royal ministry:

> Christ is king throughout His earthly life, for He came to establish and to announce the kingdom of God (Mt 4:17). However, the highlights of His royal ministry are the cross itself (for, according to Saint John Chrysostom, Christ dies as the king who offers His life for His subjects); the descent into Hades to announce salvation to 'those who were asleep there from all ages' (Troparion of Holy Friday); the Resurrection, through which Christ 'tramples down death by death, bestowing everlasting life to the dead' (Resurrection hymn); Christ's Ascension into heaven, through which He re-enters into the Father's glory; and Christ's glorious coming again.[11]

Christ, the New Adam, not only originates a new "being" in His deified humanity; He introduces a "well-being," through His saving work, his sufferings upon the Cross and the washing away of human sin through shedding upon the Cross His precious blood; upon humankind He also bestows life of immortality, "eternal being" through His glorious resurrection from the dead (Saint Maximos the Confessor).

Objectively speaking, salvation in Christ is an *efapax* once for all given in the one event of Christ, that is His person, His life, and His work. How does this salvation in the *human nature* (and by extension, in all the *cosmos*) become *a personal* reality for created human persons?

This requires the mission and involvement of another divine hypostasis, the work of the third, hidden hypostasis of our Triune God, who reveals Christ to us, forms Christ in us, bestows upon humankind Christ's messianic gifts, without revealing Himself. He is the source of new life in Christ, the "source of sanctification" (Saint Basil). For every blessing comes to us from the Father through the Son, in the Holy Spirit. In a similar manner, our ascent to God happens in the light and enlightenment and the life-creating and life-giving activity of the Holy Spirit; the Spirit takes us to the incarnate Son of God; and it is in Him and through Him, the Door and the Way, that we are led to the Father, our final destination.

SALVATION AS SANCTIFICATION: THE WORK OF HOLY SPIRIT

Salvation is not only redemption from sin and its consequences, death and the dominion of Satan. Salvation is also life in communion with God, participation of abundant life in Christ and sanctification through participation in the life of the Holy One. This sanctification is only possible through the mission and work of the Holy Spirit, "source of sanctification."

Let me quote my summary:

> *The Mission of the Holy Spirit*
> The last part of the plan of salvation (divine economy)
> is fulfilled by the Holy Spirit of God (economy of the
> Holy Spirit).

The Spirit of God prepares for the coming of Christ in the Old Testament period, becomes the ointment of Christ's flesh the day of the annunciation, accompanies Christ throughout His mission on earth, and applies Christ's work, both saving and deifying, to each Christian individually, through the sacramental life of the Church. Christ had achieved our salvation and deification in an objective way, in our nature. The Spirit applies salvation and deification in a subjective way, to our persons. Divine grace, the Church and the sacraments are the workings of the Holy Spirit.

Divine Grace

By divine grace we understand the saving and deifying energy of God, made available through Christ's work, and distributed by the Holy Spirit, the source of grace and sanctification. Divine grace, the work of the Holy Spirit, is a free gift, necessary for our salvation, non-coercive, which requires our cooperation (*synergy*). Our response to the grace of God is our works of love, which are the fruits of God's grace working in us. We are justified by God's grace. However, this justification is not real, unless it produces the 'works of righteousness.'[12]

Justification and Sanctification

Saint Paul tells us that God (the Father) is the source of our lives "in Christ Jesus, whom God made our wisdom, our righteousness and sanctification and redemption" (1 Cor 1:30). "Wisdom" is certainly referring to the person of Christ, whereas "righteousness, sanctification, and redemption" refer to His saving work. The three are taken together as synonymous; which means that redemption is righteousness (or justification) and sanctification.

The same Saint Paul also tells us that God "predestined us to be conformed to the image of His Son, in order that he might be the first-born among many brethren. And those whom he predestined he also called; and those whom he called he also justified; and those whom he justified he also glorified" (Rom 8:29-30).

In this second text, Saint Paul introduces a distinction between four things: *predestination, calling, justification,* and *glorification.* However, even here these various "stages" of our life in communion with God can only be seen as part of only one and unique process, that of sanctification. God predestines and calls all men to salvation in Christ and conformity with His glorious humanity. Then He justifies and glorifies them in a sole redemptive act, in the Holy Spirit, who is the "perfecting cause" and source of sanctification. The spirit applies salvation in Christ to each human person who is a brother or sister of the Lord Jesus.

In other words, *justification* is not a separate act of God, but is the *negative* aspect of salvation in Christ, which is freedom from sin, death, and the devil; whereas *sanctification* is the *positive* aspect of God's saving act, that of spiritual growth in new life in Christ communicated by God's Holy Spirit.[13]

Humanity's *justification* as forgiveness of sins is not "a mere covering over man's sins, but a real destruction of them. It is not a mere external decision but a reality. Sins are forgiven truly and really. God does not declare someone to be justified if he is not really free. We understand this teaching better if we remember the relation between Adam and Christ.

As we became not only apparently but really sinful because of Adam, so through Christ the Second Adam we become really justified."[14]

In other words, darkness and light cannot exist together, for when light arrives, it chases away the darkness. So it is with justification in Christ: When it happens, through participation in the *restored* life in Christ, sinful life disappears, exactly as darkness flees the presence of light. Man in communion with Christ's humanity, "conformed to the image of Christ," cannot be at the same time "sinful and righteous," with a mere "imputed" righteousness, that is a "pseudo-righteousness." Once justified, man is also *sanctified* by the life of Christ in the Holy Spirit.

In quoting Saint Cyril of Alexandria, Dr. Dratsellas says of *sanctification:*

Man's sanctification in Christ is mainly participation in the Divine Nature. When the Holy Spirit communicates Himself to a creature He makes the nature of that creature holy. To be without sin, as it is possible for man, and to be transformed to the creator's image are two inseparable ideas. This tranformation and sanctification of man takes place in man not only by the grace of God, but through the Holy Spirit Himself, who 'forms Christ in us' and who 'renovates us to (conforms us with) God.' The Holy Spirit is God and for that reason man's sanctification takes place not… through something like a ministerial grace, but as participation in the Divine Nature that the Spirit gives to those who are worthy.[15]

This "Divine Nature" in which man participates, is obviously, *not the essence* of God, but God's *divine energies*, as described above.

Justification by Faith: Faith and Works

Objectively speaking, salvation (to be understood both as justification and sanctification) is a *given* in Christ and the Holy Spirit. *Justifcation* in our *nature* is more appropriate for Christ's work, *sanctification* in our *persons* is most appropriate for the work of God's Holy Spirit. Both are the gift of God, a *gratia gratis data*.

However, in order for justification and sanctification to be real, human freedom of choice is required. God does not want to save humankind in spite of human free will and human freedom of choice.

True, a true "freedom of choice" according to humanity's "natural will" is the only possible choice for authentic human nature, which, as in the case of Christ, always submits itself to the divine will. However, because of what Saint Maximos calls man's "gnomic will," which can also choose not to submit itself to God's holy will, both the possibility of fall and the possibility of not receiving God's free gift of salvation in Christ also exist. At the very end, not all humankind will be saved in spite of God's desire for "everyone to be saved and to come to the knowledge of truth" (1 Tim 2:4).

The Spirit of freedom sets men free, to freely choose salvation in Christ as justification and forgiveness of sins. Their *faith* is enough, in order for this justification to come about.

Dr. Dratsellas quotes Saint Cyril of Alexandria as saying: "We are freely justified through the grace of Christ, and we have not offered anything in exchange for our lives, nor have we bought the glory of our freedom, but we gain this gift through the gentleness and *philanthropia* (love for man) of our Lord." Dr. Dratsellas comments: "Having been justified by grace we do not offer, or rather, we cannot offer anything in exchange for this great and unique gift. Man cannot offer anything to God. Man only receives from God, who always offers."[16]

Dr. Dratsellas continues: "speaking about justification on man's part Cyril teaches that true faith is the condition for the personal application of the divine gifts of Christ's sacrifice, and therefore for obtaining justification. 'It is in Christ that our access (to God) is realized, and we who are infected (by sin) come near to God, yet we are justified through faith.'" Now, *this faith* is true knowledge of God, not only of an intellectual, but also moral character; it is connected with repentance; it is inseparable from Christian love. It always operates through Christian love. Otherwise it cannot be true faith; otherwise, it is a "dead faith," which cannot justify humanity.[17]

Sanctification as Theosis

This faith which justifies a person, is also the gift of God's Holy Spirit, as is the gift of love, inseparable from this faith. Thus, God's Holy Spirit, in whom sins are forgiven (justification), also begins the process of sanctification and growth in the life of sanctification. This life of sanctification is the life of Holy God, shared by the Holy One of God (Christ), and communicated by God's Holy Spirit to each created person.

The process of sanctification in God's Holy Spirit, which is participation in the life of Holy God, and which includes not only human life, but the entire *cosmos*, is called *theosis* in the theological language of the Greek Fathers. It is a transfiguration of the human nature through participation in the deifying energy of God.[18]

Acquisition of the Holy Sprit, and life of *theosis* in communion with God, healing and transfiguration of the human nature, is the ultimate purpose of Christian life. The grounds upon which this process is possible and actually takes place, is the grounds of the Church of Christ.

THE CHURCH OF CHRIST –
ARK OF SALVATION AND COMMUNION OF SAINTS

Let me quote my summary of doctrine regarding the church:

> The place where the saving and deifying grace of the Holy Spirit is at work is the Church of Christ. The Church is at the same time the image of the Holy Trinity, the people of God, the Body of Christ, and the Temple of the Holy Spirit. All these aspects are necessary for a complete image of the Church.
>
> The Church is the great sacrament of salvation that Christ has instituted in the World. It is the Ark of Salvation, and the inaugurated kingdom of God. Its unity is not affected by schism and heresy; its holiness is not affected by sin; its catholicity and truth is not affected by partiality and falsehood. Founded upon the Apostles, she continues the apostolic mission and ministry in the world, being the 'pillar of truth,' never failing in accomplishing her mission.[19]

Called by God the Father as his holy people, being in Christ and the Body of Christ justified by Him, sanctified by God's Holy Spirit whose temple it is, the Church of Christ is founded on the life of the three divine hypostases, the life of the all blessed and Holy Trinity. As a sacred society of members, constituted as such by this communion with the three divine persons, the church is a reflection of the life of the Holy Trinity.

Mediating salvation to the world on behalf of its founder, Christ, the church sanctifies and transfigures the world, leading it to a life of *theosis* in communion with God, and leading it to God's holy kingdom, of which the church is a partial manifestation, epiphany, and inauguration.

The Ark of Salvation

The one, holy, catholic and apostolic (missionary) church, which teaches the truth of Christ, leads to salvation in Christ, and sanctifies the world through the means of grace in God's Holy Spirit (sacraments), is the new Ark of Salvation, in which salvation in Christ is to be found.

In quoting Saint Cyril of Alexandria, Dr. Dratsellas says:

> The whole soteriology is inevitably united with the doctrine of the church because... her significance in the work of man's salvation is great. Cyril asserts that the church was founded not by any man but by Jesus Christ Himself, and that this church as a community of people who are united through the same correct faith in and love for Christ is not merely a natural, but a spiritual unity, which came to exist because of Christ's redemptive work and of the power of the Holy Spirit.... The Spiritual purpose of the church is the salvation of people, of her members.[20]

The sacraments, signs of the Kingdom of God, bestow Christ's grace to its members through the operation of God's Holy Spirit. *Institution* and *event* in the life of the church do not contradict one another, but complement each other.

From the Christological point of view, as the Body of Christ and the grounds of organized sacramental life, the church is a sacred institution; from the Pneumatological point of view, as the Temple of the Spirit and the field where the Spirit of God operates, the church is a continuous Pentecost, with continuity of Pentecostal life and gifts of the Spirit, who "blows where He wills" (Jn 3:8). Both aspects are inseparable from one another, and completely interdependent.

Some of the major sacraments are: the sacrament of incorporation into the life of the church, participation in Christ's death and Resurrection, and beginning of the new life in Christ, the Sacrament of Baptism, our personalized *Pascha*; the sacrament of the gifts of the Holy Spirit, our personalized Pentecost, the sacrament of Confirmation; the sacrament of Christ's mystical presence amongst God's holy people, through which the deifying energies of Christ are shared with the believers who receive it, the Holy Eucharist; the sacrament of forgiveness of sins committed after baptism, which is the Sacrament of Confession or Penance; the sacrament which both constitutes and unites the church as an apostolic community, guaranteeing the preaching of Christ's truth and the celebration of God's sacraments, which is the Sacrament of Holy Orders (also known as Ordained Ministry or Holy Priesthood); the sacrament of perpetuation of life, Holy Matrimony; and the sacrament of Healing (Holy Oil, Oil of the Sick).

All these sacraments, means of sanctification of God's holy people, make of the church, which is a communion of human persons reflecting the Holy Trinity, a "communion of saints."

The Communion of Saints

> The Church thus conceived is not just another human organization; it is a gathering of people who profoundly share the life of faith, the new life in Christ, the life in the Holy Spirit, the life of God. The Church can best be characterized as a 'communion of saints.' For all its members are called to holiness, through their rite of incorporation into the Holy Body of Christ, the Temple of the Holy Spirit, the people of God. Militant on earth and triumphant in heaven, the Church is only one family sharing in the same means of grace, the holy sacraments.[21]

A communion (*koinonia*) of saints, the church is constituted as such by God's Holy Spirit, who sanctifies its life as a whole and operates through its means of sanctification, the Word and the sacraments.

As in a continuous Pentecost, the Spirit keeps the *harmony* and peace amongst the members of the church, keeping them in *koinonia* (communion) with God and with one another. The Spirit endues and endows the church with His personal gifts for each one of the members, laying stress on their variety and plurality, whilst keeping the unity. The Spirit endows the church with true

collegiality and "synodality" at all levels, with interdependence and
mutual enabling of all the church members. The Spirit directs the
mission of the church toward the world, making of the church the
great sacrament for the world's sanctification and ultimate transfiguration through the saving work of Christ and the deifying and
sanctifying operation of God's Holy Spirit.[22]

FULFILLMENT OF SALVATION IN CHRIST –
ORTHODOX ESCHATOLOGY

In commenting on the completion of salvation in Christ at the
end-time according to Saint Cyril of Alexandria and the Fathers
of the Church, Dr. Dratsellas writes:

> In patristic theology the doctrine of salvation is in-
> separably connected with eschatology because the state
> of salvation of man is not limited to this life only. On
> the contrary, the work of man's salvation will be per-
> fect and permanent in the world of eternity. The Second
> Coming is in several aspects the completion of what
> Christ had already initiated in the First Coming. The
> Judgment of the world will be completed in this Sec-
> ond Coming and God's time of waiting will come to
> an end. Man's glorious state will be in its completion
> in the world of eternity since the saved will be partici-
> pating in the eternal glory of God.[23]

To reflect the general doctrine on salvation in Christ as being
fulfilled in the eschatological times, I conclude with my summary
of the Orthodox eschatological doctrine:

> The Holy Spirit of God, working through the Church
> and its sacramental life, leads the plan of salvation in
> Christ to completion and final fulfillment. The final
> battle with evil that operates in the world will occur
> just before the coming again of the Lord. In the mean-
> time, the struggle against evil and dark forces in the
> world continues, with some victories on behalf of the
> Church, and with some failures on behalf of some of
> its members. This is the normal condition of the life of
> the Church, which is the inaugurated kingdom of God,

and which, however, has not yet come fully. Two distinct stages are to be recognized, in terms of Christian Orthodox eschatology: that of a 'partial judgment,' of a 'partial' or 'realized' eschatology, and that of a 'final judgment,' at the coming again of the Lord, which will come at the end of time.

Partial Judgment - The Hour of our Death
Our physical death, a consequence of the first man's sin that we still suffer, can be seen in two ways: (1) negatively, as a kind of catastrophe, especially for those who do not believe in Christ and life everlasting in Him; and (2) positively, as the end of a maturation process, which leads us to the encounter with our Maker. Christ has destroyed the power of the 'last enemy,' death (1 Cor. 18:26). A Christian worthy of the name is not afraid of this physical death insofar as it is not accompanied by a spiritual or eternal (eschatological) death.

A partial judgment is instituted immediately after our physical death, which places us in an intermediate condition of partial blessedness (for the righteous), or partial suffering (for the unrighteous).

Disavowing a belief in the Western 'purgatory,' our Church believes that a change is possible during this intermediate state and stage. The Church, militant and triumphant, is still one, which means that we can still influence one another with our prayers and our saintly (or ungodly) lives. This is the reason why we pray for our dead. Also, almsgiving on behalf of the dead may be of some help to them, without implying, of course, that those who provide the alms are in some fashion 'buying' anybody's salvation.

General Judgment - the Coming Again of Christ
The early Church lived in expectation of the 'day of the Lord,' the day of His coming again. The Church later realized that the time of this day is known but to

God; still, some signs of Christ's second coming were expected: (1) The Gospel will be preached everywhere in the world (Mt 24:14; Lk 18:8; Jn 10:16); (2) The Jews will be converted to Christ (Rom 11:25-26; cf. Hos 3:5); (3) Elijah, or even Enoch, will return (Mk 9:11); (4) The anti-Christ will appear with numerous false prophets accompanying him (1 Jn 2:10; 2 Thess 2:3; Mt 24:5); (5) Physical phenomena, upheavals, wars, suffering will occur (Mt 24:6; Mk 13:26; Lk 21:25); and (6) The world will be destroyed by fire (*ekpyrosis*: see 2 Pet 3:5). All these signs are expected to be given in due time; without them, the end-time will not occur.

The resurrection of the dead is a miracle that will happen at the second coming of the Lord. According to the Creed: 'I await the resurrection of the dead.'

This resurrection will be a new creation. However, our physical bodies as we know them now will be restored, in a spiritualized existence like that of the Lord after His Resurrection.

The final judgment will follow the resurrection of all. Some will rise to the resurrection of life, and some to the resurrection of judgment and condemnation. Christ will be our Judge on the basis of our deeds, our works of love or our acts of wickedness.

The end-time will follow, with a permanent separation between good and evil, between those who will be awarded eternal life of happiness and bliss in heaven, and those who will be condemned to the fire of eternal damnation, to the eternal remorse of their conscience for having rejected God and authentic life in Him and having joined the unauthentic life invented by the devil and his servants.

A new heaven and new earth will be established, indwelt by righteousness (2 Pet 3:13). The kingdom of God will be fully established; the Church will cease to exist. Finally, the Son of God will turn the kingdom over to God the Father, 'that God may be everything to every one' (1 Cor 15:28).[24]

CONCLUSIONS

Here are some keys to understanding Orthodox soteriology:

1. Orthodox soteriology does not limit itself to the discussion of the saving work, and especially the sacrifice on the cross of the Savior. Instead, Orthodox soteriology considers salvation as basically given in the person of the Savior, with His work only completing what is already given at the incarnation of the Word-of-God-made-flesh: *theosis,* communion between man and God, and reconciliation of man (and the world) with God.

2. With regard to the understanding of the "essence" of salvation in Christ, Orthodox soteriology lays stress on "communion in the risen body of Christ; participation in divine life; sanctification through the energy of God, which penetrates humanity and restores it to its 'natural' state, rather than justification, or remission of inherited guilt."[25]

3. With regard to the understanding of the sacrifice of Christ on the Cross, Orthodox soteriology does not favor the Anselmian doctrine of "satisfaction." Instead, it lays stress on the "cosmic event" of the death of a divine hypostasis, the Word-of-God-who-became-flesh, so that another "cosmic event," that of human failure, sinful condition and death may be reversed.

4. Salvation in our nature, and transfiguration in it of the whole cosmos, is achieved by the person, life and work of Christ (economy of the Son of God). However, this same saving and deifying work of Christ should be applied to every human person, a work which requires the mission of another divine person, God's Holy Spirit ("economy" of the Holy Spirit).

5. The grace of the Holy Spirit, freely given to all, invites and incites man's faith to receive salvation in Christ as justification and sanctification. In order for this faith to be real and achieve justification, this faith should "operate through love."

6. The Church, as the "ark of salvation" and the "communion of saints," is the *locus* where salvation in Christ and the Spirit is to be found and be accomplished. To this end the sacraments, signs of the kingdom of God – and especially the sacrament of communion (*koinonia*) with God and one another, the Holy Eucharist – are of paramount importance.

7. Finally, salvation in history finds its fulfillment in the eschatological times, when Christ will return to "judge the living and the dead," rightly awarding or not awarding everyone according to his or her life and acceptance or rejection of God's salvation in Christ. This final judgment will complete the whole salvation process, which begins with the Incarnation of the Son of God and ends with the submission by Him of God's Holy Kingdom to His eternal Father.

Endnotes

[1] The above is a paper presented to the 6th meeting of the Orthodox-Lutheran dialogue in the USA, at Luther Northwestern (Theological) Seminary, Saint Paul, Minnesota, November 29-December 2, 1989.

[2] John H. Leith, *Creeds of the Churches* (New York: Anchor Books, 1963) p. 33.

[3] Maximos Aghiorgoussis, "The Dogmatic Tradition of the Orthodox Church," in *A Companion to the Greek Orthodox Church* (New York: Greek Orthodox Archdiocese, 1984) pp. 160-1.

[4] M. Aghiorgoussis, "Dogmatic Tradition," pp. 161-2.

[5] Ibid., pp. 162-4.

[6] John Meyendorff, *Byzantine Theology* (New York: Fordham University Press, 1974) pp. 151-2.

[7] Constantine Dratsellas, *Questions of the Soteriological Teaching of the Greek Fathers* (Athens: [reprinted from *Theologia*] 1969) pp. 9-10.

[8] See C. Dratsellas, *Questions*, pp. 58-64; Meyendorff, *Byzantine Theology*, pp. 159ff.

[9] M. Aghiorgoussis, "Dogmatic Tradition," p. 164.

[10] J. Meyendorff, *Byzantine Theology*, pp. 160-1.

[11] M. Aghiorgoussis, "Dogmatic Tradition," pp. 164-5.

[12] Ibid., p. 165.

[13] See C. Dratsellas, *Questions*, pp. 98-103.

[14] Ibid., p. 98.

[15] Ibid., pp. 101-2.

[16] Ibid., p. 103.

[17] Ibid., pp. 104-5.

[18] Ibid., pp. 106-10.

[19] M. Aghiorgoussis, "Dogmatic Tradition," pp. 165-6.

[20] C. Dratsellas, *Questions*, p. 114.

[21] M. Aghiorgoussis, "Dogmatic Tradition," p. 166.

[22] See J. Meyendorff, *Byzantine Theology*, pp. 173-6.

[23] C. Dratsellas, *Questions*, p. 123.

[24] M. Aghiorgoussis, "Dogmatic Tradition," pp. 166-8.

[25] J. Meyendorff, *Byzantine Theology*, p. 146.

Seven

"Sister Churches:" Ecclesiological Implications[1]

On November 6, 1963, *Apostolos Andreas*, the official bulletin of the Ecumenical Patriarchate, published a letter from Pope Paul VI to Patriarch Athenagoras, under the title: "The Two Sister Churches."[2] This was the first public modern use of an old expression used to describe the profound relations between the Churches of Rome and Constantinople.[3] The expression entered the vocabulary of the Second Vatican Council[4] and was repeatedly used in the official correspondence between the two sister Churches, Rome and Constantinople.[5] The expression, constantly used in the ecumenical dialogue since then, became the object of theological reflection at an important ecclesiological colloquium between Orthodox and Roman Catholic theologians in Vienna, April 1-7, 1974. Frs. John Meyendorff and Emmanuel Lanne presented position papers on the topic.[6]

Given the importance of this expression for the ongoing theological dialogue between the two sister churches, we will summarize the historical antecedents of the expression, beginning with the Holy Scripture, and tracing the expression through the tradition of the fathers, through the Middle Ages and to our contemporary times; following the historical overview, we will deal with the profound ecclesiological meaning of the expression as applied to the two major Christian Churches, Eastern Orthodox and Roman Catholic, which are established by history and called today to be "sister churches," in full communion with one another.

THE SCRIPTURAL ANTECEDENTS

The expression "sister church" is not explicit in the Holy Scripture. However, there are expressions which suggest the teaching about "sister churches" as a legitimate teaching. Thus, in the Septuagint, Jerusalem is called the "mother" of all [Psalm 87(86):5]. Galatians 4:25-26 reflects this teaching, as comparison is made between the present Jerusalem, a "slave like her children," and "Jerusalem above," which "is free and is our *mother.*"

This image of "Jerusalem above," that is the *church*, as the *mother of all*, is an image which was later used by the church writers to indicate first of all the "motherhood" of the Church of Jerusalem with regard to *all* the other churches (including Rome); secondly, this image applies to the church of Christ in general, as the "mother" of all believers.

The (spiritual) "motherhood" of the Church of Jerusalem implies a "sisterhood" of all the churches "born" of her: for all the churches which received the Gospel, salvation in Christ through the apostolic preaching, faith, life and practice, are considered as (spiritual) "daughters" of Jerusalem.

Even if this idea of (spiritual) "motherhood" of the (local) Church of Jerusalem is not an explicit one in the Holy Scripture, there is no doubt that the idea of "sister churches" in the Holy Scripture is no longer contested by contemporary biblical scholars.[7]

According to Father Lanne, the "mysterious expression which concludes 2 Jn 13: "Greetings to you from the children of your *sister* (ἀδελφή), the chosen one," is usually interpreted today as "the Church of the Elder, author of the letter."[8] Confirmation of this interpretation is given by the notion of "brotherhood" (ἀδελφότης) in 1 Pet 2:17 and 5:19. Even more explicit is the use of the term "συνεκλεκτή" (the community of those who are chosen along with you), in 1 Pet 5:13. The "sister [church] in Babylon" is the Church of Rome, whence the epistle is written.[9]

It is of special significance that modern English translations not only express the idea of "sister church," but that they introduce the expression itself into the text of the Bible, at least in the specific instance of 1 Pet 5:13.[10]

The personification of the local churches, to which salutations are addressed at the end of an epistle, was already established in the Pauline letters. See, for example, Romans 16:16: "Greet each other with a holy kiss. All the churches of Christ send greetings" (cf. 1 Cor 16:19-20).

It is noticeable that "greetings" and "holy kiss" (ἀσπασμός, ἅγιον φίλημα) are not merely "ceremonial." They have a "sacramental character," especially when exchanged among "sister churches."[11]

It is important to notice that Saint Paul and the other authors of letters are not always consistent in their addresses. Most of the time they use the expression "to the church of God which is in ...." (1 Thes 1:1; 2 Thes 1:1; 1 Cor 1:23; 2 Cor 1:1; Gal 1:2; 1 Pet 1:1; and 1 Jn 1.1) an expression which characterizes the local church as the full expression of the "catholic" church, as "the church of Christ in its plenitude and everywhere" will be called later. But also the names "saints," (Rom 1:7; 2 Cor 1:2; 2 Cor 1:1; Eph 1:1; Phil 1:1; Col 1:2; and Jd 1:l) "chosen ones," (Rom 1:7; 1 Cor 1:2; 1 Pet 1:1; and Jd 1:1) and "sojourners" (1 Pet 1:1) will be used to indicate the Christian brothers of the local, sister churches.

Finally, the book of Revelation speaks of personified local churches in Asia Minor in a female form (Rev 1:1; 2:1; 8, 12, 18; 3:1, 7, 14). Each of these churches is governed by an "angel," a local bishop who represents them. The same pattern will be found in 1 Clement and the Apostolic fathers of the Church.

"SISTER" AND "MOTHER" CHURCHES
IN THE EARLY CHRISTIAN CHURCH

In the early Christian literature, each local community is normally personified with the name of its main city as a church. This church is closely related to the other local churches as a "sister church." These churches exchange sisterly greetings as a form of communion with one another, and, at times, feel free to extend sisterly admonitions to one another. Also the terms of church-mother, mother-city, and mother-church appear during these early years of the life of the Christian church. Let us review some of the literature.

Clement of Rome

The classic example of the attitude of a "sister church" writing to another sister church is that of the Church of Rome addressing the Church of Corinth in 1 Clement. Saint Clement feels free to represent his church in writing to the Church of Corinth on her behalf. The "church of God sojourning in Rome" (παροικοῦσα ἐν Ρώμῃ) writes to the "church of God sojourning in Corinth" (παροικούσῃ ἐν Κορίνθῳ).[12] Unlike the comments of some western commentators, who see in this letter an "authoritative document by Saint Peter's successor" addressing a "daughter church," the tone and scope of the letter is diametrically different: The Church of Rome, a sojourning sister and pilgrim church writes to another sojourning sister and pilgrim church, the Church of Corinth, in the hope that its *sisterly* counsel will be heeded by its sister church, lest she disobey the word of God in the Holy Scriptures, abundantly expounded upon by Saint Clement.

Ignatios of Antioch

The martyr bishop of Antioch exemplifies the same teaching with regard to "sister churches" in his many letters. These local churches are "autonomous moral persons (juridical entities?) which entertain sisterly relations with one another."[13]

Saint Ignatios greets the churches in the "traditional" way of the New Testament epistles. As we have stated, these "greetings" (ἀσπασμός) have a liturgical and sacramental connotation, being an expression of the communion existing between local churches.

Saint Ignatios uses the word "love" to mean the local church, or even the church of Christ in general. Love, as taught and exemplified by Christ, expresses "the most profound and authentic life of the community, and the most complete manifestation of the sisterly relation which unites this community to another."[14] Thus, the church can easily be called "love" as we see it in Saint Ignatios' letters.[15]

Finally, even if the expression "sister church" is not present in Saint Ignatios' writings, there is an equivalent expression, which results in the same meaning: that of "love of the brothers" (the *love of the brothers* who are in Troas salute you; *Letters to the Philadelphians,* 11:2, and *Smyrnæans,* 12:1).[16]

Polycarp of Smyrna

The *Letter to the Philippians* of Saint Polycarp of Smyrna reflects the same teaching found in 1 Clement and the Ignatian letters regarding sister churches. "Polycarp and the elders with him" address their letter "to *the church of God sojourning* (παροικούσῃ) *at Philippi.*" Filled with biblical quotations, the letter is a brotherly admonition to persist in the faith, be *"affectionate to the brotherhood,* devoted to one another, united in the truth, serving one another in the gentleness of the Lord."[17] The expression "sister church" is not present, but the idea is certainly implied and equivalent expressions are used.

The *Martyrdom of Polycarp,* a letter from the Church of Smyrna to the Church of Philomelium in Asia Minor, repeats the same teaching. In the address of the letter we read: "To the church of God *sojourning* (παροικούσῃ) in Philomelium and to all the communities (παροικίαις) of the holy and universal (καθολικῆς) church *sojourning in every place* (κατὰ τόπον, local churches): mercy, peace, and love of God the Father...".[18] This passage represents one of the most explicit texts of the early church with regard to the theology of the "local church" in its relationship to the "universal church": each local church is a concrete manifestation of the one, "holy and catholic church" of God, fully present in each of those local, "sojourning" and pilgrim churches, which are only one communion with the rest of the other local, "sister" churches. Again, the expression "sister church" is not here, but the reality certainly is.

Letter of the Martyrs of Lyons

The *Letter of the Martyrs of Lyons,* probably written by Saint Irenaios of Lyons, introduces a new idea into the relationship of the local church and its members: the church-mother. The main topic of the letter, partially preserved by Eusebios, is that of the church as virgin-mother, giving birth to her children in martyr-

dom. The apostates, afraid of martyrdom, are the "miscarriages."
However, there is hope for them to have a change of heart and to
be saved: the "living" (the martyrs) may, through their example,
instill life in the dead (the lapsed), and make them return to the
womb of the virgin-mother, the church.[19]

Saint Irenaios

Saint Irenaios gives a similar idea of "motherhood," applied to
the Church of Jerusalem, "the mother of all churches." Jerusalem
is the mother of all churches, for she gave them birth through the
preaching of the Apostles which originated in Jerusalem. In his
Adversus Haereses, Saint Irenaios says regarding Jerusalem: "These
are the voices of the church, which is at the origin of every church;
these are the voices of the mother-city (μητροπόλεως) of the citi-
zens of the New Covenant; these are the voices of the disciples of
the Lord" (III, 12:5).

The text implies a reference to Psalm 87(86):5, quoted above. It
is to be noticed that when Saint Irenaios speaks of "all churches" as
being derived from Jerusalem, the "mother-city" of Christendom,
he actually means *all* churches, including Rome, Smyrna, and
Ephesus, which Saint Irenaios mentions in the same book.[20]

Tertullian

A teaching similar to that of Saint Irenaios is proposed by
Tertullian in his *De Prescriptione Haereticorum,* XX and XXI. Without using the expression, Tertullian established a theory of "sister
churches." All the churches are apostolic, because they are the off-
shoot of apostolic churches; "all of them are primitive, and all
apostolic, because they are only one church. To manifest this unity,
the churches share the peace, exchange the name of *brother* [sis-
ter], practice hospitality, rights and obligations which are
regimented by the unique tradition of the same mystery" (XX, 8-9).

Tertullian calls the apostolic churches "wombs and sources of
the faith" (*matribus et originalibus fidei,* XX, 4). Tertullian repeats
and develops the teaching of Saint Irenaios regarding the primitive community of Jerusalem as "the mother of all churches."[21]

Firmilian of Caesarea

A predecessor of Saint Basil the Great, Firmilian of Caesarea in Cappadocia, found himself involved with the baptismal controversy between Carthage and Rome. Firmilian sides with Saint Cyprian. He appeals to the authority of the church of Jerusalem as being higher than that of the church of Rome. He dismisses the claim of Stephen of Rome that he is the successor of Peter and Paul the apostles. In his *Letter to Saint Cyprian,* Firmilian says:

"What Stephen dares to do... is an insult to the blessed apostles Peter and Paul" (VI, 2). Rome has innovated "with regard to the celebration of Easter, and many other points of religion (*circa celebrando dies Paschae et circa multa alia divinæ rei sacramenta*). Rome does not keep the traditions as does Jerusalem *(nec observari illic omnia æqualiter que Hierrusolimis observantur)*" (VI, 1).

Fr. Lanne observes: "For Firmilian, Jerusalem is the guardian par excellence of the traditions of ecclesial life, and not Rome. Is there a theory of Mother Church? For this bishop of Caesarea, it does not seem accurate; according to his baptismal theology, the Catholic Church as such is the Mother. Wherever she is, she is the only one to give birth to children for God."[22]

"MOTHER" AND "SISTER" CHURCHES DURING THE FOURTH AND FIFTH CENTURIES

The golden age of Christian patrology gives us at least two good examples for the use of the expressions "mother" and "sister church" which are unequivocal and unique. They are given by two of the most prominent fathers in patristic literature, Saint Gregory the Theologian, and Saint Basil the Great.

Also, years later, we have at least one clear example of the use of "sister churches" by a Western author, Innocent I, Pope of Rome. Let us review these cases.

"Mother" and "Sister Church" in the Fourth Century

Mother Church. The first case involves Saint Gregory of Nazianzos, regarding the expression "Mother Church" (μήτηρ ἐκκλησία). The expression appears three times in Saint Gregory's letters.

The first letter (XLI), dated July-September, A.D. 370, is sent to the prominent clergy and laity of the Church of Caesarea, Cappadocia. Its purpose is to promote the candidacy of the priest Basil to the metropolitan throne of Caesarea. Basil is the best and most capable of all the priests in Caesarea. This city deserves a good bishop, for the good reason that it is the central, important city of Cappadocia, looked upon as a kind of "mother" by the area Christian community. Saint Gregory says: "Caesarea is more important than any area church: for since the beginning she was the mother of almost all the churches (ἡ μήτηρ σχεδὸν πασῶν τῶν ἐκκλησιῶν); she continues to be this; she continues to be regarded as such; she attracts the attention of the Christian community (πρὸς ἣν τὸ κοινὸν ἀποβλέπει) which surrounds it with her as the center."[23] The reasons for this attraction are very clear: "This role [of motherhood] belongs to her not only because of the sound faith which she has always propagated to all; but also because of the onemindedness (χάριν τῆς ὁμονοίας) which God grants her in a very evident manner."[24]

The *second letter* (XLIV), dating also July-September, A.D. 370, is addressed to Eusebios of Samosata. Its purpose is the same as that of the previous one, that is to ask Eusebios to cast his vote for Basil. The reason is also the same, that is the importance of Caesarea, the "mother church" of Cappadocia: "our *mother church*, that is the church of Caesarea."[25]

The *third letter* (L) is addressed to Saint Basil. It is written on behalf of Saint Gregory's father, Gregory senior, to assure Basil of the support of the bishop of Arianzus against the claims of Anthimos of Tyana. Anthimos claims that his new diocese of "Second Cappadocia" is more important than that of Saint Basil because it is a larger one than old Cappadocia. Gregory answers Anthimos: "If you feel that your diocese is larger, why, then, do you try to include our town into your circumscription? Are we too not part of this church (of Caesarea) which is truly the mother of the other churches from the very beginning?" (...καὶ τὴν ἐκκλησίαν, ὡς ὄντως ἐκκλησιῶν μητέρα, καὶ ἄνωθεν).[26]

Two more contemporary witnesses confirm this traditional perspective regarding "mother churches." The first is that of the synod of Constantinople, A.D. 382. In transmitting the Acts of the Second Ecumenical Council (First of Constantinople, A.D. 381), the Synod acknowledges Cyril as the bishop of the Church of Jerusalem, "the mother of all churches" (μητρὸς πασῶν τῶν ἐκκλησιῶν).[27] The expression is not to be seen as "polemical," opposing the Roman primacy, as some have tried to interpolate. It just expresses a reality of the life of the church of Christ present in it since its very inception.

The other witness is the inscription which Pope Damascus (of this same era) put on the tomb of Hippolytus of Rome. In that inscription, Rome is regarded as *"mater et magistra omnium ecclesiarum" (mother* and teacher of all the churches). This expression should be seen in the light of the general teaching regarding "mother churches," as delineated above, and especially in the light of the *Letter of the Martyrs of Lyons,* quoted above.

Sister Churches. Finally, we have a clear-cut case where the expression "sister church" is unequivocally used. It is that of Saint Basil the Great.

Saint Basil writes to the priests of the church of Neocaesarea in Pontus, asking them to circumvent their bishop Atarbios, a Monarchian, and defend orthodoxy. He reminds them that the two churches, Caesarea and Neocaesarea, are the biggest in the area, and they have always behaved as "sister churches" in their relationship to one another. They have always shared in the one Christian faith and life; and they have always kept the peace and harmony that reigns among "sister churches," a peace and harmony which is now threatened by heresy. Saint Basil says:

> Don't force me to divulge the things I now hide in my heart, as I am in anguish by myself and lament the misery of our times: that is, that *the most prominent among the churches,* which from an old time were *sisters with one another* (αἱ μέγισται τῶν ἐκκλησιῶν, καὶ ἐκ παλαιοῦ πρὸς ἀλλήλας ἀδελφῶς τάξιν ἐπέχουσαι), for no reason now find themselves to be in dissention... it is better for us to disappear, in order for the churches to keep in harmony with one another...[28]

"Sister Churches" in the Fifth Century

Thirty years following Saint Basil's expression of "sister churches," we find a similar expression in the West. In A.D. 415, Pope Innocent I called the Church of Antioch "sister of the Roman church" *(velut germanam ecclesiae romanae).* The justification for this appellation is that both churches are honored by the presence of the apostle Peter, and eventually share in his doctrine. Innocent writes to a priest by the name of Boniface: "The Church of Antioch, which the blessed apostle Peter honored with his presence, before he came to Rome, *as she is like a sister of the Roman church,* could not stand being separated from her any longer."[29]

"Sister Churches" from the Fifth to the Twentieth Centuries

To bridge the gap between the fifth century and our contemporary times regarding the expression "sister church," we refer to the summary made by the well known scholar and ecumenist, Fr. Yves Congar:[30]

1. In A.D. 415, Pope Innocent I calls the Church of Antioch a *"sister of the Roman church."*[31]

2. In A.D. 429, Nestorios of Constantinople wrote to Pope Celestine I: "We owe each *other fraternal* and *reciprocal information."*[32]

3. Patriarch John II of Constantinople A.D. 518-520, wrote twice to Pope Hormisdas of Rome that *"the church of Constantinople and that of Rome make only one church."*

4. In A.D. 1136, Nicetas of Nicomedia said to Anselm of Havelberg that the Eastern Orthodox bishops do not deny the primacy of the Roman church among its sister churches: *"Qui nos quidem inter has sorores primatum non negamus."*

5. In the twelfth century, Patriarch John X (Camateros) of Constantinople (1198-1206) writes to Pope Innocent III of Rome with regard to his claims of authority and supremacy over the entire church, Eastern and Western:

> Where do you find in the Holy Gospels that Christ said that the church of the Romans is the head and

universal mother and the most catholic of all the churches at the four points of the compass; or by what Ecumenical Council was what you say about your church decided?... It is not, then, for these reasons that Rome is the mother of the churches; but, as there are five great churches adorned with patriarchal dignity, that of Rome is the *first among equal sisters* of the *same dignity* (πρώτην ὡς ἐν ἀδελφαῖς ὁμοτίμοις τυγχάνειν αὐτήν). So the church of the Romans has the first rank (πρώτη τῇ τάξει); it is the first of the other churches which, as sisters (ἀδελφῶν) equal in honor (τιμή) are born of the same heavenly Father...

6. In A.D. 1853, N. A. Muraviev called the Western Church the *sister church* of the Eastern Church.

7. At the First Vatican Council (1870), which was not characterized by openness to "ecumenism," Msgr. Papp-Szilegyi, who was opposed to the declaration of papal infallibility, recalled that the Church of the East has been our *sister.*"[33]

8. In A.D. 1884, the Metropolitan of Kiev, Plato (died 1891), called the Western Church the *sister* of the Eastern Church.

9. In A.D. 1927-8, Georges Calavassy, "Greek Rite" bishop in Athens, Greece, in his correspondence with the Archbishop of Athens, Chrysostom Papadopoulos, called the latter "head of a *sister church.*"

10. In July A.D. 1948, in Moscow, Patriarch Alexis I called the Roman Church a *"sister church."*

"SISTER CHURCHES" IN CONTEMPORARY OFFICIAL DOCUMENTS

We now come to our contemporary times. Both the expression "sister church" and what goes with it, that is the name of "brother" used by bishops as they recognize one another as brothers in the one episcopacy of the church are abundantly used in the modern documents and the official correspondence between the two sister churches, Eastern and Western. Let us review some of the most important documents of this abundant literature.

"Sister Churches" in Unitatis Redintegratio

The *Decree on Ecumenism [Unitatis Redintegratio (U.R.)]* of the Second Vatican Council uses the term "sister churches" to speak of the Eastern Orthodox Churches in their relationship to one another. However, the same Decree lays the foundations for "sisterly" relations between them and their Western counterpart, the "sister church" of Rome.

In number 14, section on the Eastern Churches,[34] the Decree acknowledges that "for many centuries, the churches of the East and of the West went their own ways, *though a brotherly communion of faith and sacramental life bound them together."* In the same number, the Eastern Orthodox Churches, being of independent apostolic origin, and keeping the apostolic life and faith, are acknowledged as relating to one another as "sister churches." It is easy to realize that what makes the Eastern Churches "sister churches" is the sharing of the one apostolic faith and life. The same principle can be applied to the relationship of the two churches, Eastern and Western, and the same name can be applied to them, that of a "sister church."

The whole effort of the Decree on Ecumenism is to establish that the two churches, Eastern and Western, share in the same treasures, liturgically (number 15), canonically (number 16) theologically (number 17), and spiritually (number 18). Even if the expression "sister church" is not explicitly present with regard to the relationship between the Eastern and Western Churches, the teaching regarding this relationship is well established by the Decree.

"Sister Churches" in the Brief Anno Ineunte, *July 25, 1967*

The most important of all the documents regarding both the theology, ecclesiological teaching and significance, and also the expression itself of "sister churches" applied to the Eastern and Western Churches, is the papal Brief *Anno Ineunte.*[35] The Brief was handed by Pope Paul VI to Patriarch Athenagoras on July 25 1967, at the conclusion of an ecumenical service at the Latin Cathedral of the Holy Spirit in Pera, Istanbul.

In the Brief, the Pope calls himself "the head of the Catholic Church," to be understood as the Roman Catholic Church. He and his counterpart as the ranking bishop of the Eastern Orthodox Church, the Ecumenical Patriarch, share in the responsibility of reestablishing the visible unity of the "Universal Church of Christ."

The Pope establishes the profound *brotherhood* of the two bishops, based on "divine filiation, the gift of the Father through His beloved Son, Jesus Christ the Lord." After the brotherhood is established among the bishops, it is time for the *sisterhood* of the churches which they represent to also be established. The Pope says: "In each local church, this mystery of divine love is enacted, and surely this is the ground of the traditional and very beautiful expression *sister churches* [italics my own], which local churches were very fond of applying to one another (cf. Decree, *Unitatis Redintegratio*, 14)." The expression "sister churches," which in the Decree applies to the Eastern Churches amongst themselves, is now about to be also solemnly applied to the relationship between Eastern and Western Churches in the solemn papal document.

The Pope continues: "For centuries we lived this life of 'Sister Churches', and together held Ecumenical Councils which guarded the deposit of faith against all corruption. And now, after a long period of division and mutual misunderstanding, the Lord is enabling us to discover ourselves as 'sister churches' once more, in spite of the obstacles which were once raised between us." However, these obstacles are not insurmountable, because a basic communion still persists between the two sister churches: they share in the apostolic succession of their clergy and the true sacraments, with the Holy Eucharist as their center (cf. *Unitatis Redintegratio*, 15). The Pope continues: "In the light of Christ we see how urgent is the need of surmounting these obstacles in order to succeed in bringing to *its fullness and perfection* the already very *rich communion* which *exists* between us."[36]

The Pope suggests that it is important to educate our clergy and laity, as it is also very important to establish a "sincere theological dialogue, itself made possible by the re-establishment of fraternal love, to come to know and respect one another amidst the legitimate variety of liturgical, spiritual, disciplinary, and theological traditions (cf. *U.R.* 14-17), in order to reach agreement in a sincere profession of every revealed truth."

The Common Declaration of Pope Paul VI and Patriarch Athenagoras, October 28, 1967

Only three months after their encounter in Istanbul and the promulgation by the Pope of *Anno Ineunte,* the heads of the two sister churches met again, this time in Rome. At the end of the Patriarch's visit, the two brother bishops signed and issued a common declaration, which is of great significance in terms of the theology and practice of "sister churches."[37] The two bishops were thankful that they were able to meet again, "to greet one another with a kiss of peace, and to talk in a spirit of charity and fraternal openness."

They recognize that the way to restoration of full communion, which presupposes unity in the faith, "is still a long way to go." But they rejoice that their meeting has played a part in the way of further discovery of their two churches as "*sister churches.*"

They realize that the unity between the Orthodox and the Roman Catholic Churches can only be found "within the framework of a renewal of the church and of Christians, in fidelity to the traditions of the Fathers and to the inspirations of the Holy Spirit."

They expect the "dialogue of charity," which should underlie a possible theological dialogue, should lead them to "unselfish collaboration and common action upon pastoral, social, and intellectual levels." Among the practical problems that should be resolved are the regulations regarding marriages between Orthodox and Catholic faithful.

The two leaders recommend cooperation between Orthodox and Roman Catholic scholars as they study the common tradition of the church. In a general way, the spirit which should inspire all efforts of rapprochement should be "a spirit of loyalty to the truth and of mutual comprehension, with a desire to avoid rancors of the past, *and every kind of spiritual and intellectual domination.*"[38]

Joint Declaration of Pope John Paul II and Patriarch Dimitrios on the occasion of the Inauguration of the Theological Dialogue, November 30, 1979

Following in the footsteps of Pope Paul VI, his predecessor, Pope John Paul II visited Constantinople and Patriarch Dimitrios on the feast of Saint Andrew, November 30, 1979. At the conclusion of the papal visit, the two leaders promulgated a common declaration of readiness to move into theological dialogue.[39]

The two leaders expressed their thankfulness to God because they were able to celebrate together the feast of the Holy Apostle Andrew, "the First-Called and the brother of the apostle Peter." They express their determination to do everything in their power for the restoration of full communion between their two sister churches.

They are happy to realize that the preparation of the theological dialogue has reached such a state, that they can announce this dialogue, and make public the list of its members on both sides.

The purpose of the dialogue is *restoration of full communion* between the two *sister churches.* But there is even more: "This Theological Dialogue envisages not only an advance towards the re-establishment of full communion between the Catholic and Orthodox *sister Churches,* but also a contribution to the multiple dialogues that are pursuing their course in the Christian world as it seeks its unity."

The two leaders praise the "dialogue of charity" and they rejoice at its results: "The dialogue of charity (cf. Jn 13:34; Eph 4:1-7), rooted in complete faithfulness to the one Lord Jesus Christ and to his overriding will for his church (cf. Jn 17:21), has opened up the way to *better understanding* of our *respective theological positions* and thereby to *new approaches to theological work,* and to a *new attitude* with regard to the common past of our Churches."[40]

John Paul II and Dimitrios also suggest that the "dialogue of love" has produced one more important fruit: the "purification of the collective memory of our Churches is an important outcome of the dialogue of charity, and an indispensable condition for future progress." Thus, the importance for the "dialogue of love" to continue in full strength together with the Theological Dialogue: "The Dialogue of Charity itself *must continue with might and main* in the complex situation which we have inherited from the past, and which forms the real order of things in which our enterprise must be conducted today."

ECCLESIOLOGICAL IMPLICATIONS

Let us now come to the ecclesiological implications regarding the expression and theology of "sister churches" as delineated above.

Before I give my own, personal evaluation, let me summarize the positions of three leading theologians who have dealt with the same topic. As one will see, there is significant consensus in their evaluation.

Ecclesiological Implications of "Sister Churches" according to Fr. Y. Congar

We begin with Fr. Congar, even if his article was written seven years later than those of Fr. E. Lanne and J. Meyendorff for the simple reason that it is more focused, and certainly takes into account, at least, Fr. Lanne's article.

Fr. Congar sees the following as the theological (and ecclesiological) implications of "sister Churches," not only applied to "local Churches" within the Roman Catholic or the Orthodox Churches (such is the explicit use of *U.R.* quoted above). Fr. Congar applies (as did Frs. Lanne and Meyendorff) this expression to the relation between Roman Catholic and Eastern Orthodox Churches. These are his assumptions:

1. *"It is the same church,"* that is, the Roman Catholic and the Eastern Orthodox Churches were, and continue to be, the One Church of Christ (One, Holy, Catholic and Apostolic: *the Una Sancta!*).

Fr. Congar finds this to be "presupposed by a number of historical facts, or is implied by canonical theological positions." Fr. Congar gives two examples: (a) The consciousness in the church of the East that there cannot be held an *ecumenical* council in the absence of the Roman Patriarchate; and (b) In Florence, the effort of the Council was to heal a "schism," actually a *de facto* separation within a church which was meant to be one: "There was not a church on the one side and a group which was not the church on the other. The church was split in two."

To corroborate this argument, let us not forget that the bishops on both sides had no problem recognizing one another as bishops of the church. They could not agree on many issues because of their *estrangement* (Fr. Congar's own word coined on some other occasion); but they were in agreement that on both sides there was real episcopacy representing the One Church of Christ.

Let me quote the rest of Fr. Congar's text regarding the still existing unity between the two sister churches:

> Many of us would hold that on the level of the ancient conception of the church as a unity of faith, a sacramental reality, and spiritual organism, which the Orthodox retain, it is the same church. I have often suggested this and more than once have wished that the church *would begin to breathe through its two lungs,* an image which His Holiness John Paul II has also used several times. Fr. Christopher Dumont, for a long time a specialist in Orthodoxy and ecumenism, has often expressed his basic conviction of the real unity between the two churches. But it is Fr. Louis Bouyer who, in the framework of a positive doctrine, and by virtue of his excellent knowledge of Eastern theology, has most explicitly affirmed 'that *the Orthodox Church and the Catholic Church,* although both sorely tempted by the spirit of division, *remain a single church,* and do so as of right, despite appearances which are so contrary.' Do the Orthodox accept that? Certainly not all do. But when he received members of the joint Orthodox-Roman Catholic commission at Rhodes on 30 May 1980, Metropolitan Spyridon twice called them '*brothers of the Eastern and Western sections of the only, holy, catholic and apostolic church.*[41]

2. *"According to two different traditions,"* Fr. Congar emphasizes the same thing that *Unitatis Redintegratio* emphasized, as well: that the traditions of the two churches are *different* at many points. Of course, difference and variation "in secondary things" is not

contrary to the unity of the church, of which Fr. Congar spoke above. Fr. Congar states that he spoke and wrote about this repeatedly.[42] He concludes: "All is common between Orthodox East and Catholic West; and *yet it is all different,* even what is essentially the same thing!"[43]

3. *The common inheritance of the two churches to them directly from the Apostles.* In other words, Rome is not the "mother Church" of the East. Let us quote Fr. Congar:

> The substance of faith and sacramental reality which is common to the Orthodox Church and the Roman Catholic Church does not come from the Roman Church, as is the case with the Protestant communions of the Reformation. *Unitatis Redintegratio* links it with apostolicity. So it is that the churches are *sisters, not daughters.* Paul VI went so far as to speak of a 'universal and holy church of Christ' embracing the *two sister churches.* All these texts seem to me to raise a serious question when we think not only of all the quarrels that can now be relegated to the past but basically of the age-old ecclesiological opposition between the East and Rome. It was in fact a basic criticism of the Byzantines that the Roman Church put herself in the position of *mater et magistra, mother and mistress,* and then went on to treat the other churches, particularly those of the East, not *as sisters but as daughters and infants.* One need only recall the protest of Nicetas of Nicomedia in dialogue with Anselm of Havelberg in 1136: *quae fraternitas, seu etiam quae paternitas haec esse poterit? (…) sola Ecclesia Romana (…) jam non pia mater filiorum, sed dura et imperiosa domina servorum videritur esse... non contemnat fratres suos, quos veritas Christi non in servitutem sed in libertatem in utero matris Ecclesiae generavit:* 'What brotherhood, or even fatherhood could there be?... Only the Roman Church... would not be a tender mother of her sons, but an authoritarian and harsh mistress of slaves... let her not scorn her brothers whom the truth of Christ has engendered, in the bosom of the church, not for servitude but for liberty.'

The comments of John X Camateros were more precise still, since they were in response to equally precise affirmations by Pope Innocent III. Writing to the emperor and the patriarch, the pope had spoken of the Roman Church as *Cunctorum fidelium mater et magistra,* and of the return of the daughter to her mother. After a first reply and a new letter from Innocent, amounting to a treatise on the view that Rome had of its primacy at this time, John X Camateros replied again. He said in particular: 'It is not because of the martyrdom of Peter at Rome that this Rome seeks to be the mother of the other churches. *There are five great patriarchal churches: the Roman Church is the first among sisters of the same dignity (proten hos en adelphais homotimois tynkanein auten...).* The church of the Romans is the first in order (*te taxei*); it has only this prerogative of being the first of the other churches which are, like sisters, of the same dignity and the same father, he of whom it is said that all fatherhood in heaven and on earth comes from him... But we have never learnt that she is mistress and head.[44]

Fr. Congar then asks the hard questions:

> After that, we can see that to speak of sister churches raises a serious question. What do we mean by this expression? The idea of John X. Camateros, taken up a hundred times by the Greeks? Athenagoras I once called the Church of Constantinople "younger sister," *neotera adelphe.* Has Rome revised, adjusted, sharpened up the conception of what she is to the other churches, particularly to the Eastern Churches? *How can she, why should she, continue to be mother, mistress, and head?* Replying on 30 November 1969 to Patriarch Athenagoras, Cardinal Willebrands spoke of the ministry of Peter, coryphaeus of the college of apostles, being transmitted to his successors, and he said: 'This service of authority for unity must be looked at again in the light of the gospel and the authentic apostolic tradition, in a dialogue of love and truth between our churches as

being all churches and ecclesial communities of Christianity.'

This new study is taking place. It presupposes patient and profound historical and ecclesiological rethinking.[45]

We cannot express ourselves better than Fr. Congar, with whom
we fully share his feelings. Our only reservation is regarding the
comments that Cardinal Willebrands made on November 30, 1969
at the Phanar. The Cardinal spoke of the need "to recognize one
another as sister churches, and to proclaim the fact officially."[46] He
spoke of the need for "a restored unity between sister churches."[47]
He also spoke of the need for unity and harmony, and the need for
the *Petrine ministry:* "We believe that in this land of the Apostles
(where unity reigned) Peter was the first leader, and that he was so
not only in Jerusalem but that he continued this ministry in Rome,
and that he handed it on to his successors."[48] And then follows the
quote given by Fr. Congar.

The questions that the Orthodox raise are not regarding the
"Petrine ministry" as a "ministry of unity" in itself. The questions
are with regard to the ministry of Saint Peter himself (Did he
actually continue his ministry in Rome? Was he given the time?
Was it possible for him to do it? Did he leave a successor in Jerusalem? And in Antioch? And in Alexandria? And to what other
places?); and also, the question is asked regarding the *way* of his
succession, that is: how is one a successor of Peter? Is it through
"juridical" succession? Through canonical appointment and installation? Or is it on the basis of one's ordination into Holy Episcopacy
in general? What have we done with Saint Cyprian's understanding of the Petrine ministry being present in *every bishop,* thus
making *every bishop* a successor of Peter? Or is the Pope the *only*
successor of Peter?

Of course, these are the questions to be asked with regard to
our *differing* perceptions regarding our common tradition, and these
are precisely the questions of our Theological Dialogue.

Ecclesiological Implications of "Sister Churches" according to Fr. E. Lanne
    Ten years earlier, Fr. Lanne was expounding upon the theology

behind the phrase "sister churches," in terms very similar to those presented above by Fr. Congar.

After he reviewed the biblical and patristic foundations of this theology, he came to the two main instances of contemporary usage of the terms: *Unitatis Redintegratio* and that of *Anno Ineunte,* presented above.

Unitatis Redintegratio. With regard to *Unitatis Redintegratio,* Fr. Lanne points out that the Decree uses the term "brothers" to refer to *all Christians,* who, as sons of the one Father of the Lord Jesus, are brothers to one another (I.3). The second reference of special importance is that regarding *"mutual brotherhood,"* based upon communion with the three persons of the Holy Trinity, and promoted by living according to the Gospel: "Let all Christ's faithful remember that the more purely they strive to live according to the Gospel, the more they are fostering and even practicing Christian unity. For they can achieve depth and ease in strengthening *mutual brotherhood* to the degree that they enjoy profound communion with the Father, the Word, and the Spirit."[49]

This "brotherhood" among all Christians is based upon the common basic faith in Christ and upon the common Christian baptism. But there is more regarding the Orthodox Christians, as *U.R.* states in Ch. III, 14-18, and as we saw above.

However, in the case of the Orthodox churches, that "mutual brotherhood" passes on from individual persons (Christians) to *churches:* the relation between Roman Catholic and Eastern Orthodox *Churches* is that of a *fraternal communion* ("brotherly communion of faith and sacramental life" which "binds together" the "Churches of the East and of the West")[50], and which continues to "bind them together" even today, in spite of the apparent division ("same apostolic succession, same sacraments, same priesthood, same Eucharist whereby they [the Eastern Orthodox] are still joined to us in a very close relationship").[51]

Thus, the relationship between Eastern and Western churches is basically that of "sister churches," even if the expression is not used. It is that relationship which the Decree describes in II.14 as being that of the Eastern Church between themselves, all of their "local churches," most of *apostolic origin,* relating to one another "in a communion of faith and charity," and exemplifying "those family ties which ought to thrive between local churches, *as between sisters.*"

It is obvious that this "fraternal relationship" between "sister churches" excludes "dependence and filiation," which is the relationship between "mother" and "daughter" churches.[52]

On a positive note, through the celebration of the *one* Eucharist of the church in each local Eastern Orthodox Church, the church is built up and the fraternal communion grows not only between the local churches of the East, but also those of the West.[53] On the "canonical-sacramental" level of communion, it is not yet possible for that profound communion (the "profound and mysterious communion" of *Anno Ineunte),* expressed in the concelebration between bishops in the case of the Eastern local churches, to find expression between the local churches of East and West. This is precisely the purpose of the Theological Dialogue, as the exchange of speeches and correspondence between Rome and Constantinople has indicated over the many years of growth of sisterly relations between the two sister churches.

Fr. Lanne expounds upon the "close," fraternal ties between Eastern Orthodox and Roman Catholic Churches, based upon the celebration of the one Eucharist of the Church, celebrated by the one priesthood of apostolic foundation, succession, faith, and saintly life.[54]

He highlights the importance of the independence of the Eastern Churches when it comes to church structure, organization, and discipline, of which the honor and respect by the West is absolutely required: "the strict observance of this traditional principle is among the prerequisites for any restoration of unity."[55]

Finally, Fr. Lanne highlights the connectedness between liturgy, spiritual life, and theology as lived and experienced by the church of the East, and as presented in *Unitatis Redintegratio.* All these realities create close ties between Eastern and Western Churches, *very different,* yet well connected in the one Christian life and experience of the one Christian Church, the variety of which does not impair, but rather enhances the unity of the church in a diversity of gifts and voices. This diversity is meant to create harmony in the one Spirit of God who inspires and guides the lives of both sister-churches.[56]

Fr. Lanne offers this conclusion of his remarks on the theological implications of "sister churches" in the *Decree on Ecumenism:*

> [Thus, through this analysis,] we have indicated that not only the teaching of the conciliar *Decree* authorizes us to speak of churches in the full meaning of this term when we speak of the churches of the East, with which we have not yet restored (refound) full canonical communion; but it also offers us a number of indications which all go in the direction of an ecclesiology of communion which is based upon fraternity among the Churches.
>
> This brotherhood is to be understood in the way which we have indicated as we traced the history of the concept (of sister churches) through the life of the early church: all these churches are sisters, because all of them are apostolic; but also, because in each of them the one and only Church is built up and grows. In other words, the churches are sisters because each of these churches, through its function in the transmission of the apostolic faith; through its sacramental life; and through its experience of saints which inspires it [makes it alive throughout the generations] is at the same time a *sister* of the other Churches and a *mother*. The one and only Church is built up and grows in each of these Churches of East and West.[57]

Anno Ineunte. Father Lanne gives the next and last text of his analysis, which he now sees in the light of some more recent documents[58] and points out some further theological (ecclesiological) implications.

Following the *Decree on Ecumenism* which is repeatedly quoted, the Brief bases the communion between the *sister churches* of East and West on the "most profound level." Fr. Lanne says:

> In the document under study, Pope Paul VI founds the brotherhood between the [two] Churches [Orthodox

and Catholic] upon the Christian brotherhood of children of the same Father in heaven; but [he] also [bases the brotherhood] upon apostolic faith, baptism, and before all upon the priesthood and Eucharist which, in spite of the absence of canonical communion, establish between the two churches, Catholic and Orthodox, a 'profound and mysterious' communion, by which they can already rediscover themselves as sister churches.[59]

Fr. Lanne finds in the Pope's welcoming address to Patriarch Athenagoras at Saint Peter's Basilica on October 26, 1967, a new, important element added to the list already given: the life of holiness, and the "witness of the lives of the saints."[60] Fr. Lanne reminds us that "this communion of saints through the ages, and their spiritual experience which is transmitted from generation to generation, constitute one of the criteria upon which the Orthodox Church is based in order to recognize the authenticity of the doctrine, seen in the light of eschatology."[61] This "life of holiness" is, according to Fr. Lanne, the "only one necessary thing" which is sought by both churches, according to the conclusion of *Anno Ineunte*.[62]

The fact that in this Brief there is no mention of the teaching on Roman primacy, or other teachings developed in the West after the separation between East and West, raises the question: "Does this ecclesiology of brotherhood of sister churches imply a renunciation of what constitutes the unacceptable singularity of the Roman see?" In order to answer this question, Fr. Lanne considers the following:

1. Being fully conscious that he acts as the Bishop of Rome, but also the head of the [Roman] Catholic Church, through the terms which he utilized in this Brief, the Pope has indicated in principle that the ecclesiological perspectives developed in the West were not applicable to the Churches of the East. This is in total agreement with the exhortation addressed by the [Second Vatican] Council at the end of no. 14 of the *Decree on Ecumenism* that we have analyzed above: the relations between the Churches of the East and the See of Rome, even during the time of full commun-

ion between the two Churches, *were never identical* with those between Rome and the rest of the churches in the West.

2. On the occasion of the visit of Patriarch Athenagoras to Rome,
in the address mentioned above, the Pope made a discrete allusion
to the particular [special] position of the Church of Rome within
Christendom with regard to the Synod [of Roman Catholic Bish-
ops] which at that moment was meeting in Rome. To do so, he
repeated the terminology of Saint Ignatios of Antioch: "The
Church of Rome which presides in love."[63] This is an implicit reference to the special role that Rome had before the separation.[64]

3. But, at the same time, in the *Common Declaration* composed
by the Pope and the Patriarch during the latter's visit to Rome, it is
very explicitly affirmed that the new spirit which animates the
relationship of the two Churches which have rediscovered one another as *sister Churches,* intends to avoid "any kind of domination,
spiritual and intellectual."[65] This affirmation is not a fortuitous
one: everyone knows that it is neither Rome, nor the West, which
might fear spiritual or intellectual domination from the other party.
On the other hand, to the Church of the East this domination
seems to be the unavoidable consequence – not to say the veritable, yet unavowed origin – of the Roman Catholic ecclesiology
regarding [Roman] primacy.

Thus, the rediscovery of an ecclesiology of fraternity between
Rome and the Churches of the East, implies that, as a prerequisite
in its dealings with the East, the Church of Rome will renounce
the forms taken by the exercise of the Roman primacy following
the rupture of canonical communion [between East and West].

Fr. Lanne certainly makes a very courageous statement at this
point. It is the hope of the Eastern Churches that such a statement will be heeded by all those involved, and not lost in the tons
of literature that pay "lip service" to the real cause of true unity,
and possible restoration of unity between East and West, the "venerable" Church of Rome, and its "venerable" sisters of the East.[66]
To support his statement, Fr. Lanne continues:

In fact, since the beginning, the Christian East has al-

ways recognized an authority without comparison attributed to the See of Rome.[67]

But, as time evolved, this authority in the West took
shapes which the East has ignored, and which are
strange to its own ecclesiological development [evolu-
tion]. This is precisely the fact that the *Decree on
Ecumenism* of Vatican II, chapter II, 14 recognized; and
this is what Pope Paul VI has implicitly sanctioned by
his authority in the brief *Anno Ineunte* and in the two
other documents mentioned above.

Thus, the ecclesiology of brotherhood [sisterhood?]
among sister churches requires, as Paul VI recognized,
a new view regarding the relations between Rome and
the Orthodox Church of the East: this rediscovery
implies that we *rethink together,* and not in the absence
of Orthodoxy [the Orthodox Church], *what is the nature of the particular authority* that the East recognizes
[as belonging] to the 'See of Peter.'[68]

In what follows, Fr. Lanne makes the boldest possible statement, which I hope can be accepted on both sides of the two sister
churches, as an incentive to move the dialogue on in its pursuit
towards "full communion," and full restoration of the already existing unity and communion between the two sister Churches. Fr.
Lanne concludes his penetrating study on sister churches:

The ecclesiology of brotherhood among sister
Churches, which the Pope, following the Second
Vatican Council, took in its more profound meaning
implies also that from *the [Roman] Catholic side, in principle nothing impedes the immediate return to the relations
of canonical communion* between the two parties, with
only one condition: that the Orthodox Church may be
willing to reciprocate with the same theological implications. In other words, if the entire Orthodox Church
is willing to acknowledge the [Roman] Catholic
Church as she is, to be the true Church of Christ and
a church which is fully a sister of the Orthodox Church
[which means acknowledgment of the Roman Catholic faith to be the same with that of the Orthodox

Church, acknowledgment of the sacraments as identical, and acknowledgment of an identical experience of (the life of) sainthood in both churches], then there will be no obstacle, according to the viewpoint developed here, to resume complete canonical relations between the two churches.[69]

Finally, Fr. Lanne responds to some final questions: How does one interpret Vatican I, or even Vatican II, regarding Papal authority and Primacy? How can one have unity of the Churches with a double ecclesiology? And, last, but not least, was Pope Paul VI serious in his statements and acts, or was he merely trying to be polite? Fr. Lanne answers these final questions:

Contrary to what some people may think, there is no question here for the Roman Catholic Church to erase the past. The dogmatic definitions made by Vatican I are mandatory for the [Roman] Catholic faith, and they should not be abolished. They should be acknowledged for what they are: definitions which were made without the participation of the sister church of the East. Consequently, on the one hand they require adhesion of the [Roman] Catholics of the West and, on the other hand, *they demand to be rethought in the light of the development of the Tradition which is proper to the East,* as acknowledged by the *Decree on Ecumenism* and as Pope Paul admitted when, on his part, he sanctioned a consistent theology of sister churches.

Long fraternal explanations will certainly be necessary in order to achieve a reciprocal understanding in the domain of this double ecclesiological tradition. But these explanations may take place gradually *following resumption of full canonical communion.* This is so because in spite of the differences of the theological traditions, one would recognize that *common faith, common sacraments, and common [life of] sainthood* would already permit us to *accept one another as sister churches.* If the theology of sister churches is to have a meaning; if it is not a matter of kind words, but devoid of meaning; if the acts of Pope Paul VI are more than gestures of human courtesy; but if, to the contrary, they were accomplished in a solemn way and in full consciousness of their meaning: then, from the [Roman] Catholic side, the brotherhood [sisterhood] between the Catholic and the Orthodox Churches supposes that *there is no insurmountable obstacle for the resumption of full canonical and sacramental communion with the sister church of the East.*[70]

Ecclesiological Implications of "Sister Churches" According to Fr. J. Meyendorff

Finally, let us also hear from a leading contemporary Orthodox Christian theologian and scholar, Fr. John Meyendorff, of blessed memory.

As Fr. Lanne, Fr. Meyendorff also addressed the topic of ecclesiological implications of the expression "sister churches."[71] His approach differed form that of Fr. Lanne. However, it was not less important nor was it less courageous. Actually, it both sharply criticizes and complements the position of Fr. Lanne.

As a good historian, Fr. Meyendorff places himself from the viewpoint of the history in the relations of the two churches. This, for him, is of utmost importance in order to understand and evaluate the present.

The lifting of the anathemas, at the conclusion of the Second Vatican Council, has a *symbolic* value only! He can only establish that, if he goes back to history, to realize that: as the *Common Declaration* of the lifting of the anathemas "from the midst and the memory of the church" already states, these anathemas were not addressed against the churches of East and West, but against *persons:* Humbert de Silva Candida excommunicated Michael Cerularios and his close co-workers, but not the Emperor and the pious people of the Church of Constantinople, whom he found "very Christian and Orthodox." And Cerularios returned the excommunication against Humbert and his co-workers. From the Roman point of view, it can even be debated whether Humbert still had the authorization and the right to act as he did, as the Pope had meanwhile died in Rome.

The meaning of these anathemas is, then, more *symbolic* than real. The *Common Declaration* has captured this meaning.

In any case, if there were real anathemas, these were rescinded on the Roman side in 1089: Pope Urban II had lifted any excommunications in his dealings with Alexis I Commenos, Emperor of Constantinople; on the other hand, the Emperor asked for documents concerning these anathemas. They could not be found in the archives of the Church of Constantinople. Thus, the Emperor asked for the Pope's name to be restored to the diptychs (commemoration at the Divine Liturgy) of the Church of Constantinople (the sign of *communion* between sister churches in the East). This happened automatically.[72]

The question is: what is it, then, that has occurred in the life of the two churches for the actual separation (schism) to have happened? What is the *nature* of the schism?

Fr. Meyendorff uses the word "estrangement," a word that Fr. Y. Congar created and all ecumenists have now accepted, in order to qualify the *nature* of the schism. This *estrangement* goes back to the fourth century, and it took a thousand years for it to happen: "there was a polarization in Trinitarian theology and there were the beginnings (in the 4th century) of an ecclesiological divergence: the Latin West attributed a very particular importance to the "apostolic" sees; the Roman see became conscious of its "Petrine" character; in the East, "apostolic" sees were so numerous, that they could not have any administrative importance whatsoever; the East established the primacy of Constantinople, based on factors solely empirical: it made the capital of the Empire the true center of the life of the church.[73]

Fr. Meyendorff traces the "estrangement" through history; he indicates that a conflict between Pope Nicholas I and Photios I of Constantinople, regarding claims of intervention of the first in the affairs of the East, and the introduction by the Franks of Charlemagne of the interpolation of *Filioque* into the Creed. The conflict was finally resolved at the Council of 879-80 at Saint Sophia in Constantinople. Communion was restored, until the end of the eleventh century (1100), when the "Gregorian reform" substituted in the place of this council the "Ignatian" Council of ten years prior (869-70).

Regarding the date of the schism, Fr. Meyendorff finds that the year 1204, with the Fourth Crusade and the sack of Constantinople by the Crusaders, is the actual date of the schism. From a canonical point of view, a schism is duplication of hierarchy: the usurper establishes his own jurisdiction parallel to the legitimate hierarchy of apostolic succession and tradition. Unfortunately, the establishment in Constantinople and other cities of the East of a Latin hierarchy, parallel to the canonical one of the Eastern Church, is evidence of the presence of schism.[74]

In spite of this uncanonical situation, the East remained magnanimous enough to not immediately break communion with the West. The East continued to see the Latin Church as part of the Christian *Ecumene*, and, certainly, still a sister church. The proof is in the "union councils" of Lyons and Ferrara-Florence where the Eastern bishops came to try to heal the schism between them and their Latin counterparts.[75]

It seems that the failure of the last of these Union Councils (A.D. 1438-9) was the cause of the hardening of the ecclesiological and canonical positions and dispositions on both sides. As of the fourteenth century, the Latins in Hungary and Poland began to rebaptize the Orthodox. Following Florence, the Greeks received the Latins through chrismation "second degree heretics!", and even re-baptism (Council of Constantinople of A.D. 1755).[76]

How can we heal this schism in order to restore communion between the two churches?

Fr. Meyendorff knows that mere canonical acts and dispositions cannot heal a schism. He said that with regard to the lifting of the anathemas. These canonical acts *sanction* an already existing situation. However, canonical acts are also *necessary*, he says.[77] Then, he suggests an idea which will help the two churches to overcome and heal the division and schism. This division and schism can only be healed if "dogmatic relativism" is avoided, and if there is "union of spirits and agreement on the institutional forms of unity."[78]

Fr. Meyendorff finds such an instance of "union of spirits and agreement" regarding the "institutional forms of unity" in the "Eighth Council" of A.D. 879-80 at Saint Sophia. This Council can be used as a model for our future relations. A "return" to the unity which existed on the basis of that Council, the last that can be mutually recognized as an "Ecumenical Council," would have healed the schism much more than any other "canonical act," including the "lifting of the anathemas."

Fr. Meyendorff reminds us what that Council had accomplished:

1. On the canonical and disciplinary levels, the two churches mutually recognized one another as the highest instances [authorities] in their respective territories; thus, there is no papal "jurisdiction" in the East (Canon 1); the primacy of honor of Rome is, naturally upheld, and so are the traditional limits of the Roman Patriarchate, including Illyricum.

2. On the dogmatic level, the Council affirms unity of the faith, expressed by the keeping of the original text of the Nicaean-Constantinopolitan Creed by both churches; any "addition" to the Creed was formally condemned. It is obvious that this addition is that of *Filioque,* which, however, does not affect the authority of the Church of Rome; Rome had not yet adopted the interpolation; this stand was taken with regard to the Frankish clergy, which promoted the interpolated Creed in the lands of the Slavs.[79]

Fr. Meyendorff then moves to today's perspectives, as delineated in *Tomos Agapis (Healing of Schism),* and especially the Brief *Anno Ineunte.*

The gestures and words of Pope Paul VI and Patriarch Athenagoras were interpreted in different ways, and at times misinterpreted. However, there are some gestures and words which go far beyond "ecclesiastical diplomacy," and are situated at a profound ecclesiological level. Fr. Meyendorff stops on two of these gesture-events, or words of ecclesiological wisdom: (1) the *image* of the Pope as the *brother* of the Patriarch, and (2) the significant Brief *Anno Ineunte.*

With regard to the Pope's *image,* the Pope gives the impression of being the *equal* in episcopacy of another bishop, exchanging the

brotherly kiss of peace with a bishop who does not owe his episco-
pal dignity, his teaching authority, and his patriarchal jurisdiction
to Rome. What does it mean, in terms of ecclesiology? The Pope's
image is very much that of a *primus inter pares* of Eastern Orthodox ecclesiology. Was that intended by the Pope? And is this
attitude of Pope Paul VI (and, by now, Popes John Paul I and John
Paul II) in agreement with the teaching of Vatican I regarding the
primacy of the Bishop of Rome?

This new image of papacy, as witnessed in Pope Paul VI, is "a
symbol," "to which a process of ecclesial and theological 'reception' has now the obligation to give content."[80]

Fr. Meyendorff then discusses *Anno Ineunte,* a document which,
"without yet possessing all the necessary clarity, is the second important element which can be used as a dialogue basis."[81]

Fr. Meyendorff stops at "the contrast" of titles given to the Pope
and the Patriarch; He feels that those given to the Pope are "absolute," whereas those given to the Patriarch are "reserved" ("most
qualified"). He is "shocked" that the Pope used the title "head of
the Catholic Church," which eventually reminds us of the "papal
claims." Fr. Lanne has already established that, to the contrary, the
Pope used the title in a "confessional" way [head of the (Roman)
Catholic Church]; Fr. Lanne establishes that the titles that the
Pope gives himself are parallel with those of the Patriarch, who is
called "Ecumenical Patriarch." The Brief, let us be reminded, distinguishes between the "Catholic Church" (in a confessional way)
and the "Universal Church," to the benefit of which both the Pope
and the Patriarch exercise their ministry.

Then, Fr. John goes to the important statement on "sister
churches," which he finds to be a statement of Orthodox
ecclesiology, indicating the *local* church. However, here the expression is applied to the (Roman) Catholic and the (Eastern) Orthodox
Churches.

"According to the text, the theological basis of this affirmation
resides in the mystery of the sacramental presence of Christ. This
mystery 'is present [operating] in each local church,' and, consequently, 'the communion [between our churches] exists already,
even if it is imperfect.'"[82]

In Fr. Meyendorff's estimation, this text implies two things:

1. The *rapprochement* between East and West should be understood as a mutual progressive recognition between local churches; it is certainly not a *"return"* to the *canonical obedience* of Rome!

2. The dogmatic definitions of the Latin Church, promulgated after the separation between East and West thus rejected by the Orthodox (*Filioque*, the Council of Trent, the Assumption of the Virgin) are, so to say, put in parentheses. The fact that the Orthodox do not accept them is not an obstacle in order for an "almost complete communion" to exist between East and West. The same teaching is present in the *Decree on Ecumenism*. How can one interpret this?

Some Roman Catholic theologians have already drawn the conclusion, on the basis of *Anno Ineunte,* that "there is no obstacle for the resumption of canonical relations between the two churches."[83] Practically, even from today, the churches could return to full canonical and eucharistic communion, without Rome renouncing these new dogmas, and without the Orthodox Churches having to accept them.

Fr. Meyendorff raises some questions regarding this interpretation.

Theological pluralism is not only acceptable, but also, to some extent desirable in the united church. There always were, and are now present, the so-called *theologoumena* (theological opinions) in the life of the church. However, a *theologoumenon* can be accepted, or even rejected as a false teaching. Can we treat the Latin definitions after the separation as *theologoumena*? Aren't we condoning not mere theological pluralism, but conflicting doctrines? It seems to Fr. Meyendorff that some of the modern and recent Latin dogmas present a conflict with opposing doctrines of the Eastern Church, and are not mere theological opinions, but doctrinal definitions binding for the West. Can one reestablish the union between the two churches without having resolved this problem of conflict?[84]

The next question that Fr. Meyendorff asks is: is it possible to consider that dogmatic definitions may have a meaning which is *geographically* limited? What is the idea for a dogma to be mandatory for the West, but to be "rethought" in the light of the Eastern tradition?[85]

Fr. Meyendorff says:

> Even the fact of asking such a question implies that the Westerners should exercise their reservation and circumspection regarding these dogmas, because these dogmas were not received by their 'sister church.' Are these 'dogmas' truly dogmas, in the full sense of the term? On the other hand, don't the Orthodox have a responsibility toward the West, and especially the Protestants? In 'rethinking' the Roman definitions, don't they have the obligation to consider the problems not only in the light of their own Eastern tradition, but also in the light of the conflicts which they created in the West? And, finally, what is 'East' and what is 'West' in 1974?[86]

In what follows, Fr. Meyendorff expresses both his appreciation of the expression "sister churches" in terms of creating the right climate for the theological dialogue between East and West. But he also cautions against the statement that the churches are already united. He cautions against an ecclesiological and doctrinal relativism. He trusts the discernment of the church, exercised by its bishops, who, under the guidance of the Holy Spirit, discern both what is positive in the "remarkable events of these past fifteen years;" but the bishops also discern what is negative, as, for example, the problems which resulted in the bosom of the Roman Catholic Church because of its recent openness. Fr. Meyendorff finally blames the Orthodox, as well, for the "estrangement," and for not playing their role to witness against pervasive movements ("the recent ravage of secularism") which operate in the West.

He finally urges that we promote theological rapprochement with the West without compromises and the deception that the unity already exists. He finally repeats his solution to all these problems and the answer to all these questions, which is restoration of the Ecumenicity of the Council of 879-80 as the Eighth Council, and "return" to the faith commonly accepted at that time, as the way of healing the schism: "There would have been not a symbolic gesture, but a true ecclesial act, which would have made possible a veritable communion between the two churches."[87]

In his conclusion, Fr. Meyendorff indicates some of the difficulties for the dialogue, both on the Roman Catholic and the Orthodox side. With regard to the latter, he once more promotes an idea dear to him regarding the position of the Church of Constantinople, which has a real "Petrine" ministry and role to play among the sister churches of the East. "That is the road leading not only to an authentic renewal of historical Orthodoxy, but also making possible a dialogue with Rome which will be truly representative."[88]

CONCLUSIONS REGARDING THE THEOLOGY OF "SISTER CHURCHES"

Let us now draw some conclusions from this rich presentation of sister Churches. We again depend on Fr. Lanne, for the first part of these conclusions.[89]

1. Sisterhood among (local) churches is based upon the New Testament. It is an expression of the communion of faith and love which unite the communities.

2. The notion of "motherhood" of a (local) church follows the notion of "motherhood" of the church as such. The church gives birth in baptism, but also in martyrdom.

3. This "motherhood" applies to local churches founded by the apostles, especially those where the apostles were martyred *(Letter of the Martyrs of Lyons)*. From this point of view, Rome has a special place (especially in the West) because of the Martyrdom of Saints Peter and Paul, who "poured on her all their doctrine with their blood."

But from another point of view (besides being the place of the martyrdom of Christ and of Saint Stephen and Saint James, the brother of the Lord), Jerusalem, the first Church of Christ, has a very special place among the churches, for it is the first community of believers, which gave birth to *all* the rest, including Rome.

4. Firmilian of Caesarea (Cappadocia) makes reference to the "motherhood" of the church of Jerusalem; this "motherhood" of

Jerusalem is confirmed by the First Council of Constantinople (381).

5. Saint Gregory of Nazianzus creates the phrase "mother church" for the church of Caesarea in Cappadocia. Saint Basil the Great creates the term "sister church" for the Church of Neocaesarea. In both cases, the criterion of motherhood, or sisterhood, is that of the common Orthodox faith and relation of communion in charity (love).

6. Rome is aware of this terminology, and applies it to the Church of Antioch: the latter is a "sister church" with Rome, because the apostle Peter stopped there before he went to Rome.[90]

7. The phrase "sister church" is to be traced throughout the history of the church; it is used mostly in a positive way to describe the relationship of communion in the faith and sacramental life of the church among local churches, especially East and West.

At times (in the polemics with the West) the expression is used to counteract the appellation of the Church of Rome as "mother church" in its relations not only with the West, but also with the churches of the East. These churches have a "sisterly" relationship with Rome because their faith, life, and practice comes to them through direct apostolic succession from Jerusalem.

8. The contemporary use of "sister churches" appears repeatedly in the abundant literature of *Tomos Agapis (Decree of Love,* translated into English as *Healing of Schism).*

9. The *Decree on Ecumenism* uses the term in reference to the Eastern Orthodox Churches (and all the Oriental Churches). But it also lays down the *teaching* behind the phrase "sister churches" as it applies to the Roman Catholic and Orthodox Churches.

10. The Brief *Anno Ineunte* presents a coherent doctrine behind the expression sister churches as it applies to the churches of East and West. Their "sisterhood" is based on their "profound and mysterious communion" in Christ, the faith, sacraments (priesthood and Eucharist); later the life of sainthood will be added to the list of realities which unite the two churches.

11. The same teaching is present in the *Common Declaration* of Pope Paul VI and Patriarch Athenagoras at the end of the Pope's

visit to Istanbul; the teaching is repeated in the documents exchanged between John Paul II and Dimitrios, and especially their *Joint Declaration* in Istanbul, as they were announcing the beginning of the official theological dialogue.

12. Fr. Congar sees strong theological and ecclesiological implications in the expression "sister churches" applied to the Roman Catholic and the Eastern Orthodox Churches: they are the One Church of God in Christ and the Spirit; they are also different; and Rome is not the "mother" church of the Eastern Orthodox Churches. He hopes that the Theological Dialogue will lead to the healing of the relationship between these two sister churches.

13. Fr. E. Lanne is enthusiastic regarding both the teaching of the Decree *Unitatis Redintegratio,* and the Brief *Anno Ineunte.* Both documents establish the "deep and mysterious" relationship of "almost complete communion" between the two churches, communion which allows for the immediate restoration of canonical communion between them. With regard to the doctrinal developments of the church of Rome following the separation, Fr. Lanne suggests that they should not necessarily be abandoned, but rethought in the light of the tradition of the East.

14. Fr. J. Meyendorff has his own solution for the healing of the schism between East and West: the two churches will be rediscovered as fully, canonically, and ecclesiologically "sister churches," and communion (which now does not exist) can be restored, if the two churches mutually recognize the ecumenicity of the Council of A.D. 879-80 in Constantinople.[91] This acceptance will resolve the problem of "dogmatical and ecclesiological relativism," which he sees in the position of "union now, no matter what the differences."

My Response

And now, this in my own response to the theology of "sister churches," as applied to the Eastern Orthodox and the Roman Catholic Churches: There is no doubt that the two churches are not yet in "full communion." But to say that there is no communion at all is also inaccurate.

In spite of the division, the separate ways of the two churches, and the dogmatic formulations in the West following the separation, the one Eucharist of the church is always celebrated on both sides, and in the same ecclesial context. Can we say that this does not keep our churches profoundly united?

I agree with the late Fr. John Meyendorff that, full agreement in the faith should be restored, before we share our communion. Also that, there should be no theological and ecclesiological relativism, and also that, the council of A.D. 879-80 should be restored as the council that can still unite our two churches. This is precisely the work of the Theological Dialogue.

But, meanwhile, on the road to the restoration of full communion between our two churches, in the fullness of the apostolic faith, life, practice, and witness, being in constant communication[91] with one another, let us enjoy the abundance of God's gifts, offered to both of our sister churches by our one heavenly Father through Christ the Lord, in the communion of God's Holy Spirit.

ENDNOTES

[1] Paper presented in the Orthodox - Roman Catholic Theological Consultation of North America.

[2] E. Stormon, S. J., ed. and trans., *Toward the Healing of Schism: The Sees of Rome and Constantinople; Public Statements and Correspondence Between the Holy See and the Ecumenical Patriarchate, 1958-1984* (New York: Paulist Press, 1987) p. 11.

[3] Actually, the first modern use of the expression "sister churches" is to be found in a letter of Patriarch Athenagoras to Cardinal Bea, dated April 12, 1962. See E. Stormon, *Healing of Schism*, p. 35.

[4] *Decree of Ecumenism, Unitatis Redintegratio.*

[5] See, for example, *Anno Ineunte, Healing of Schism*, pp. 161-3, and *Common Declaration*, ibid., pp. 181-2.

[6] Emmanuel Lanne, O.S.B., "Eglises-soeurs. Implications ecclésiologiques du Tomos Agapis", ibid., pp. 35-46. Fr. E. Lanne followed his presentation with an article in a recent *festschrift* offered to J. J. von Allmen: "Eglise-soeur et Eglise-mère dans le vocabulaire de l'Eglise ancienne", in *Communio Sanctorum,* Mélangers offerts a Jean Jacques von Allmen (Geneva: Labor et Fides, 1982), pp. 86-89.

[7] E . Lanne, *Eglise-mère*, p. 87.

[8] Ibid.

[9] *The Jerusalem Bible* (New York: Doubleday and Company, 1966), p. 406.

[10] *Holy Bible, New Revised Standard Version (NRSV) with Apocrypha* (New York-Oxford: Oxford University Press. 1989), p. 254: "Your *sister church* in Babylon."

[11] E . Lanne, *Eglise-mère*, pp. 87-88.

[12] Jack Sparks, ed., *The Apostolic Fathers* (Nashville: Thomas Nelson Publishers, 1978), p. 18.

[13] E. Lanne, *Eglise-mère*, p. 88; also *Eglises-soeurs*, p. 53.

[14] E. Lanne, Ibid., p. 88; also *Eglises-soeurs*, p. 54.

[15] See Trallians, 12:1, and 13:1; see also Philadelphians 11:2 and Smyrnaeans 12:1.

[16] E. Lanne, Ibid., p. 88.

[17] *Polycarp to the Philippians*, 10:1, in J. Sparks, ibid., p. 134.

[18] *The Martyrdom of Polycarp*, Salutation (inscription), in J. Sparks, ibid., p. 139.

[19] Eusebios, *Church History*, V, 1, 3ff.

[20] E. Lanne, *Eglise-mère*, pp. 849-90; *Eglises-soeurs*, pp. 56-8.

[21] E. Lanne, Ibid., p. 90; *Eglises-soeurs*, pp. 58-9.

[22] E. Lanne, Ibid., p. 91.

[23] Letter XLI, 6.

[24] Ibid.

[25] Letter XLIV.

[26] Letter L, 5.

[27] Theodoret, *Ecclesiastical History*, V,9,17.

[28] Letter CCIV, 7.

[29] Letter XXIII, P.L. XX, 546A. E. Lanne, Ibid., pp. 96-7; cf. Yves Congar, "The Orthodox Church and the Roman Catholic Church", in *Diversities and Communion* (Mystic, Connecticut: Twenty-third Publications, 1985), p. 86. The French original was published three years earlier: Yves Congar, "Eglise Orthodoxe et Eglise Catholique Romaine," in *Diversités et Communion* (Paris: Editions du Cerf, 1982), pp. 126-141.

[30] Yves Congar, *The Orthodox Church*, pp. 86-7, and 90-1.

[31] P.L., XX, 546A.

[32] Mansi 4, 203.

[33] Mansi 52, 601.

[34] W. M. Abbot, S. J. editor, *The Documents of Vatican II* (America Press, 1966), pp. 357-361.

[35] E. Stormon, *Healing of Schism*, pp. 161-3.

[36] Emphasis added.

[37] E. Stormon, Ibid., pp. 181-2.

[38] Emphasis added.

[39] E. Stormon, Ibid., pp. 367-8.

[40] Emphasis added.

[41] Y. Congar, *The Orthodox Church*, pp. 89-90.

[42] Fr. Congar lists some of these studies of his: *L'Ecclésiologie du Haut Moyen Age*, 1968; *I Believe in the Holy Spirit*, III; *The River of Life flows in the East and in the West*, ET, 1983.

[43] Y. Congar, *The Orthodox Church*, p. 90.

44 Ibid., pp. 90-91.

45 Ibid., p. 91.

46 E. Stormon, *Healing of Schism*, doc. no 275, p. 225.

47 Ibid., p. 226.

48 Ibid., p. 227.

49 *U. R.*, II.7.

50 *U. R.*, II.14.

51 *U.R.*, II.15.

52 E. Lanne, *Eglises-soeurs*, p. 65; see the rest of the pointed Analysis of the Decree by Fr. Lanne, ibid., pp. 62-71.

53 Ibid., p. 66.

54 *U. R.*, II.15.

55 *U. R.*, 16.

56 Regarding the difference in theology, Fr. Lanne indicates that *U.R.* presents its boldest statement on the legitimacy of a variety of theologies in the One Church of Christ. He repeats the six affirmations characterizing the theology of the Eastern Orthodox Churches, a theology which is sanctioned by the "living magisterium of these churches": the authentic theological traditions of the Orthodox churches are: (1) rooted in the Holy Scripture "in a truly excellent way"; (2) developed and expressed in the liturgical life (of the Church); (3) are nourished by the living apostolic tradition, and (4) by the writings of the Fathers and the spiritual writers; (5) they lead to the correctness of "saintly" life, and, even more (6) to the full contemplation of the Christian truth" (ibid., p. 70).

57 Ibid., p. 71.

58 Namely doc. nos. 195, and 311, in *Healing of Schism*, respectively on pp. 174-8; 181-2; and 259-61. No. 190 is the address by Pope Paul VI in the Basilica of Saint Peter as he welcomed Patriarch Athenagoras on October 26, 1967; no. 195 is the *Common Declaration* by Pope Paul VI and Patriarch Athenagoras at the end of the Patriarch's visit on October 28, 1967; and no. 311 is the address by Patriarch Dimitrios in the patriarchal Cathedral of Saint George in response to the address of Cardinal Willebrands, on November 30, 1973.

59 E. Lanne, *Eglises-soeurs*, p. 71. See also our comments above, as we presented *Anno Ineunte*. The expression "profound and mysterious communion" is repeated by Pope Paul VI three months later in his address to Patriarch Athenagoras in the Basilica of Saint Peter; see doc. 190, *Healing of Schism*, pp. 176-7: "What kind of renewal would it be that did not revive our faith in this deep and mysterious communion, established between us by a same obedience to the Gospel of Christ, by the same sacraments and above all by the same Baptism and the same Priesthood which offers the same Eucharist – the unique sacrifice of Christ – by a same episcopacy received from the apostolic times to guide the people of God towards the Lord and to preach his word to it (cf. *U.R.* 15-17)? There are so many ways used by the Holy Spirit to make us tend with our whole being towards *the fullness* of that *communion*, already *very rich* but still *incomplete*, which *unites us* in the *mystery of the church.*"

60 *Healing of Schism*, doc. 190, pp. 177-8.

61 E. Lanne, *Eglises-soeurs*, p. 72.

[62] Ibid.

[63] Saint Ignatios, *Letter* to *the Romans, ad init. Healing of Schism*, p. 175. It is obvious that when Saint Ignatios speaks of the Roman Church as "the Church of God which sojourns in Rome," which "presides in the land of the Romans," and which "presides (there) in love," it is the *local* church of Rome to which he refers.

We cannot forget that Saint Ignatios, the theologian of the "monarchical episcopate," is also the theologian of the "local church," which goes along with it. As he leaves his church, he calls upon a neighbor church, that of Philadelphia (see, *Letter to the Philadelphians*, X) to send a *deacon* (not a bishop, for his own church will elect a bishop to preside over it), to help his church, an "orphan" church because of his departure. He does not call upon the church of Rome to send a bishop... much less the deacon he has requested is of Philadelphia. He only asks the Church of Rome not to interfere with his martyrdom *(Letter to the Romans, IV)*.

Patriarch Dimitrios has made repeated references to this quotation in his own speeches and letters to Pope Paul VI. The question is, how has the Eastern Orthodox Church always understood this "presidency in love" of the Church of Rome? In his address quoted here, the Pope himself utilizes the expression "presiding in love" to speak of his presidency over the bishops of his own Church in the West. Does this not remind us of Saint Ignatios' other reference in the same letter to the Romans, according to which the church of Rome "presides in the land of the Romans;", i.e., the West? The expression, "the church which presides in love", follows the statement that the Church of Rome presides in the West. Is it possible to understand "presiding in love" as a further specification of "presiding in the land of the Romans"? Even if one understands "love" as "church", why should this "church" be anything other than the Church of Rome?

[64] We tend to disagree with this interpretation. See previous note.

[65] The direct quotation of Document 195 in *Healing of Schism* (p. 182) says: "The spirit which should inspire these efforts is a spirit of loyalty to the truth and of mutual comprehension, with a real desire to avoid the rancors of the past, *and every kind of spiritual or intellectual domination.*"

[66] "Venerable" is one or the titles given to canonical sister churches, both in the East and the West. It is a title that recurs often in the official documents of *Tomos Agapis*, or *The Healing of Schism*.

[67] This Statement is subject to interpretation. As a student of Saint Basil, I remember his harsh words regarding the non-intervention (actually no help) from the West (Pope Damasus and the Bishops of Italy) when Saint Basil *requested* such help. Saint Basil begged the West to help the Eastern Churches in their struggle against Arianism. He reminded them that "as Christianity came to you from us, so too can heresy." He received no reply. Instead, against Saint Basil's recommendation, Pope Damasus and the Italian bishops supported Paulinus, a usurper, against the legitimate bishop of Antioch, Meletios. In his exasperation, Saint Basil wrote: If God does not come to our aid, "what can one expect from Western pride (τῆς δυτικῆς ὀφρύος)?" [*Letter* 239, 2; *P.G.* 32, 893B; *Greek Fathers of the Church* (ΕΠΕ, Saint Basil. Vol. 1, p. 304)].

[68] For the Orthodox, the first question is: Which see is the "see of Peter." Did

the Apostles (missionaries, on *constant mission: apostle* is someone who is *sent!*) have a "see" at all? Were they "bureaucrats", administrators of a given diocese, "diocesan bishops"? How can one make such anachronisms?

However, the question of the primacy itself in the life of the Church is a very pertinent question, and its relation to the figure of Saint Peter is a valid one.

This same idea of studying the Petrine ministry *together* in the light of our *common* Christian tradition ("in thc light of the Gospel and of the authentic Apostolic tradition in a dialogue of charity and truth") has already been suggested by Cardinal J. Willebrands (see above, and *Healing of Schism*, Doc. 275, p. 227).

[69] E. Lanne, *Eglises-soeurs*, p. 73.

[70] Ibid., p. 74.

[71] J. Meyendorff, *Eglises-soeurs*, pp. 35-46.

[72] Fr. Meyendorff notes that the Patriarch Nicholas II, wrote to the Pope to ask for a declaration of faith, "in a very discrete and irenic way." He addressed the Pope in the way Orthodox bishops in full communion address one another: Μακαριώτατε καὶ Σεβασμιώτατε [ἐν Χριστῷ] ἀδελφέ, Most Blessed and Most Reverend Brother [in Christ]. Ibid., p. 37.

[73] Ibid., pp. 36-37.

[74] It is known that Pope John XXIII abolished the Latin Patriarchate of Constantinople. At the time, Roman canonists tried to downplay the ecclesiological importance of that event. In the light of the "sister churches" ecclesiology, and as an extra gesture of good will and in an effort to "heal the schism," Rome could abolish the Latin Patriarchate of Jerusalem, as well, for it still remains as a vestige of the old schism that we continue to try to heal.

[75] See details in Fr. Meyendorf's article, Ibid., pp. 37-8.

[76] Meyendorff, ibid.

[77] Ibid., p. 38.

[78] Ibid., p. 40.

[79] Ibid., p. 39. See rest of Fr. Meyendorff's comments Ibid., pp. 35-40.

[80] Ibid., p. 41-42.

[81] Ibid., p. 42.

[82] Ibid., p. 42.

[83] It seems that Fr. Meyendorff had read Fr. Lanne's paper, for the expression is his.

[84] Fr. Lanne has responded to this question, as we have seen above: the conflict can be resolved through the healing effect of restoration of communion. The West will feel compelled to see all these recent doctrines in the light of the doctrine of the Eastern Church, which, in our estimation, reflects the doctrine of the undivided church of apostolic life, practice, and continuity.

On the other land, Fr. Meyendorff's question with regard to "dogmatic relativism" sounds very pertinent.

[85] This is a clear reference to Fr. Lanne's paper, which suggests that the Western dogmas may be "rethought" in the light of the Eastern tradition.

[86] Meyendorff, Ibid ., pp. 41-42. 1974 was the year of the *Symposium*.

[87] Ibid., pp. 44-45.

[88] Ibid., pp. 45-46.

[89] E. Lanne, *Eglise-Soeur et Eglise-mère*, p. 97.

[90] Ibid.

[91] Curiously enough, there are documents in *Tomos Agapis/Healing the Schism* speaking a similar language, in terms of a "return" to restoration of full communion as it was experienced by our two churches during the first millennium of our Christian era (see doc. No 127, p. 128, and doc. 334, p. 288).

[92] I still remember the statement of Fr. Olivier Rousseau, O.S.B. (the nephew of Dom Lambert Beauduin and a monk of Chevetogne, Belgium) who once (back in the late 50's) told me: "As we cannot be in communion with one another, let us, at least, be in *communication*." These were the times of pre-Vatican II, and pre-"sister churches" ecclesiology. We certainly have progressed in "communication," as we have rediscovered that "deep and mysterious communion" which still unites our two sister churches, in spite of the apparent division and separation.